THE FAMILY LEGAL COMPANION

Thomas Hauser

ALLWORTH PRESS, NEW YORK

93-602

For Ruth, Peter, Alison. and Lenny

3 40
Hau

Published by Allworth Press, an imprint of Allworth Communications, Inc., 10 East 23rd Street, New York, NY 10010.

Distributor to the trade in the United States: Consortium Book Sales & Distribution, Inc., 287 East Sixth Street, Suite 365, Saint Paul, MN 55101.

Distributor to the trade in Canada: Raincoast Books Distribution Limited, 112 East 3rd Avenue, Vancouver, B.C. V5t 1C8.

Book design by Douglas Design Associates, New York, NY.

Library of Congress Catalog Card Number: 92-071565

ISBN: 1-880559-04-8

Contents

Introduction

*E*very day the law shapes our lives. People get married, drive cars, buy houses, and go to work—all in conformity with the law. Things we take for granted, like consumer rights and a safe place to live, are ours because of the law. Some laws are extremely complex; others are simple. But stripped of its Latin terminology, the law is relatively easy to understand.

The Family Legal Companion is not a do-it-yourself legal guide. Rather, it's designed to give you, the reader, enough information to make intelligent decisions regarding legal issues you are likely to face in everyday life. Not every issue will pertain to every reader. But I suspect that, at one time or another, virtually every situation covered in these pages will be of concern to you, a relative, a co-worker, or a friend. The book won't solve all of your legal problems, but it will make you more aware of your legal rights and how to enforce them.

The questions and answers that follow have been grouped into seventeen chapters according to subject matter. I've tried my best to make *The Family Legal Companion* entertaining and informative. Properly used, it will guide you in understanding what you are entitled to, and what is expected of you, under the law. However, a few words of caution are in order:

1. Legal battles are best avoided. When a conflict arises, try to see the other side's point of view. Be willing to compromise if a fair compromise is possible.

2. This book offers general guidelines—not advice that fits every situation like a glove. Many laws vary from state to state, and specific fact patterns are crucial in determining who wins and who loses a particular piece of litigation.

3. The law changes—often. New statutes and new court decisions make it imperative that you check the copyright date of this and every other legal guide to see how current the advice you're receiving really is.

4. Major legal decisions that affect your financial condition and personal life should be made with the advice of a lawyer. If you don't have an attorney, your local bar association—which is listed in the telephone directory—will provide you with a list of counsel able to handle legal matters at reasonable rates outlined in advance.

Some knowledge of the law is essential to getting along in today's society. The more you know, the better able you'll be to protect yourself and your loved ones.

Chapter 1

Your Job

Am I entitled to extra pay when asked to work overtime?

Q. I work at what is supposed to be a nine-to-five job. However, several days a week my boss insists that I stay overtime without extra pay. Am I entitled to additional wages?

A. Quite possibly, yes. Approximately 50 million Americans are employed in jobs covered by the Fair Labor Standards Act. Among its many provisions, this act provides that for any time worked in excess of forty hours in any given work week, employees must receive overtime pay at a rate of not less than one-and-a-half times their regular pay. Moreover, the act does not permit employers to average the hours worked over two or more weeks. An employee who works thirty hours one week and fifty hours the next must receive overtime pay for the extra ten hours worked in the second week, even though the number of hours worked in each of the two weeks averages forty.

You should be aware, though, that certain jobs are not covered by the act's overtime provisions. Workers who fall under the Department of Labor's definition of "executive," "professional," and/or "administrative" personnel are not covered, nor are employees in some small businesses and several other categories of employment.

The Fair Labor Standards Act is administered by the Wage and Hour Division of the United States Department of Labor. If you have questions about whether or not you qualify for protection under the act, check your telephone directory for the department's nearest office. A division compliance officer will answer any questions you have and investigate any complaint you make. Should a violation be found, the division will file suit on your behalf for the payment of back wages and, in cases of severe misconduct, will institute criminal proceedings against your employer. Upon request, the division's local office will also mail you a copy of its free pamphlet *Handy Reference Guide to the Fair Labor Standards Act.*

If health problems keep you from getting a job

Q. My husband has been treated for a serious illness, which is now in remission. But although he is willing and able to work and his doctors say there is no reason why he should not be working, several prospective employers have refused to hire him. Is this legal?

A. Maybe not. Many states have laws that protect the handicapped. And in 1973 Congress passed the Federal Rehabilitation Act, which states, "No otherwise qualified handicapped individual shall, solely by reason of his handicap, be excluded from participation in, be denied the benefits of, or be subjected to discrimination under any program or activity receiving federal financial assistance." Under this law, a handicapped person is any person who has, has had, or is considered to have a physical or mental impairment that substantially limits a major life activity. This includes people (such as your husband) with a history of cancer, heart disease, and other serious illnesses.

Insofar as employment is concerned, the Federal Rehabilitation Act applies to the following employers: the federal government, businesses that have contracts with the federal government for goods and services worth more than $2,500, and all employers who receive federal financial assistance—for instance, federally subsidized mass-transit systems or schools. Among other things, the statute covers everything from recruitment, hiring, promotions, firings, rates of pay, and fringe benefits. Even employer-sponsored social and recreational programs must take the needs of the handicapped into consideration.

Moreover, in 1990, Congress passed the Americans With Disabilities Act. Among its many provisions, this statute prohibits employers with 25 or more employees from discriminating against qualified physically disabled individuals in the areas of hiring, advancement, job training, compensation, and other terms and conditions of employment.

If your husband believes he has been discriminated against because of his condition, his best first step would be to write to the Department of Labor, Washington, D.C. 20210, within 180 days of the alleged discrimination incident. This office will examine his complaint and, when warranted, take action. Your husband might also write to the attorney general's office in your state for a list of local antidiscrimination statutes.

How to see your personnel file

Q. I've worked at the same job for a number of years, and, since my personnel file will have an obvious bearing on promotions, salary increases, and the like, I've asked to see these records. But my employer has denied me access to them. Am I legally entitled to review my employment file?

A. You might be, depending on the kind of job you have and the state in which you work. Virtually all employees of the federal government have right of access to their records under the regulations of the agencies they work for, as well as the 1974 Privacy Act. And quite a few workers in the private sector can review their employment files under contracts negotiated by their unions.

But otherwise, a worker's right to review employment records depends on the law of the state where he or she works. For example, the California Labor Code requires employers to make a copy of each employee's personnel file available at the place where the employee reports for work, within a reasonable period of time after a request to review the records has been made. Access is given by law to all records "which are used or have been used to determine that employee's qualifications for employment, promotion, additional compensation, termination or other disciplinary action." Letters of reference and records relating to the investigation of possible criminal offenses are exempt.

Many states have statutes similar to the California law, and at least one—Oregon—requires employers to keep personnel records available to employees for a minimum of sixty days after the termination of employment.

To find out what the law is in your particular state, contact the state

Department of Labor, which is listed in the telephone directory along with other divisions of your state government.

Suing a boss for negligence

Q. My husband was recently injured in an accident at work. Can he sue his employer for negligence, or does workers' compensation limit the amount of money he can be awarded?

A. That will depend to a large degree on the law of the state in which your husband works.

Workers' compensation is insurance, paid for by the employer, that provides cash benefits and medical care for workers who become disabled due to injury or sickness related to their job. If death results, benefits are payable to the surviving spouse and dependents as defined by law. The system is designed to eliminate the issue of negligence and guarantee payment to the injured party regardless of who was at fault. However, in most states, there is a trade-off. In return for the security of knowing that fixed benefits will be paid, the worker is precluded from suing his employer for a greater monetary award. However, a worker can collect workers' compensation and, at the same time, sue any third party whose negligence contributed to the accident.

Workers' compensation programs differ radically from state to state. In some areas of the country, employers can choose not to be in the system but, if they are not in it, they are fully liable to employee lawsuits for negligence. Seriously disabled workers may be entitled to Federal Disability Insurance Benefits in addition to state payments. And Congress has enacted a federal workers' compensation statute, which preempts state laws in certain industries, such as maritime and interstate railroad employment.

Whenever a worker has been injured on the job, he should notify his employer as soon as possible. I assume your husband has already done this. He should then get in touch with local workers' compensation authorities, who will provide him with detailed information concerning his obligations and rights. Generally, employers will assist in this process. If your husband belongs to a union, the shop steward should also be able to furnish helpful advice. And, of course, your husband should feel free to consult a lawyer if the injury is serious or he is for any reason uneasy about the outcome of his claim.

Is there any way to force an employer to correct dangerous working conditions without risking your job?

Q. My husband works in a factory. For the past few months he has been increasingly troubled by dust, fumes, and the noise level of the machinery. Is there any way he can force his employer to alter these dangerous conditions without risking the loss of his job?

A. Yes, there is. In 1970, Congress passed the Occupational Safety and Health Act. Three quarters of all civilian workers in the United States are covered by it. The only major exceptions are workers protected by other statutes (such as coal miners). Whether or not your husband has a union to turn to, this act will offer support and assistance.

The act is enforced by the Occupational Safety and Health Administration of the United States Department of Labor (200 Constitution Avenue, N.W., Washington, D.C. 20210). If your husband sends the department a letter, outlining the conditions he believes to be unhealthy or unsafe, department personnel will investigate his complaint. These investigators have the power to conduct on-site inspections, subpoena witnesses, and examine all records relevant to the case. Also, they will keep your husband's name in confidence if he so requests.

In the event safety or health violations are found at the factory, the Department of Labor is empowered to order that they be corrected. Civil fines can be levied against the factory owner for willful or repeated violations, and, if the violations are not corrected within a reasonable period of time, an additional per diem fine can be charged. Also, in certain instances, criminal fines of up to $20,000 and sentences of up to one year in prison can be meted out.

Can I sue an employer who promised me job security—and then fired me?

Q. Several months ago I left a secure job I had held for years to take a position with another company. It was a difficult decision, but I felt that the advancement possibilities offered by the new firm would make the change worthwhile. Also, at the time I switched jobs I was told that, whatever else happened, my new job would be "just as secure" as my old one. Then, after eight weeks, my new boss told me "things hadn't worked out," and I was fired. My old position, which

I liked very much, is now filled. I have no job, very little money, and feel as though I have been taken advantage of. Are there any grounds on which I can file suit against my second employer?

A. There might be. Your position would be stronger if you had entered into a written contract with the second employer since, in many states, unwritten promises of employment for a period of more than one year are difficult to enforce. However, you might have a successful lawsuit for breach of contract.

To prove your case, you must show that your employer reneged on a specific promise or that you were dismissed for an unlawful reason. For example, if you and your new boss clearly agreed that under no circumstances would you be dismissed in less than a year, you would probably be entitled to monetary damages of some sort. Or, if your employer made romantic overtures and you were fired because you didn't respond favorably, you could file suit for sexual harassment. But, on the other hand, if you misrepresented your credentials and your new boss hired you expecting certain work-related skills that you were unable to provide, your dismissal would be neither unlawful nor unjust.

There is always some element of risk involved when a person changes jobs. However, if you feel that the circumstances of your case go beyond this normal risk and amount to misrepresentation or other unlawful conduct by your employer, you should consult an attorney about the possibility of filing suit. Also, if you belonged to a union at your most recent place of employment, you should speak with union officials about the matter. Quite possibly they will be able to achieve your reinstatement without turning to the courts.

My paycheck is too large—must I report the error?

Q. My most recent paycheck included $100 more in overtime pay than I was entitled to. If I don't report the overpayment to my company and the error is discovered, what steps can be taken against me?

A. If the error is discovered without your reporting it, the company may have a cause of action against you for "unjust enrichment."

The law of unjust enrichment is based on the belief that one should not be allowed to profit unfairly at the expense of another person or organization. Both fairness and the law look askance at a person benefiting from mathematical errors to the detriment of someone else. Thus, where a paycheck has been erroneously computed in your favor, you will not be allowed to knowingly profit from your employer's mistake. No doubt, you would be outraged if your employer accidentally underpaid you and then kept silent upon discovering the mistake. Indeed, were it to happen, you would probably march into his or her office and demand the full salary to which you are entitled.

Report the overpayment.

When you make less money than a man

Q. I'm employed full time, but I make $20 less a week than a male coworker who does precisely the same work I do. Isn't this unlawful sexual discrimination?

A. It might be. Salary differentials between men and women are permitted for reasons other than sex—say, seniority or the quality of a worker's performance—but otherwise the Equal Pay Act, which applies to most American workers, requires that men and women employed under similar working conditions in the same establishment receive equal pay (including fringe benefits) for jobs that involve similar skill, effort, and responsibility. The actual duties need not be identical, but merely "substantially equal," for the act to apply. (Job titles are not taken into consideration in determining whether two jobs are comparable.)

The Equal Pay Act is administered by the Equal Employment Opportunity Commission (1801 L Street, N.W., Washington, D.C. 20507), which has offices throughout the country. To file a complaint, contact the commission's nearest office (check your local telephone directory). A specialist in equal-pay-discrimination complaints will interview you and advise you regarding your rights. Then, if the situation calls for it, the commission will discuss the matter with your employer—without disclosing your identity. If a violation is found and your employer refuses to promise future compliance with the Equal Pay Act as well as payment of back wages, the commission will file suit on your behalf.

If, for any reason, the commission decides not to take on your case, you can file suit on your own for back pay, plus court costs and reasonable attorney's fees. You must sue within two years of the equal-pay violation or, in the case of intentional discrimination, within three years. If a violation is found, your employer will not be able to lower your male counterpart's salary to make the pay equal. Rather, he will have to increase your salary to a higher level.

Is it legal to fire an employee for a drinking problem?

Q. My husband lost his job recently as the result of a drinking problem. Since then, he has sought professional help and stopped drinking. However, his former employer would not pay for any medical-disability benefits while he was ill and now refuses to rehire him, even though he is cured. What are my husband's legal rights?

A. Alcoholism affects all levels of America's work force, from corporate executives to unskilled workers. For many years, it was looked on as a social problem, and those who suffered from it were considered morally deficient. Within the past decade, however, a growing number of people in authority have begun to recognize that heavy drinking is a disease that requires understanding and treatment, not ridicule and scorn.

Several states now have laws that regard alcoholism as a disability and restrict employment discrimination against alcoholics. Perhaps the most progressive approach has been taken by the State of New York, which has the following rules:

1. An employee cannot be fired simply because he or she is an alcoholic. The burden is on the employer to prove that alcoholism prevented the employee from performing safely and properly.

2. An employee who has been fired for alcoholism is generally entitled to twenty-six weeks of medical-disability benefits. (Permanent payments are rarely allowed, since alcoholism is considered "curable.")

3. Prospective employers cannot inquire whether a job applicant has ever been treated for or suffered from alcoholism. However, they can ask whether the applicant has a drinking problem at present that would affect his or her ability to perform the job applied for.

4. An employer is generally not obligated to rehire an employee who has been properly dismissed for a drinking-related problem.

Your husband might also be protected under the Federal Rehabilitation Act, which applies to most companies in the country that have contracts with the federal government for goods or services in excess of $2,500. Under this act, a company cannot discriminate in any way against persons suffering from alcoholism; it must employ them on the same basis as other workers, unless their condition prevents them from properly performing their job or directly threatens the safety and property of others. Additionally, the recently passed Americans with Disabilities Act might be relevant to the situation.

Thus, resolution of your husband's case will depend on several factors, including the state in which he was employed, whether his company does business with the federal government, and whether his condition interfered with his work performance. Also, it is possible that his employment contract or union rules would have a bearing on the matter.

Perhaps your best first step would be to contact a regional office of the National Council on Alcoholism and Drug Dependence, whose headquarters is at 12 West 21st Street, New York, New York 10010. A council representative will be able to advise your husband about his legal rights.

Are there legal steps I can take against a boss who makes sexual advances?

Q. Several times within the past year, my supervisor at work has made sexually explicit comments to me, which I've tried to ignore. Last month, when I asked to be promoted to an available job, he suggested that I go to bed with him. When I refused, the position I was seeking went to someone else. Do I have any legal grounds on which to file suit?

A. Quite possibly, yes. For many years, no federal statute specifically banned job harassment based on sex, and only the Wisconsin legislature enacted an applicable state law. However, in recent years, many states have followed Wisconsin's lead. And in 1980, the federal Equal Employment Opportunity Commission issued a set of guidelines that might apply to your case. These guidelines apply to all federal, state, and local government agencies, as well as virtually all private employers with fifteen or more employees. They are based on the premise that sexual harassment—whether physical or verbal—is wrong, and that employers have the obligation to keep a workplace free of such behavior.

Specifically, the guidelines outlaw "unwelcome sexual advances, requests for sexual favors, and other verbal or physical conduct of a sexual nature" when any of the following conditions exist: 1) Submission to such conduct is made either explicitly or implicitly a condition of employment; 2) submission to or rejection of such conduct is used as a basis for employment decisions affecting the individual; or 3) such conduct substantially interferes with an individual's work or creates an offensive work environment (or is intended to do so).

In your case, the best first step would probably be to complain directly to your supervisor or his boss about the matter. Then, if the problem is not remedied, you can call your local office of the Equal Employment Opportunity Commission (listed in the phone book under "United States Government"), or write the EEOC at 1801 L Street, N.W., Washington, D.C. 20507. The commission is empowered to investigate complaints of this nature and negotiate with employers regarding awards of back pay for past discrimination, promotions, and other types of relief. Also, if your employer refuses to settle the complaint, the commission can file suit in federal court asking for relief on your behalf.

When people don't get paid for their work

Q. My eighteen-year-old son and two friends have been painting houses to earn money this summer. On their most recent job, the homeowner made numerous additional demands that forced them to work longer than expected. But then when the job was done, the homeowner refused to pay the agreed-upon amount. Despite all the extras, he claimed he was dissatisfied with the job. What can my son do?

A. Your son's first step should be to send a letter to the homeowner, demanding that he specify in writing exactly what was deficient about the paint job. Then, if a fair settlement can't be reached, your son and his friends can file suit in small claims court for breach of their oral contract.

No lawyer will be necessary, and your son and his friends will be able to seek not only payment of the amount originally agreed upon but also extra compensation for the additional work the homeowner demanded. They can all testify as plaintiffs on their own behalf, and all three of them should—three witnesses are better than one. Photographs of the finished job will also help.

In the future, though, your son and his friends should get their house-painting agreements in writing. At the least, these contracts should specify the exact work to be done, the type of paint to be used, the dates the work will be performed, and exactly when they will be paid. The contract should also spell out who is responsible for miscellaneous costs. Then, any "extras" can be written into the contract as "modifications," clearly requiring extra payment.

If you're fired and replaced by a younger person, can you get your job back?

Q. My father worked at the same job for twenty years. Recently, he was fired and replaced by a younger man who will be paid a much lower salary because of his lack of seniority. Does my father have any legal recourse to get his job back?

A. He might. In 1967, Congress passed the Age Discrimination Act, designed to prohibit arbitrary discrimination and promote the employment of older persons based on their ability, not age. The act protects individuals between the ages of forty and seventy, and applies to virtually all businesses with twenty or more employees. In relevant part, it states, "It shall be unlawful for an employer to discharge any individual or otherwise discriminate with respect to his compensation, terms, conditions, or privileges of employment, because of such individual's age, or to limit, segregate, or classify his employees in any way which would deprive or tend to deprive any individual of employment opportunities or otherwise adversely affect his status as an employee, because of age."

In your father's case, the employer might argue that the firing had nothing to do with age; that it was based solely on the economics of seniority. But the fact is that seniority and age go hand in hand, and an "adverse impact" against your father resulted. Thus, the primary issues to be determined will be whether there was a nondiscriminatory business justification for the employer's actions, and whether there was a reasonable alternative to the firing. (For example, could the company have terminated a less-experienced, less-skilled worker and let your father assume the other worker's duties and salary rate?)

The Age Discrimination Act is administered by the Equal Employment Opportunity Commission (EEOC), which has branch offices throughout the country. If your father wishes to pursue the matter, he should contact a commission office. An EEOC representative will then investigate the case and, if conditions warrant, file a lawsuit on your father's behalf. Or, if your father so chooses, he can retain an attorney himself and begin legal proceedings on his own. Should the employer be found guilty of unlawful age discrimination, your father will be entitled to reinstatement of his job plus back wages.

Not content to rely on federal legislation, many states have laws that further protect the jobs of older workers. Thus, you might also contact your local state attorney general's office for advice. And, last, keep in mind that employment contracts (whether or not negotiated by a union) often contain provisions for generous severance pay or out-and-out prohibitions against firings of this type. Accordingly, your father should carefully review any documents that relate to his employment.

Can my boss make me responsible for business losses?

Q. I work as a saleswoman, and part of my duties include operating the cash register. If a customer's check bounces or the cash drawer is short at the end of the day, the money lost is deducted from my salary. Are these penalties legal?

A. They might be. Whenever a person takes a job, certain terms and conditions are agreed upon as part of the employment contract. The most obvious of these are salary, hours, and job performance, but other miscellaneous contract provisions always exist between labor and management.

In your case, however unfair it might be, your boss has chosen to put the burden of several business risks on your shoulders. And, unless his rule conflicts with a specific statute (such as bringing your salary below the minimum wage set by Congress), he is entitled to do so.

One partial solution to your problem would be to ask your boss if you can refuse to accept checks from customers. If that is not possible, when you accept a check, you should always require several pieces of identification. Also, if your boss will not agree to a better arrangement than the one you have now, you have the option of resigning and taking a new job with better working conditions.

Will I still have seniority at work when I return from pregnancy leave?

Q. I've been working at my job for eight years, and will soon be taking a pregnancy leave of several months. Will I retain all of my seniority benefits when I am able to resume working?

A. Most likely, yes. In 1978, Congress passed the Pregnancy Discrimination Act, which prohibits employment discrimination because of pregnancy or related conditions. The basic principle of the act is that women must be treated the same as other employees on the basis of their ability to work. Thus, women cannot be laid off from their jobs because they are "showing"; abortion remains an entirely personal matter, not to be considered in employment decisions; and a woman who is unable to work for pregnancy-related reasons is entitled to disability benefits or sick leave on the same basis as any other employee who is unable to work for medical reasons.

The law provides that, unless a woman on pregnancy leave informs her employer that she does not intend to return to work, her job must be held open as it would be for other employees on sick or disability leave. This, of course, leads to the question of whether your employer must honor your seniority rights if you take a leave for child-care purposes after you are medically able to return to work. Here again the act comes into play. It requires that child-care leave be granted on the same basis as leave for other nonmedical reasons. For example, if employees can retain their seniority while on leave for personal travel or educational purposes, you must be accorded the same right.

If you feel that your rights are being violated, you can write to the Equal Employment Opportunity Commission's Office of Policy Implementation, 1801 L Street, N.W., Washington, D.C. 20507. A commission representative will assist in the enforcement of your rights.

If you belong to a union, a union representative should be able to offer additional help. Also, many states have laws that supplement the federal guidelines. Your state attorney general's office, which is listed in the telephone directory, will be able to advise you about local laws in the state where you work.

How can I get a former boss to change a poor job reference that is unfounded?

Q. I was recently turned down for a job even though my qualifications were good and the prospective employer seemed to like me. When I inquired as to the reasons why, I was told that a former employer had given me an extremely negative recommendation, saying that I was untrustworthy and dishonest. I worked for this man for three years and his remarks are totally unfounded, but every time I apply for a job I'll be expected to list him on my résumé. Is there any way I can force him to tell the truth?

A. The first thing I would recommend is that you confront your former employer and ask for specific examples of dishonesty and untrustworthiness on your part. It is possible that his belief stems from an inaccurate report received from someone else, in which case he might willingly set the record straight.

If this fails, you should explain the situation fully to prospective employers. Ask them to weigh your side of the story and consider such questions as why your former boss kept you on the payroll for three years if you were untrustworthy and dishonest. Job references from other employers will also bolster your cause.

Should these alternatives prove unsatisfactory, there is a third, but not very desirable, option. You can file suit against your former employer for libel (if the negative comments were in writing) or slander (if they were verbally given). In order to win such a lawsuit, you would be required to prove that your former boss actually made derogatory statements, and that they were false.

Moreover, in some states, courts have held that a "qualified privilege" protects employers who furnish information about their workers. In these states, employers who show that they responded in good faith to a reasonable inquiry by a proper party (such as a prospective employer) cannot be held liable for libel or slander. Thus, you might also be required to prove some sort of ill will or malice on the part of your former boss.

Should a lawsuit prove necessary, your local bar association can provide you with a list of attorneys qualified to act on your behalf. However, since filing a suit would most likely further alienate your former employer, it should be viewed as a last resort.

Are employee dress codes legal?

Q. My employer has a dress code forbidding female employees from wearing pants to work. Is this legal?

A. Because clothes make an impression, employers have a legitimate interest in regulating what their employees wear to work. But it is discriminatory and unlawful for employers to institute dress codes only for female employees.

The key question in your case is whether your employer has equal standards for men and women. If casual clothes are forbidden for all personnel, with male employees required to wear jackets and ties to work, then your employer's dress-code standards are probably lawful. However, if men can dress any way they want at the office while women are required to wear dresses or skirts, then, most likely, you have a legitimate grievance.

For more information, or to file a complaint against your employer, get in touch with the Equal Employment Opportunity Commission at 1801 L Street, N.W., Washington, D.C. 20507, or one of its field offices located throughout the country.

Are free-lancers entitled to employee benefits?

Q. I work an average of 40 hours a week on a free-lance basis. Am I entitled to the benefits received by regular full-time employees?

A. You might be, depending on several factors. Under federal law, most people who provide services to a company are classified as either "employees" or "independent contractors." Generally, you will be considered an employee if you perform services subject to the control of your employer as to how your work should be done. If your employer supplies you with tools and a place to work, that also weighs in favor of your being considered an employee. Whether you work full time or part time is not a factor in determining if you're an employee for federal purposes.

If there's a union at your place of work, the shop steward should be able to offer advice as to your best course of action. Regional offices of the United States Department of Labor, Internal Revenue Service, and your state attorney general can also be helpful. Once you've spoken with these authorities, you'll be in a better position to judge whether you're entitled to reclassification as a full-time employee and how much you'll gain by it. Keep in mind, though, that your employer might have the option of terminating your employment altogether, rather than reclassifying you and increasing your benefits. This possibility too must be weighed in your decision-making process.

If you're fired, do you get severance pay?

Q. I've just been fired from a job I held for several years. Am I entitled to severance pay?

A. Often an employee can be dismissed without severance wages at the discretion of the employer, but several exceptions exist.

If you belong to a union, it's possible the union contract requires your employer to make severance payments. Your union representative can advise you regarding this aspect of your rights.

Also, if you had your own employment contract, oral or written, that provided for severance pay, you would be entitled to payment on termination.

Furthermore, if your dismissal violated your contract, or some other legal right—for example, if you were fired because of unlawful discrimination—you may be entitled to back wages as well as the return of your job.

Finally, even without severance pay, unless you were fired because of improper conduct on your part, you'll probably be covered by unemployment insurance. For more information about your rights, contact your state Department of Labor.

What are my rights as a nonsmoker at work?

Q. I am a nonsmoker and work in an office with two chain smokers on either side of me. Do I have the legal right to work in a nonsmoking area?

A. You might. Smoking in confined places such as elevators and buses has been banned for decades in many areas of the country. Cities and states have also come under pressure to restrict smoking in the workplace, and a number of such ordinances have been enacted.

The first comprehensive no-smoking law was Minnesota's 1975 Clean Indoor Air Act. This law provides that "no person shall smoke in a public place, except in designated smoking areas." A "public place" is defined by the act as "any enclosed, indoor area used by the general public or serving as a place of work, including, but not limited to, restaurants, retail stores, offices and other commercial establishments." The act further provides that "where smoking is designated, existing physical barriers and ventilation systems shall be used to minimize the toxic effect of smoke in adjacent non-smoking areas." Factories, warehouses, and similar places of work need not be divided into smoking and nonsmoking sections, but, in such workplaces, the Minnesota State Department of Labor and State Commission of Health have established rules that "restrict or prohibit smoking where the close proximity of workers or the inadequacy of ventilation causes smoke pollution detrimental to the health and comfort of nonsmoking employees." Employers must enforce the Clean Indoor Air Act, and failure to do so is a misdemeanor.

Many other states and municipalities now have similar laws. In San Francisco, for example, employers are required to provide nonsmoking employees with a smoke-free environment. And, regardless of where you work, federal and state laws require certain minimum ventilation standards.

To determine the law in the area where you work, contact Action on Smoking and Health, 2013 H Street, N.W., Washington, D.C. 20006, or a local unit of the American Cancer Society. These organizations will explain your rights and how they can be enforced.

If I'm on jury duty, will my employer pay me?

Q. I missed two weeks of work last month because of jury duty. Will my employer pay me for the days I missed?

A. He might. Most states have laws prohibiting an employer from reducing sick days or vacation time—or otherwise discriminating against an employee—simply because he or she has taken time off from work to be a juror. And some states (such as Alabama, Hawaii, Massachusetts, Nebraska, and Tennessee) require employers to pay employees for the time they missed while on jury duty. However, in some of these states, the employer may deduct the employee's fee for being a juror—usually less than $20 per day—from his or her salary.

If you don't live in a protected state, you'll be entitled to compensation from your employer only if it's specified in your employment contract. You can, of course, keep the money you're paid for serving as a juror. The clerk in the court where you served will be able to advise you of your rights regarding payment.

Chapter 2

Landlords

Can our landlord refuse to return our security deposit when we move?

Q. My husband and I recently moved from an apartment we had lived in for several years. We naturally assumed the landlord would return our security deposit, which we were required to leave with him when we signed our lease. But he has refused, saying the apartment was a mess when we left. The landlord's claim is not true. My husband and I were clean, responsible tenants, and the only "mess" left behind was the normal residue of a couple moving. How can we get our security deposit back?

A. The purpose of a security deposit is to compensate a landlord in the event his property is damaged by a tenant. Thus, if you had left behind a smashed window or broken plumbing fixtures that were damaged by misuse or abuse (rather than normal wear and tear), you might not be entitled to the return of your deposit. However, some landlords take advantage of this protection by withholding security deposits without cause, and your problem is a common one. In recent years, a number of state legislatures have enacted laws to deal with it.

In California, for example, a landlord must return a tenant's security deposit, or provide an itemized written statement that explains why it has been withheld, within two weeks of the tenant vacating the apartment. Violation of this law subjects the landlord to a penalty of up to $200, plus return of the security deposit. And even if the landlord has provided an itemized statement, he or she will be found in violation of the law if a court determines that the landlord's claim was unfounded and made in bad faith.

Similarly, many states have now adopted the Uniform Residential Landlord and Tenant Act. Under this law, if a landlord fails to return a security deposit rightly owed to the tenant, the tenant may sue to recover triple damages, as well as court costs and reasonable attorney's fees from the landlord.

Whatever the particular form, all states offer some type of protection to tenants. Your first step should be to write your former landlord protesting his action. Ask him to specify in writing exactly what damage he claims the apartment suffered or, in the alternative, to return your deposit. If you do not receive a satisfactory response, check with your state attorney general's office to find out the full extent of tenant protection offered in your state. Then you can take your case to small claims court, where you will be able to proceed without need of a lawyer.

Should litigation prove necessary, it would be helpful if you brought along friends or business associates to testify to the care with which you kept your old apartment. If any witnesses were present on the day you moved, they should be your first choice. Also, if you are aware of other instances where the landlord improperly withheld security deposits, ask the tenants involved to appear in court on your behalf. If the judge sees a pattern of landlord misconduct, he or she will be even more likely to decide the case in your favor.

Is it legal to break a lease?

Q. My husband and I recently signed a two-year lease for an apartment, but now we have found a larger apartment in a better neighborhood and would like to move. Can we break our lease, or are we obligated to stay until it expires?

A. Most likely you will be able to move. You should first ask your landlord for written permission to break the lease. If he agrees, the problem is solved. If he refuses, you still have several options. For instance, you might find a subtenant—someone who will live in the apartment and pay rent on the unexpired portion of your lease. This would enable you to fulfill your obligations to the landlord without living in the apartment and paying rent yourself.

Subletting, of course, does pose several dangers. If the subtenant damages the apartment or fails to pay the rent at any time during your lease, you can be held liable. In some states, landlords can forbid subletting. However, in all cases, it is an established legal principle that landlords must take all reasonable steps to "mitigate their damages" (make up for lost income) when a tenant breaks a lease. If you tell your landlord that you plan to move, he must either accept a responsible subtenant offered by you or find a replacement. If he refuses to do either, it is unlikely that a court will honor his claim against you for reimbursement on the unexpired portion of your lease.

Sharing a summer house

Q. I would like to purchase a share in a weekend vacation house for the coming summer. What steps should I take to protect my legal rights?

A. Sharing a weekend vacation house can be a delight or a disaster. There is nothing you can do to guarantee good weather, but you can take several steps to help safeguard your legal rights. Before any final plans are made, I suggest:

1. Examine the house in person to make certain that it has the facilities you want. For some people, a rustic cabin in the woods is perfect. Others prefer the luxury of a swimming pool and modern kitchen. Do not rely on the assurances of an owner without seeing the place.

2. No matter how reliable the landlord seems, get your lease in writing. Make certain that it specifies which months the house will be available to you; how much it will cost; and whether gas, electricity, water, and facilities such as tennis courts and beach rights are included. The lease should also state that there are no "hidden expenses," such as garbage removal or beach fees, and specify a date for the return of your security deposit.

3. Some towns have passed ordinances to prevent group rentals. Contact local authorities in the area where the house is located to make sure that municipal zoning ordinances do not interfere with your renting plans. Also, make certain that the names of all persons renting with you are on the lease.

4. Should any of the people who share the house with you fail to pay their portion of the rent or damage the landlord's furniture, you as a cotenant may be held liable. It is important, therefore, to think seriously about your cotenants' reliability.

5. Just prior to occupancy, examine household appliances and furnishings, and call to the attention of your landlord existing damage. Ask him to acknowledge this damage in writing so you won't be blamed for it later. Get a written inventory of household items so there is no later allegation of theft.

6. Work out an agreement in advance with your cotenants regarding guests, cash expenditures, and the like. If you don't want a steady stream of your summer roommates' friends visiting for the weekend, that should be understood at the beginning. Similarly, an agreement about who pays for food and other household items will prevent future misunderstandings.

7. Make certain that the house is properly insured, either by you or the landlord, for possible personal injury and property damage.

A cabinet falls and breaks your china—must your landlord pay the damages?

Q. I rent an apartment and keep my dishes in a built-in cabinet above the kitchen sink. Last week, without any warning, the cabinet fell off the wall, smashing virtually all of my china. The landlord says he'll repair the cabinet but refuses to pay for the dishes, because the cabinet was installed thirty years ago and, in his words, "everything breaks sometime." Must he reimburse me for the broken china?

A. Probably, yes. Like closets, cabinet space is a factor that attracts tenants to rent an apartment. If you had known the cabinet was unusable, you might not have chosen the apartment. Once you became a tenant, you were entitled to assume that it was functional.

Needless to say, if you abused the cabinet by filling it with cement blocks, your landlord would not be liable for the loss of your china.

Likewise, if you knew the cabinet was coming loose but failed to ask for repairs, a court would probably decide against you. However, in the absence of such circumstances, the odds are against your landlord escaping liability even though "everything breaks sometime." If he felt the cabinet might break, he had an obligation to check regularly on its condition. Your claim for broken dishes is just as sound in theory as a claim for a broken arm would be if the cabinet had fallen on you and caused injury.

What landlords must do about crime

Q. Last month my husband was robbed in the lobby of our building. Neither of us knows how the assailant got past the front door, as it is supposed to be locked at all times. But we do know that security in the building is extremely lax, and the landlord has refused numerous requests by us and our neighbors to do something about it. Can the landlord be held liable for our losses?

A. Quite possibly, yes. Landlords used to be considered immune from liability for this type of incident, but rising crime rates, coupled with landlord neglect, have led many courts to reevaluate the matter. The law still leans toward the landlord, but a growing number of judges have held that, when a landlord fails to take reasonable precautions to protect tenants from crime, he can be held liable for the damage that results.

Keep in mind that the law does not require a landlord to turn his building into an armed fort. Only *reasonable* standards—such as working locks and adequate lighting—must be adhered to. Costs must be in keeping with foreseeable harm. For example, a landlord is not required to hire doormen for what was previously a nondoorman building. But, conversely, if a building intercom or front-door lock is broken and the landlord fails to make repairs, he is considered negligent and may be held responsible for any crimes that result. (The tenant's case will be strengthened considerably if the landlord had written notice of the defective condition before the crime and failed to fix it.)

In addition to negligence, your landlord might also be held liable on grounds of breach of contract. For example, tenants in a doorman building or in a building with a particularly advanced security system are entitled to have these services maintained until the lease expires or, in some areas, even after the lease has been renewed. Should these services be discontinued, the landlord will have violated the lease, and the tenant will be entitled to damages from any crimes that result.

Your case involves a rapidly changing area of the law. If the loss suffered by your husband was great enough, he should consult a lawyer about the possibility of filing suit or start an action himself. Also, you and your neighbors should consider banding together and hiring an attorney to sue for a court order requiring the landlord to improve building security immediately.

Penalty charges for late payment of rent

Q. I rent an apartment. My lease states that the rent is due on the first day of each month and that a penalty charge will be added for each day it is late. Is this charge lawful?

A. Maybe not. A lease is a contract between a landlord and a tenant, de fining the rights and obligations of each party. If the lease requires that the rent be paid on the first of the month, the tenant is required to pay on that date. However, this requirement does not mean that the landlord can automatically levy a penalty charge. And, in some cases, no matter what the lease says, a penalty charge is not lawful.

In areas such as New York City, where rent-stabilization and rent-control laws strictly limit the rent a landlord can charge, the general rule is that landlords may not impose administrative fees, interest charges, or any other financial burden for late payment without a court order.

Even without rent-control laws, the penalty charge may be illegal. Under the federal Truth in Lending Act, the terms of a finance charge must be "clearly and conspicuously" disclosed to the consumer before it can be levied. If your lease (or almost any other credit agreement, for that matter) falls to spell out the conditions, timing, and amount of an interest penalty, the law will lean in your favor.

I should add that virtually all states have laws that prohibit "usury"— the charging of unconscionably high interest rates on money owed (the lawful amount varies from state to state). If the penalty is excessive, it might also violate these statutes.

Forcing landlords to make repairs

Q. I live in an apartment and am constantly frustrated by my landlord's slowness in making repairs. If the oven breaks down, it takes ten days to fix it. I've waited as long as a month for the superintendent to repair a leaking faucet. Are there any legal steps I can take to speed things up?

A. When you signed the lease for your apartment, you entered into a contract with your landlord that entitled him to receive rent and provided you with certain guarantees. One of these guarantees, known as a "warranty of habitability," requires that everything necessary for an apartment to be safe and livable be provided. And, whether or not it's specifically stated in your lease, this guarantee requires that faulty fixtures will be repaired by the landlord at the landlord's own expense, unless you have caused the damage through misuse. These guarantees do not mean that all repairs must be made within twenty-four hours—obviously, some distinction must be made between the danger of a gas leak and the inconvenience of a broken dishwasher—but all repairs must be made within a "reasonable" period of time.

If they aren't, there are several steps you can take. First, most municipalities have special housing courts where tenants can file a complaint without a lawyer. You could also send your landlord a letter by certified mail warning him that, if the repairs aren't made immediately, you will hire a contractor yourself and deduct the cost from your monthly rent. If you choose to follow this route, make certain that you get a receipt from the contractor and find out if he would be willing to appear in court, if necessary.

Under particularly damning circumstances, you might even be justified in withholding rent altogether. For example, if facts indicate that your landlord has made it a policy to refuse repairs in order to force tenants to leave the building, he might not be entitled to further rent until all broken items are fixed. However, withholding rent might expose you to the risk of eviction, and thus you should not take this step without getting legal advice first.

When the landlord says clogged plumbing is your fault

Q. The bathtub drain in my apartment frequently clogs up. The landlord claims it's due to my hair and shampoo, and he refuses to make any repairs unless I pay for the plumber. What are my legal rights?

A. You are entitled to repairs free of charge. You as a tenant are required to pay rent; your landlord is obligated to make sure, among other things, that the plumbing can accommodate normal usage. If the clogging was caused by your misuse—for instance, if you potted plants in the tub and allowed large amounts of soil to go down the drain—then you might be held liable. But a tenant's shampooing hair in the bathtub—a logical place to do it—is entirely within the bounds of reason.

Your best first step would be to send your landlord a letter demanding that the repairs be made immediately. Then, if he refuses, you can take your case to small claims court or to the housing tribunal in the area where you live. Most likely, you'll be able to proceed without hiring a lawyer. And, if complaints of this nature are common in your building, consider joining together with other residents to form a tenants' committee. This will enable all of you to pursue your legal rights more effectively.

Landlords who refuse to rent to families with children

Q. My husband and I have two children, ages three and five. Recently, a landlord refused to rent to us, saying that he wanted to limit the number of young children in his apartment complex. Is this legal?

A. Maybe not. Traditionally, landlords were allowed to discriminate at will in apartment rentals. However, over the past two decades, numerous state and federal laws have made discrimination on the basis of sex, race, religion, and comparable factors unlawful for most apartments in most areas of the country. Some states have outlawed discrimination on the basis of marital status, and the practice of refusing rentals to parents with young children has now been challenged.

In New York, for example, the state legislature has passed a law declaring that landlords who refuse to rent to a family solely because there are children are guilty of a misdemeanor. In addition to the criminal penalties that can result from violation of this statute, an aggrieved party can institute civil proceedings demanding monetary damages and obtain a court order entitling the family to tenancy in the apartment or a comparable dwelling. The prohibition against discrimination does not apply to one- and two-family owner-occupied apartments. Certain federally funded senior housing units are also exempt. Additionally, recent amendments to the federal Fair Housing Act outlaw discrimination based on "familial status" in many instances.

Your best first step would be to contact the attorney general's office in the state where you live. Someone there will advise you more fully regarding your legal rights.

Bugging the landlord to de-bug a building

Q. The building I live in is infested with bugs, and despite my efforts to keep a clean apartment, I'm frequently besieged by cockroaches and other insects. I've complained to the landlord on several occasions, but he has done nothing. Are there any legal steps I can take?

A. The law requires that every landlord provide tenants with safe, sanitary, livable housing. This requirement is a contractual guarantee implied by law in every residential lease. And, depending on the area where you live and the circumstances of your case, if the warranty is breached, you can 1) withhold rent, 2) pay the rent and sue for damages, or 3) break the lease and move elsewhere.

In determining whether the insect problem in your building is serious enough to constitute a breach of warranty, you should consider these factors: Has the landlord violated local health-code regulations? How serious is the effect of the situation on your health and safety? How long has the condition existed? What steps has the landlord taken to remedy the matter? Are you in any in any way responsible? (Are you prone, for instance, to leaving food out on the kitchen counter overnight?)

If, after weighing these considerations, you continue to feel that the landlord is at fault, you should report him to the board of health as well as to local housing authorities. The latter will advise you regarding the most effective way to pursue your case.

Operating a business in your home

Q. Several months ago I began operating a part-time business from my home. Now my landlord is threatening to evict me on grounds that my lease restricts use of the apartment to "strictly residential purposes." What are my legal rights?

A. That will depend on several factors. First, you should look at the specific wording of your lease. Despite your landlord's claim, it might not prohibit use of the apartment for business purposes. Moreover, even if it does and your landlord goes to court, the judge may well decide in your favor. Many people conduct business at home. Teachers prepare lesson plans in their apartment; authors write; lawyers confer with clients. As long as your business activity is unobtrusive and causes no harm to the landlord or other tenants, the court could find that the lease was not violated in substantial enough fashion to constitute breach of contract on your part. And, in any event, it is unlikely that a court will order your eviction. If the conduct of business is deemed improper, the judge would be far more likely to simply order that the offending conduct cease.

If your landlord persists in threatening you, you should consult with an attorney regarding the law in the area where you live. Then, armed with legal advice, you will know how to proceed best.

Emergency apartment repairs—who pays?

Q. I rent an apartment. Last month a pipe in my kitchen burst, flooding the floor. Both the landlord and the superintendent were unavailable, so I called a plumber to shut the water off. Without his quick help, the entire apartment would have been flooded. Now the landlord is refusing to reimburse me for the $30 I spent. He says I'm the one who has to pay the plumber since I hired him. Is he correct?

A. Unless you have left some relevant fact unmentioned, this is a case where the law is on your side. Running water is an essential service, and your landlord has a duty to keep the plumbing in your apartment in working order. Had you not been available to call for help, the resulting damage to your carpets, furniture, and so on, could have equaled thousands of dollars, and the landlord would have been liable. By calling a plumber, you decreased the damage considerably. Your landlord should be thankful for your action, and—whether he is or not—he must reimburse you for the amount you paid the plumber.

Keep in mind, though, that I am presupposing that the pipe break was not your fault. If you were chipping away with a chisel at some rust on a pipe and your hand slipped, breaking the pipe in two, it would hardly be fair to hold the landlord responsible. Likewise, if you installed heavy-duty kitchen appliances in breach of a clause in your lease that warned of limited plumbing and prohibited the installation of a dishwasher or similar equipment, the law would be against you.

The best forum for your case will probably be small claims court. You may proceed there without hiring a lawyer, and you'll be reimbursed for your expenses as provided by the law. Also, some localities have special landlord-tenant courts or housing tribunals. If you live in an area that does, you will also have the option of filing a complaint with one of these bodies. Then, should you prevail, you will be allowed simply to deduct the $30 from your next month's rent check.

What should I do to stop my landlord from overcharging me?

Q. I live in an apartment and learned recently that my landlord has been charging me $15 a month more than he is entitled to under our local rent-control law. Is there anything I can do to get my money back and prevent my landlord from overcharging me again?

A. Yes, there is. You can file a civil suit and also, possibly, institute criminal proceedings against the landlord.

The means for enforcing rent-control laws vary from state to state. However, if you contact municipal housing authorities or the state attorney general's office in the area where you live, they will tell you how best to proceed.

In a civil suit, you will be entitled to a refund of past overpayments plus a court order that the landlord not overcharge you in the future. Moreover, in some areas, such as New York City, a landlord who overcharges can be held liable for triple the amount of the overcharge, court costs, and the tenant's attorney's fees, if a lawyer has been retained.

In addition, if your landlord has intentionally overcharged you, he would appear to be guilty of larceny or fraud—both criminal offenses.

My advice would be for you to write a letter to your landlord requesting a full refund and rent adjustment. Then, if he refuses, report the matter to your local district attorney's office for investigation, and take whatever civil steps are recommended by local authorities.

Is it legal for a landlord to refuse to rent an apartment to a woman just because she is single?

Q. Our daughter graduated from college recently, has a steady job, and would like to rent an apartment. Last month she found one that was attractive and well within her means, but the landlord refused to rent to her because she is a single woman. Is he legally entitled to do this? And if not, what can our daughter do about it?

A. Most states have laws that prohibit sex discrimination in the rental of apartments. Thus, your daughter should first contact her state attorney general's office for advice. Then, if help is not forthcoming, she can turn to the federal government for assistance.

Under the federal Fair Housing Act, landlords are forbidden to discriminate on the basis of sex in the rental of apartments. The act does not apply to certain single-family dwellings and small buildings where the owner lives on the premises, but virtually all other apartments are covered. Moreover, in addition to outright refusals to rent, the law extends to discrimination in the terms of a lease (such as refusing to paint or charging a higher rent for women) and inequality of facilities (for example, a landlord cannot reserve the most desirable apartments for men).

The Fair Housing Act is administered by the United States Department of Housing and Urban Development (HUD). Within 180 days of the date that the alleged discriminatory practice occurred, your daughter should file a written complaint with HUD, stating the facts of her case. HUD will then investigate the matter and seek to rectify the situation "by informal methods of conference, conciliation, and persuasion." If this falls and HUD is unable to obtain voluntary compliance (or finds your daughter's claim to be without merit), your daughter still has the option of filing suit against the landlord for monetary damages and a court order that will prevent the landlord from repeating such discriminatory practices in the future.

What can I do about a landlord who refuses to paint my apartment according to the terms of my lease?

Q. My landlord is obligated to paint my apartment every three years. This month, when I reminded him that three years had passed since the last painting, he told me that there was a "backlog" of apartments in need of painting and that he would get to it "within the next six months." I'd like my apartment painted now—not every three-and-a-half or four years, which is what the landlord is trying to impose on me. Do I have a legal right to painting now?

A. Yes, you do. If you had a "backlog" of bills, you'd still be obligated to pay your rent on time and your landlord would hardly consent to payment "within the next six months." In your case as you describe it, you have a right to painting now, and you should pursue that right just as you would pursue your rights if the landlord failed to make necessary repairs.

Every municipality in the country has at least one court empowered to deal with landlord-tenant matters, and in a case such as yours the tenant can usually proceed without need of a lawyer. In some areas, special housing tribunals handle this type of case, while in others small claims court is the best place to proceed.

Your first step should be to contact local housing authorities and ask which court generally resolves matters of this nature in the area where you live. Then you should file a suit. If you are successful, the court will most likely order the landlord to paint the apartment, award you an amount equal to what it would cost to paint, or reduce your rent until the apartment is painted. Also, if the landlord's conduct is particularly egregious, the court might award punitive damages.

In some areas, you might also be entitled to conduct a one-person rent strike—that is, simply not pay your rent until the landlord paints your apartment. However, the danger here is that the landlord might argue successfully that you defaulted on your obligations under the lease. Thus, I would not recommend withholding rent unless you are specifically advised to do so by an attorney familiar with your case.

When a landlord wants you to move out because you let a friend move in

Q. Several months ago I invited a friend to share my apartment to defray, expenses. Now the landlord is threatening to evict us, claiming that my roommate is an unauthorized tenant. Is he right?

A. To find out, first look at your lease. It may say nothing about apartment sharing, in which case the law will lean in your favor. However, many leases contain a clause specifically limiting occupancy to the tenant named on the lease and members of his or her immediate family, and, if your lease contains such a provision, you'll have to look further for relief.

One possibility is that the landlord's behavior has amounted to "constructive acceptance" of your friend as a tenant. For example, if the landlord knew that your roommate was living in the apartment but did nothing about it for several months, a court might consider that to be an implied acceptance of your friend as a tenant. This would be true, to an even greater degree, if the landlord accepted checks from your roommate in payment of the rent.

Even if yours isn't a case of "constructive acceptance," a court might still rule in your favor. A decade ago, in New York, when a landlord tried to evict a tenant for having an "unauthorized" roommate, the court decided that, despite restrictions in the lease, both the tenant and his roommate should be allowed to stay because of the severe housing shortage in that city. It concluded: "In the housing field, these are not ordinary times. . . . It is simply no longer feasible or desirable to mechanically impose eviction for breach of the immediate-family clause." Other court decisions took issue with this theory, leaving the law in flux. Then the New York State legislature passed a law declaring it unlawful for a landlord to restrict occupancy of a residential unit to a tenant and his immediate family.

Your best first step would be to try to work out a reasonable settlement with your landlord. He could, for instance, agree to add your roommate's name to the lease in exchange for a higher rent. If you can't reach a settlement, consider waiting for your landlord to bring the case to court. In general, housing-court judges are extremely sympathetic to responsible tenants, and, even if your roommate is forced to leave, it is highly unlikely that you will be evicted.

How can I get my landlord to provide my apartment with adequate heat?

Q. Every winter my landlord fails to provide my apartment with enough heat. How can I get the heat I am entitled to?

A. Virtually every state in the country has laws that require landlords to provide adequate heat when the weather turns cold. In New York, for example, the Multiple Dwelling Law imposes heating requirements from October 1 through May 31. Under that law, indoor temperatures must be maintained at a minimum of 68 degrees Fahrenheit from 6:00 A.M. through 10:00 P.M. when the temperature outside drops below

55 degrees. (After 10:00 P.M., apartment temperatures must be kept at 55 degrees or above if it is below 40 degrees outside.)

Housing authorities in your area will be able to advise you about local heating requirements and are empowered to take legal action against landlords who do not comply with the law.

If their action is not fast or forceful enough, you may choose to hire a private attorney. The attorney can seek a court order that adequate heat be provided, supervise the withholding of rent until the situation is remedied, or help you break your lease and move to a better maintained apartment.

You should first send a sternly worded letter to your landlord, demanding that adequate heat be provided. State that you are prepared to enforce your legal rights and will not back down simply because he threatens or ignores you. When your landlord realizes that you mean business, he might comply with the law. If not, you will have adequate remedies available.

Can my landlord veto apartment alterations?

Q. I would like to improve my apartment by hanging wallpaper and installing built-in bookshelves, but several friends have told me that I can't make these changes without my landlord's approval. Is this true?

A. It might be, since most leases specifically require approval.

If your landlord agrees to the changes, there's no problem. Simply get written proof of consent.

If your landlord opposes changes, you can still proceed as long as you don't structurally affect the premises or make changes that constitute "alterations." For instance, improvements such as putting up wallpaper that can be removed with steam or polyurethaning the floor (which would enhance but not change the floor's essential character) would most likely be acceptable. Laying linoleum over a parquet floor would not. Renovating a bathroom would also fall into the not-acceptable category, because "improvements" like expensive fixtures might later prove difficult or costly for the landlord to maintain.

Keep in mind, however, that even with leases that do not specifically preclude alterations, tenants still have an implied obligation to leave their premises in substantially the same condition in which they found them, minus wear and tear.

Is my landlord liable when belongings stored in the basement are stolen?

Q. Several years ago, with the landlord's permission, I stored a sofa in the basement of my building. Recently the sofa was stolen. The landlord refuses to reimburse me for the loss, claiming that the storage was free and all items are stored at the owner's risk. What are my rights?

A. This is a close case, but you might be able to recover damages.

A landlord is not an insurer. Unlike a warehouse operator who charges a fee to store items for safekeeping, the landlord cannot always be held responsible for loss. He is expected to exercise a reasonable standard of care in safeguarding items that are in storage, however, and if he does not he may be liable for negligence.

First, find out what led to the theft. Did the landlord leave a regularly locked area of the basement unlocked? Were delivery men allowed to roam unattended through the storage area? If you can show that the landlord was careless in protecting your property and that this led to the theft, a court will probably rule in your favor.

Your case will be more difficult to win if the landlord made it clear when you stored the sofa that all items were stored at the owner's risk. Under those circumstances, you would be required to prove that the landlord was guilty of gross negligence in order to recover. Standards for what constitutes gross negligence are imprecise, but usually it is conduct that shocks the conscience—for example, if the landlord ignored reports that property was being stolen regularly from the basement.

You should first send the landlord a letter stating your claim and asking reimbursement from him or his insurance company. If you don't receive a fair settlement offer, you can file suit in small-claims court.

Can the landlord enter my apartment without my permission?

Q. The landlord in my building has a key to each apartment for emergency purposes. On occasion, however, he lets himself into apartments simply to make certain that no damage has been done to his property. Is this lawful?

A. No, it isn't. Even though many leases do require a tenant to leave keys with the landlord, those keys should be used only for emergency purposes, such as when a gas line breaks or a water pipe bursts. If your landlord simply wants to check on the condition of your apartment, he should make an appointment with you beforehand.

The best thing for you to do is send a letter to your landlord demanding that he limit his visits to genuine emergencies. Then, if his conduct persists, you can proceed against him in small-claims court or a special housing court, if there is one in your area.

Chapter 3

Owning Your Own Home

Do I need a lawyer when I buy a house?

Q. My husband and I are planning to purchase a house from a couple we have known for years. They have suggested that their lawyer handle the closing for both families in order to save money. Do we need our own lawyer?

A. Yes, you do. Buying a house is an extremely complex undertaking, and it is important that you be represented by someone who has your best interests in mind. If you and the seller are represented by the same counsel, unforeseen problems might arise.

For example, in purchasing a house, you as the buyer want to be sure that you are receiving "good title." Does the seller have a faulty deed? Are there any outstanding claims against the property? Does the house satisfy municipal zoning ordinances? Many of these questions are matters of subtle legal interpretation, and you will want written guarantees that you are fully protected.

Conversely, it is only natural for the seller to guarantee as little as possible. It would be extremely difficult, if not impossible, for one lawyer to represent both sides with appropriate aggressiveness and competence.

No one enjoys paying money to a lawyer. But, in this instance, it's an expense that will help safeguard your financial standing in the future.

Eight months ago our house was painted, and now the paint is peeling. Can we get our money back?

Q. Eight months ago my husband and I hired a man to paint the outside of our house. Two months after he finished the job, the paint began to peel. Six months later it looked as though our house hadn't been painted in years. The paint job cost $1,000. Is there any way we can get a refund or a new paint job?

A. There might be. At first glance, your case appears to involve a breach of contract. You hired a painter to perform a service in a professional manner, and he apparently failed to do so. However, the outcome of your case will probably hinge on the reason why the paint began to peel. If, for example, the painter used inferior-quality paint, then you would be entitled to your money back. Likewise, if he knew it would be necessary to scrape the old paint off your house before the new paint was applied and neither told you this nor did the scraping, you would be entitled to recover some money. However, if the painter recommended that the old paint be scraped but warned that this would cost an additional $500, a court might find that you assumed the risk of peeling if you told him to paint at the cheaper price without scraping.

As with most disputes, your best first step is to contact the painter to see if he is willing to settle the matter. Perhaps he will offer a fair refund or a new paint job. Should settlement prove impossible, you can always sue. To bolster your case in the event you do wind up in court, you should take several photographs that show the degenerating condition of your house. Also, it would be wise to ask your neighbors if they know of similar complaints lodged against the painter. Your local consumer affairs bureau might also have complaints on file. Obviously, a court will lean in your favor if this has been a recurring problem, and it will strengthen your claim that it is the painter's sloppy work rather than some other miscellaneous factor that has caused the peeling.

Paying the broker when you change your mind about selling

Q. Several months ago my husband and I decided to sell our house. We contacted a real-estate broker and put the house on the market at a price he recommended. One week later we had a buyer, but by then we also had second thoughts about selling and took our house off the market. Now, though no sale took place, the broker is demanding a commission. Is he entitled to one?

A. Unfortunately, he might be. When you and the broker put your house on the market, you entered into a contract. He performed his end of the bargain by delivering a buyer and now expects to be reimbursed.

In sorting out your obligations, you should first reread any written contract signed by you and the broker. What does it say about "second thoughts" or a "change of heart"? Is there an escape clause that allows you to withdraw from the agreement? If so, you might not be liable.

Otherwise, you'll have to dig a little deeper for relief. One way you could escape liability would be to show that the broker failed to perform his part of the bargain in a professional manner. For instance, if the price he recommended was unreasonably low and you later realized that the house was worth far more than he suggested, then the broker simply failed to perform as required by the contract. (Unscrupulous brokers may price a house low for the easy commission that a quick sale brings—which means that they're providing less than professional service for their clients.)

Also, it's possible that the prospective buyer did not actually have the money to buy the house and would have been unable to arrange financing. Here again, unless the broker can prove the buyer's ability to pay, you will not be liable.

The burden of suing and proving the case will rest on the broker's shoulders. However, if he was scrupulous and did a lot of work showing the house to different people, the court might award him commission. Thus, rather than wait for him to bring suit against you, the best thing would be for you or your lawyer to discuss the matter directly with the broker. In all likelihood, if both sides negotiate in good faith, a fair settlement can be reached.

Hiring a contractor

Q. My husband and I are planning to redo our kitchen completely. What steps should we take in dealing with the building contractor to safeguard our legal rights?

A. First, you will have to be careful in choosing a contractor. In many areas, home-improvement contractors must be licensed to do business. Telephone your local department of consumer affairs or Better Business Bureau to make certain his license is current and that no complaints have been lodged against him. Ask to see his certificate of workers' compensation insurance, so you won't be held liable if a worker is injured while in your home. As for the contract itself, include the following clauses in writing:

1. A binding estimate, specifying the cost and all work to be completed

2. A list of brand names and model numbers for all the materials and appliances to be installed

3. Warranties for these materials and appliances

4. A specified completion date, with penalties for late performance

5. A provision requiring the contractor to display necessary work permits

6. Guaranteed compliance with building codes and zoning ordinances

7. A provision requiring that the contractor clean up the jobsite and haul away all debris at his own expense

8. A payment schedule allowing you to withhold a reasonable amount until the job is completed

In addition, you should make certain that the contractor pays all subcontractors and suppliers. Otherwise, in the event they are not satisfied with his treatment of them, they could put a lien on your home. To protect yourself, insert a clause in the contract requiring the contractor to provide you with written proof that all of his payment obligations have been met.

Read the final contract carefully. Make sure you understand every word in it. A reputable contractor will not object to your questions and will understand your desire to protect your legal rights.

Refunds for landscaping

Q. Six months ago my husband and I paid a gardener to landscape our property. Now several of the more expensive bushes are dead, and the gardener refuses to give us a refund or to replace the bushes. What are our legal rights?

A. The answer depends on whether the gardener fulfilled his contractual obligation to plant healthy bushes in a professional manner.

If you failed to water the bushes as instructed or they were killed off by an unexpected frost, the gardener can't be held responsible. But if other factors were involved, he could be Iiable. Were the bushes poorly planted? Did he fail to give you adequate instruction about proper care? Were they a type of plant that has trouble surviving in the climate or soil of the area where you live? Were they unhealthy, with poor root systems or some disease? If the bushes died for reasons like these, the gardener would have failed to fulfill his contractual obligations, and you would be entitled to a refund or replacement.

Your best first step would be to send the gardener a letter stating your case. Then, if you don't get a satisfactory response, take the matter to your local consumer affairs bureau or pursue it in small claims court.

We recently bought a house and had to make unexpected repairs. Can we force the previous owner to reimburse us?

Q. Last year my husband and I bought a house. Two months after we moved in, we discovered that part of the furnace wall had disintegrated, leaving a large hole. The repairs will cost well over $1,000. Is there any way we can force the previous owner to reimburse us for all or part of this expense?

A. Probably not. Two states (New Jersey and Minnesota) have laws requiring limited warranty protection for the purchasers of new houses, and some houses are covered by voluntary builders' warranties. However, this protection does not normally extend to the resale of houses, and about 10 percent of the Americans who buy houses from previous owners this year will be forced to make unforeseen major repairs within twelve months of their purchase.

If you can prove that during negotiations the previous owner deliberately misrepresented the condition of the furnace, a court might rule in your favor. Also, it's possible that some unexpired portion of the original furnace warranty still exists. However, in the absence of these or other qualifying circumstances, your chances for recovery are bleak. Unfortunately, your experience demonstrates the advisability of retaining a capable attorney when you purchase a house. A well-drafted closing agreement would have, in your case, included a guarantee by the seller that the heating, plumbing, and electrical wiring were all in good shape, and thus would have better protected your legal rights.

What happens when you purchase a home—and then a highway is built nearby?

Q. When my husband and I bought a house in a quiet suburban neighborhood a year ago, we didn't know that a major highway was going to be built nearby. Now the value of our property will drop, and the noise will be intolerable. Do we have any legal recourse?

A. You might, depending on what the seller and broker knew at the time of purchase and whether they took steps to cover up that knowledge.

As a general rule, a broker works for the seller and has no duty to disclose information to the buyer. This does not mean, however, that sellers and brokers have a license to act dishonestly. If they knew that the highway was about to be built and simply didn't tell you, it will be difficult for you to win a price rebate. But, if you can prove that they actually took steps to conceal their knowledge—for instance, showing the house only on Sundays, when surveying crews were off duty—you will have a better case. And, if they out and out lied to you, you'll be entitled to void the purchase or sue for a rebate on the grounds of misrepresentation and fraud.

The purchase of a house is the largest investment most families ever make, and it is enormously important for you to safeguard your rights. The best way for you to do so is to retain legal counsel.

Unjoining a joint house purchase

Q. Several years ago a friend and I purchased a summer house together. Now I want to sell, but my friend doesn't. How can I extricate myself without losing the fair value of my holdings?

A. First, examine the deed and all papers relevant to the purchase of the house and see what they say about ownership, sale of the property, and the like. In all likelihood, these documents will provide a way for you to reach a fair settlement with your friend, the most obvious solution being for you to sell your interest in the property to her or to a third party. However, if this proves impossible, you can file an "action for partition."

Under an action for partition, the court will order your summer house to be sold, with the proceeds to be divided up between the owners. Or, if your friend should decide to purchase your interest in the house, the court will determine a fair price. Either way, you will be compensated fairly.

Real-estate transactions can be complex, however, and this is an instance in which you would be better off with a lawyer. In the future, should you decide on another joint real-estate purchase, be sure to draw up a written contract between you and your partner, including a specific "exit" clause to deal with contingencies of this nature.

House sales—exclusive listing

Q. When my husband and I put our house up for sale, we signed an "exclusive" listing with a broker. Now a potential buyer has been recommended to us by a friend. If we sell to this buyer, will we be obligated to pay a commission to the broker, who has yet to deliver a purchaser?

A. That will depend on several variables. Most homeowners utilize "multiple listings" when their house is for sale—that is, they deal with several brokers, all of whom are encouraged to bring in prospective customers. However, some sellers opt for "exclusive" listings, which limit their dealings to one broker. The advantage in an exclusive listing is that it encourages a broker to work particularly hard on the sale of a house. The disadvantage is that it forecloses potential customers from other sources.

As for the specifics of your case, much will depend on the wording of your written contract with the broker. For example, many contracts for exclusive listings contain a "private sale clause"—to wit, if the owner sells the house to someone introduced by a friend or relative, then no commission is owed to the broker. Other contracts distinguish between "exclusive listings" and an "exclusive right of sale." The latter gives greater control to the broker in that it forecloses potential customers from other sources. Also, most contracts for exclusive listings contain an expiration date at which time the broker's right of exclusivity comes to an end. Where no such date is written into a contract, the courts will infer that expiration was intended "within a reasonable period of time."

Your best first step would be to study the contract carefully to determine your rights and obligations. Then, armed with this knowledge, either you can sell the house without paying a commission or make a reasonable settlement offer to the broker. In future dealings of this kind, however, keep in mind that you as a seller have the power to dictate reasonable terms in contracting with a broker. Brokers need clients in order to make a living. And if one broker's terms aren't to your liking, you can always take your business to another.

Transfer of homeowner warranties

Q. My husband and I are planning to purchase a house. When we do, will the present owner's warranty rights against the builder, the boiler manufacturer, and other contractors be transferred to us, or will those warranty rights expire when the house is sold to us?

A. That will depend on several factors.

In the absence of a clause to the contrary, warranties may be assigned like other contracts. Thus, if they do not specifically forbid assignment, most likely the seller of the house will be able to transfer them to you. Also, since most warranties are for a limited period of time, you will want to know the point at which the warranties expire.

To secure your rights in this area, you should read all of the present owner's warranties carefully. The contract you sign to purchase the house should provide that all such warranties are transferred to you to the greatest extent possible. And, since the present owner might destroy his records or be difficult to locate at a later date, you should get copies of his cancelled checks and all other warranty-related material now. This might involve a modicum of extra work at the time you purchase the house, but it will be well worth it to you in the long run. Transferring warranty protection costs a house seller nothing, and it could save you as the buyer thousands of dollars.

A noisy factory opens nearby

Q. I've lived in the same house for twenty years. Six months ago a cement plant opened a block away and, since then, the noise has been unbearable. Trucks load and unload at all hours of the day and night. The mixer causes my house to vibrate. What are my legal rights?

A. Most likely, there will be several steps you can take. First, it's possible that the cement plant is violating local zoning regulations or "noise pollution" ordinances. If so, local authorities will pursue your case for you. If not, you still might be able to proceed against the plant, claiming that its operation constitutes a "nuisance." The law of nuisance provides that all people have the right to reasonable comfort in their homes. This does not mean that every petty annoyance and disturbance must be stopped. Indeed, factories are allowed to function and noisy airports operate day and night in many areas of the country. However, substantial interference with a person's comfort is actionable where the offending conduct is abnormal or out of place in its surroundings.

Whether or not the cement plant is being operated in a reasonable manner will be the big issue in your case, and the judge will consider several factors. What was the character of the neighborhood before the plant opened? Was it substantially residential or industrial? What has been the duration and frequency of the offending conduct? And, most important, has the cement plant taken all reasonable steps to curtail noise and diminish inconvenience to its neighbors? For example, is there any reason why the loading and unloading of trucks can't be limited to daylight hours?

Under the law of nuisance, the court will make a common-sense judgment as to whether the harm and annoyance caused by the plant are more than you as a private citizen should have to bear. This will involve balancing rights and obligations; and, in the end, you may well prevail.

Your local bar association (listed in the telephone directory) can provide you with a list of counsel qualified to handle the matter at a reasonable rate. Should you win, the court will award you damages for past inconvenience and order the cement plant to modify its operation or cease doing business altogether in your neighborhood.

Cooperatives versus condominiums

Q. My husband and I currently rent an apartment and are thinking of buying a home. What would be the difference between our buying a condominium and a cooperative apartment?

A. A cooperative is a corporation. Technically, you as a purchaser buy stock in that corporation, and sign a proprietary lease for the apartment that is designated for your shares. As a shareholder, you'd have a say in building management to the extent of being entitled to vote for co-op officers and the board of directors. You'd also be responsible for paying monthly maintenance charges to cover the building's mortgage costs, general operating expenses, and taxes.

By contrast, with a condominium, the purchaser owns legal title to his or her actual apartment, rather than shares. Should a condominium complex fail financially, the individual owners are on their own. In that respect, the situation is different from a cooperative, where individual shareholders can be held responsible for the co-op corporation's debts. However, a failed condominium is no bargain. And your own direct upkeep costs plus maintenance costs for condominium community areas such as the lobby or garden will generally equal coop maintenance payments.

Depending on the state where you live and your own financial situation, there might be certain tax advantages to owning a coop rather than a condominium — or vice versa. Talk with an accountant to find out which investment is best for you. But don't lose sight of the fact that taxes are just one component of an investment. Purchase price, monthly maintenance costs, and the desirability of your home are usually much more important considerations.

When the lot you buy is ill-suited for a home

Q. My husband and I bought an out-of-state lot from a real estate developer in anticipation of building a house on the property and moving there. Now, however, we realize that the land was overpriced and not suited to residential use. Can we get our money back?

A. Quite possibly, yes. To protect consumers, Congress has passed the Interstate Land Sales Act, administered by the Department of Housing and Urban Development. This law applies to most sellers who offer 100 or more unimproved lots for sale.

Under the act, a seller must provide potential buyers with a detailed property report, containing information on such items as the availability of utilities and sewage disposal, local schools, hospitals, transportation systems, site financing, local ordinances, zoning regulations, and development plans for the property. If you did not receive this report prior to signing your purchase contract, you may cancel and receive a full refund any time within two years of the signing date. If you did receive the report but it contained false information, you may cancel on grounds of fraud. And, even if you received an accurate property report prior to signing, federal law gives you the right to cancel before midnight on the seventh day following the signing. The law is applicable regardless of whether or not you personally inspected the lot before purchase. Violation of the law by a seller is a felony.

If you believe you've been cheated, write to HUD/ Office of Interstate Land Sales Registration, 451 Seventh Street, S.W., Washington, D.C. 20410. In your letter, state the specific details of your complaint, and include copies of the sales contract, cancelled checks, and all promotional literature. Also, prior to your next purchase, you should write HUD at the above address for a copy of the pamphlet *Buying Lots From Developers.*

What to do when your building undergoes a conversion

Q. I live in a rental apartment, and the landlord is trying to convert the building to condominium or cooperative apartments. What steps should I take to protect my rights?

A. Although laws regulating conversions vary widely, there are several steps you should take.

First, tenants must be unified and well-informed. Form a tenant's committee, and hire a lawyer who will monitor the situation and protect your rights. The lawyer should draft a "no-buy pledge" for each tenant to sign. This pledge is a binding contract among tenants who promise to negotiate as a group against the landlord and who agree that they won't buy until the landlord offers terms that satisfy a specified percentage of tenants signing the pledge.

Then, when the landlord submits a formal offering, the lawyer and other tenants' committee members should analyze its items and proceed to:

• Hire an accountant (or recruit one from the tenant roster) to examine the landlord's financial statements.

• Hire an engineer to examine the building carefully.

• Compare your apartment with other cooperative and condominium conversions in the neighborhood.

Very often, a landlord will begin coop negotiations by asking a "market price." Then—particularly if state law requires that a given percentage of tenants buy in order for the conversion to become effective and if the tenants are united—the landlord will lower the insider price to 50 percent or less of what the market might normally bear.

Be patient during negotiations. And don't sign anything the landlord offers you without the advice of your own or the tenants' committee lawyer.

Chapter 4

Marriage, Divorce, and Custody Battles

Who keeps the ring when an engagement is broken?

Q. My son and his fiancée have broken their engagement, and now she refuses to return the engagement ring. Is she legally entitled to keep it?

A. Probably not, but the answer will depend on the circumstances of their particular case.

The key issue is what your son intended when he gave his fiancée the ring. If he presented it as a permanent gift regardless of whether or not the marriage took place, then it is hers to keep. But, if her keeping the gift was contingent on their getting married, it must be returned. The problem, of course, is that newly engaged couples rarely consider breaking up at such a moment, and the issue of intent is seldom thought out, let alone spelled out. Thus, courts are likely to give considerable weight to why the engagement was broken. If your prospective daughter-in-law broke the engagement for a liaison with another man, the court would be more likely to rule against her. But if your son got "cold feet" and backed out himself, the decision might be in her favor.

Other factors will also be considered. Did the ring cost your son a large percentage of his savings? Was it a family heirloom with sentimental value? Using these guidelines, a judge will most likely do what he thinks is "fair"—something your son and his former fiancée should be able to accomplish without going to court.

I should add that, if you do take the case to court, other premarital gifts might also become part of the dispute. Generally speaking, the law distinguishes between gifts "without strings" and gifts "conditional on marriage." For example, if after the engagement your son gave his bride-to-be an expensive stereo with the words "This is for the two of us," a court might order her to return it. The same would hold true of gifts from members of the family that were clearly given with the marriage in mind.

What are the grounds for annulment?

Q. I was recently married and realize now that I've made a horrible mistake. Are there any grounds on which I can get an annulment rather than a divorce?

A. There very well may be. Unlike a divorce, which legally ends a marriage, an annulment is a legal declaration that no true marriage ever really existed.

Grounds for annulment differ from state to state. In most states, an annulment can be granted if, at the time of the marriage, one of the parties was underage, legally insane, incurably impotent, or already married to someone else. It is also generally held to be grounds for an annulment if one of the parties was forced into the marriage under duress or misled by fraud.

On the surface, this may seem like a pretty stringent list of conditions. However, in recent years, some courts have become extremely liberal in their interpretation of annulment statutes. In New York, for example, fraud has been found to exist (and a marriage thus ruled annullable) if one person misled the other before marrying with regard to his or her financial status, religious ideals, or desire to have children.

The concealment of a prior marriage, drug addiction, venereal disease, criminal convictions, homosexuality, or other circumstances has also been held to constitute fraud. In one instance, a court went so far as to annul a marriage that had lasted for over six years because, before marrying, the groom had failed to tell his bride that he derived sexual satisfaction from peeking into other people's bedroom windows. The wife claimed that, if she had known of this condition, she would never have married him. Based on her testimony, the court ruled that "fraud" existed.

Quite obviously, before you seek an annulment, you and your husband should talk things over. Then, if you still want to void the marriage, consult with a lawyer who specializes in domestic relations. It would be best if you and your husband were represented by separate counsel.

As with divorce proceedings, an annulment is more easily obtainable when both parties agree upon the break. However, your husband's cooperation is not necessarily essential, and should he oppose the annulment in court, your attorney will be able to suggest the best course of action.

Living-together contracts

Q. My boyfriend and I are thinking about living together. Both of us have responsible, well-paying jobs, but I'm still afraid of financial entanglements. Is there any type of contract that can be drawn up between us to protect our rights?

A. No set contract formula for living together exists, and needs vary from couple to couple. However, it will probably help you and your boyfriend clarify things personally if the two of you have a written understanding with regard to the following:

1. If you rent an apartment, the amount each of you will pay monthly should be clearly understood. Your agreement should also specify who will keep the apartment in the event of a split, and that person's name should be on the lease. If neither of you can afford the entire rent without help from the other, the lease should contain a cancellation clause for use in the event things do not work out between you.

2. If you buy a home rather than rent, there should be an understanding about ownership, as well as reimbursement for property improvements and other cash expenses.

3. Bank accounts may be separate or joint. As a general rule, separate accounts will help you steer clear of the financial entanglements you wish to avoid. However, you may want to consider a small joint account for day-to-day living expenses.

4. The payment of living expenses can be based on your respective salaries, divided equally, or apportioned by any other formula you choose. An understanding in advance will help avoid controversy later.

5. Ownership of major personal items, such as a car or a sofa, should be well defined, and there should be some means for dividing them fairly in the event the relationship ends.

6. Should one of you return to school or for any reason stop working, your written understanding should cover the situation where you maintain the relationship, and provide for the possibility of later reimbursement to the person who bears the financial burden during this period.

7. When a couple lives together, the possibility of pregnancy and childbirth may increase. The agreement should spell out your understanding as to the rights and obligations of you and your friend with regard to any children that may result from your union.

A "living-together contract" can be drafted by a lawyer or written in less formal fashion by you and your friend. Given the many contingencies that accompany each situation, I recommend the former. However, a self-drawn contract is usually better than none at all.

No longer living together and you want to be reimbursed

Q. For three years I lived with a man who worked for a large corporation. During that time I did not hold a steady job, but I did entertain his business associates, paint the apartment, cook, clean, take his shirts to the laundry, and run just about every other errand he asked. Last month we broke up. His career is going well, but I can't find a job. Is there any way I can force him to reimburse me for the services I performed?

A. There may be. Cohabitation without marriage has increased in recent years and, as a result, some states have begun to reexamine laws regarding situations similar to yours. For example, in California there are several ways you could win reimbursement for your services. The most obvious would be evidence of a clear understanding between you and your friend, reached before or while you were living together, that he would reimburse you in some manner if the relationship ended. Such an agreement, whether oral or written, would be as enforceable as any other contract.

In the absence of any express agreement, courts in California and elsewhere have sometimes examined the circumstances of a couple's living arrangement to determine whether reimbursement is warranted on some other ground. For example, if you had given up a well-paying job to help out at home or worked to put your friend through school, these factors would weigh in your favor and might prompt a decision on your behalf. However, even without this kind of sacrifice, a court could hold that your relationship with this man deprived you of three years' advancement in the outside world and that you were entitled to reimbursement.

Your case involves a newly developing area of the law which differs from state to state. However, you may have some chance of success and it is conceivable that the very prospect of your bringing a lawsuit with some merit to it may convince your friend to offer a reasonable compromise.

As a guide to settlement, you should know that, where reimbursement has been granted, the amount most often awarded by courts has been the value of the woman's services minus the financial support she received from her living companion. This support includes such items as rent, food, clothing, and other personal expenditures. Other courts have awarded the woman an amount that is half of the total money and property accumulated by both parties during the relationship minus their expenses.

Do-it-yourself divorce

Q. I have been separated from my husband for over a year and would like a divorce. The matter is uncontested. No children or alimony is involved, and I would like to handle things as inexpensively as possible. What is your opinion of the "do-it-yourself divorce kits" that are now on sale in some states?

A. The purpose of "do-it-yourself divorce kits" is to allow a husband and wife to obtain a divorce without having to pay an attorney. However, people who choose to "do-it-themselves" frequently regret their decision.

A typical divorce "kit" (which you can find at legal supplies stores and at some bookstores) contains an instruction sheet and copies of several legal forms to be served and filed with the court. However, domestic relations laws vary from state to state, and some kits won't apply in the state where you live or are planning to sue for divorce. Also, many kits fail to cover all of the possible problems involved in the dissolution of a marriage.

For example, you and your husband might have co-signed a loan agreement to borrow money for his college tuition. If so, even after the divorce, you might be called upon to repay whatever part of the loan your ex-husband has not repaid. Thus your divorce decree should specifically provide for payment by him. Even though such an agreement would not be binding on the lender, your ex-husband would be obligated under it. Similarly, the sale of your home or cancellation of an apartment lease could be more complicated than you think. A tax refund might be imminent or a joint investment ready to mature. It's also possible that you are entitled to alimony and don't know it.

No one enjoys paying money to a lawyer. But by the time you pay for your kit (which generally costs $10 or more, depending on the publisher and the store where the kit is sold), fill out court papers, pay the filing fee, and complete all the other steps in the divorce process, you will find that a "do-it-yourself divorce" is far more expensive than you might think. My advice would be to contact your local bar association (listed in the telephone directory) and ask for the names of several lawyers who would be willing to handle your divorce for a reasonable fee. Then, phone them and ask how much they charge. A relatively small amount paid to a competent lawyer now might save you a considerable sum of money later.

Is there any way I can force my former husband to increase his alimony payments?

Q. My former husband and I were divorced several years ago after my consenting to a separation agreement that requires him to pay me $200 a month until I remarry. At the time of our divorce, I was satisfied with this arrangement. However, since then my circumstances have changed, and I am no longer able to get by on my salary plus the $200 a month. Is there any way I can force him to increase his payments?

A. There might be, but your case will be difficult to win.

A separation agreement is a contract and, in the absence of special circumstances, courts are generally reluctant to force a change in terms once a divorce has been granted. The most frequent exception to this rule occurs when child-support payments from a former husband are inadequate. In such instances, rather than let the child suffer, a court will oftentimes intervene and reform the separation contract. Where no children are involved, court intervention is less likely.

However, there are occasions when a change in circumstances is deemed sufficient to warrant reforming the contract. If, for example, you and your husband each earned $12,000 a year at the time of your separation, and his salary has now risen dramatically while you've been forced to quit your job because of ill health, a court might intervene. Likewise, if you were coerced into signing the agreement (for example, your husband threatened to "publicly humiliate you" if you did not sign) or tricked into signing by fraud (your husband lied about the success of his financial investments at the time), a court might rule that the agreement was not voluntarily entered into and was thus invalid. The specific wording of your separation agreement and divorce decree will also play a role in determining how much leeway a court has in ordering increased alimony payments.

Your case is one that requires skilled legal advice. If you are satisfied with the lawyer who handled your separation and divorce, you should seek his help, since he is already familiar with the case.

Can I sue a woman for breaking up my marriage?

Q. My husband and I have two children and had been married for five years when he left me for another woman. I realize that our marriage was far from perfect, but my husband himself admits that if this woman hadn't pursued him, he'd still be with me today. Is there any way I can sue her for breaking up our marriage?

A. There might be. Your case appears to fall within an area of the law known as "alienation of affections."

In order for a woman to successfully sue a third party for breaking up her marriage, it is generally held that three conditions must be met. First, the "other woman" must have acted with the purpose of breaking up the relationship. Second, she must have done so in an affirmative manner (mere passive acceptance of your husband's advances would not be sufficient to sustain liability). And third, her conduct must have been a major cause of the marital break.

On the surface, this might seem like a fairly easy set of circumstances for you to prove. However, in recent years, courts have become increasingly reluctant in cases like yours to rule in the plaintiff's favor. The feeling among many judges is that they should not tell a husband whom he must love nor a woman which men she can pursue. Also, some state legislatures have enacted statutes barring lawsuits of this nature.

It might be best for you and your husband to see a marriage counselor first. Then, if the marriage appears irretrievably lost, in all likelihood your well-being will be best served by securing adequate alimony and child-support payments from your husband.

My ex-husband insists on calling me all the time—is there a way to legally stop him?

Q. My former husband and I have been divorced for over a year, but he insists on calling me at all hours of the day and night. Recently he went so far as to call my present boyfriend to ask "how I was doing." Are there any legal steps I can take to make him leave me alone?

A. Yes, there are. Your former husband's conduct appears to be both a criminal offense and a violation of your civil rights.

As far as the criminal law is concerned, your husband seems to be guilty of harassment. Definitions of this offense vary from state to state, but most states define it in a manner similar to New York, which maintains that "a person is guilty of harassment when, with intent to harass, annoy, or alarm another person, he engages in a course of conduct or repeatedly commits acts which alarm or seriously annoy such other person and which serve no legitimate purpose."

The procedure for enforcing the criminal law against harassment varies from state to state. In some instances, the matter can be reported directly to the police. In others, the person filing the complaint must report the violation to a court official, who will then issue a summons for the complaining party to serve on the violator. If you wish to press criminal charges (or simply learn more about them), the district attorney in the area where you live can provide you with additional information.

You can also file civil charges against your former husband using the same definition of harassment. A decision in your favor could entitle you to recover money for damages as well as a court order that your former husband leave you alone. In addition, it is possible that a court would find your former husband liable based on the theory that he is guilty of the "intentional infliction of mental suffering."

Civil charges can be handled by any competent attorney. As with criminal prosecution, the procedure for seeking relief varies from state to state.

Quickie foreign divorces

Q. My husband and I are separated and would like an immediate divorce. If we go to another country where a divorce can be obtained after temporary residence of only twenty-four hours, will the decree be recognized as legal in the United States?

A. It could be, with careful planning on your part.

Divorce laws vary widely from state to state, but one common standard is that a marriage can be dissolved only in a state where one of the parties resides. Each state decides how long a person must live within its borders to meet its residence requirement, and the period can run anywhere from six weeks to well over a year. To circumvent this delay, some couples seek out "quickie" divorces in foreign countries where residence requirements can be as little as twenty-four hours. Occasionally, such a divorce can be obtained through a local attorney without the parties even appearing in person. However, unless both parties consent to be bound by the court's jurisdiction, foreign decrees are generally considered invalid in the United States.

As a first step, you and your husband should consult separate attorneys regarding your rights and the merits of a foreign divorce. Then, if you wish, you may consent to have the marriage dissolved by a foreign court. But keep in mind that, even though foreign divorces are often recognized as lawful, state courts are reluctant to enforce those portions of foreign judgments relating to alimony, child support, and other financial matters. Thus, if you do decide on a foreign divorce, you and your husband should first have a carefully drafted separation agreement.

Who decides a child's religion?

Q. Just before my husband and I got married, we agreed to raise our children in his religious faith. Now we're divorced, I am the custodial parent for our two young children, and my husband still insists that the children be brought up in his religious faith. Am I legally bound by our prior agreement?

A. Maybe not. To be sure, first review the separation agreement and divorce judgment that ended your marriage. Quite often, the custodial parent is specifically granted authority to make major decisions regarding religious upbringing, education, and the like. If this is true in your case, the matter will most likely be decided in your favor.

If not, you can return to court. You would argue that appropriate religious training is an important part of a child's upbringing, and this is something that you as the custodial parent are best able to provide. The judge will then rule in accord with what he or she believes to be your children's best interests, given the present circumstances.

Protecting children from their father

Q. My ex-husband and I have three young children. Under the court's divorce order, I have custody of the children, and he's allowed to visit them once a week. However, in recent months, his behavior has been quite erratic, and I'm concerned that he might harm the children. Is there any way I can arrange for supervision by a third party while my ex-husband is with the children?

A. Children very often become pawns in battles between ex-spouses. The first thing you should do is ask yourself whether your former husband's conduct actually represents a threat or whether it may not be just irritating or distasteful to you personally. Is he truly erratic or just eccentric? Are his gestures toward the children loving or are they fraught with harmful sexual overtones? These are questions a court will ask, and you should be prepared to answer them.

If you are convinced that your ex-husband's behavior really is dangerous, you can apply for a court order that will require supervising his visit. Before making a final determination, the judge might require a psychiatric examination of all the persons involved in the case (including your children). Also, witnesses, such as relatives and friends familiar with the family situation, will be called to testify. And, while courts are generally reluctant to come between parents and their children, supervision of your ex-husband's visits will be ordered if the situation calls for it.

Who pays the bills when you're separated?

Q. My husband and I were separated several months ago. Now, pending our divorce, he refuses to pay bills for doctors' visits and department-store purchases that I made while we were still living together. Which one of us is responsible for paying these debts?

A. You both are, but most likely your husband will be considered the primary debtor. As a general rule, a husband is obligated to support his wife during the time they live together. This doesn't mean that he has to pay all her bills, but he does have to cover reasonable and necessary expenses. For instance, if you went out and bought five expensive evening gowns the week before you separated, a court would probably consider your purchases extravagant. But if the doctors' bills and department-store charges were reasonable and in keeping with your past expenditures, as well as with your husband's present financial situation, a court will be likely to rule in your favor. This may not be the case, however, if you earn a salary equal to or greater than your husband's. But outside of circumstances such as these, your husband's traditional support obligation should govern.

Most disputes of this nature are worked out as part of an overall financial settlement at the time a couple's separation agreement and divorce judgment become final. Thus, the best thing to do would be to have your attorney include this matter in the general negotiation, along with alimony, child support (if there are children), the ownership of household furnishings, and other financial issues. In the interim, unless your attorney advises otherwise, you should notify the doctors and stores involved to send the bills to your husband. Then, if he refuses to pay, they will have to wait until the dispute between you is settled. I should add that, if someone sues you directly for payment, you can sue your husband to make him a party to the suit as well.

When an ex-husband cheats on child support

Q. When my ex-husband and I were divorced, the court ordered him to pay one-quarter of his gross annual income to me for child support. Recently, however, I've come to suspect that he's understating his income to reduce the amount he pays. How can I find out if this is the case?

A. You can have your attorney file an enforcement proceeding to determine your former husband's total income and, if that amount has been understated, to recover back payments.

In essence, your attorney will notify the court that there is reason to believe that your ex-husband is violating the divorce decree. If reasonable grounds for suspicion exist—for instance, the purchase of a new house or a life-style beyond the means of his stated income—the court will order your ex-husband to turn over his tax returns, bank statements, and other financial records. If warranted, the court will also require him and/or his employer to answer questions under oath about his financial condition.

If your suspicion turns out to be correct, the amount your husband owes will be deducted from his assets. Also, a regular monitoring system will be put in place—for example, he might be required to give you his tax returns and other financial information on an annual basis.

How much say do children have in custody battles?

Q. My husband and I are separated. I want custody of our two young children, but they want to stay with their father. To what extent will a court consider our children's preference in determining custody?

A. When parents are able to agree on who takes custody, a court will almost always follow their choice. When divorcing spouses battle over the issue, however, the court has to decide what will best meet the interests of the children. And this makes things considerably more complicated.

A court has to weigh many intricate variables in ruling on a custody case, and it may seek the advice of an impartial social worker or therapist. While no state gives children a controlling voice in determining custody, their preferences will generally be considered. In fact, in at least two states—California and Colorado—courts are required to give due weight to the preferences of children who are "of sufficient age and capacity to reason so as to form an intelligent preference." No exact age is set; what is involved is the child's maturity, something that the court will assess with the help of advisers.

Thus, if you and your husband cannot agree on custody, your children may well be consulted. However, no court will give children final responsibility for the decision. And, obviously, it will be best if you and your husband can work this out on your own, rather than leaving such a vital decision to a court.

Divorce without his consent

Q. I want a divorce, but my husband is trying to stop me. Is there any way I can get one without his consent?

A. There might be, depending on where you live. In California, for example, a spouse can sue for divorce on the grounds of "irreconcilable differences which have caused the irremediable breakdown of the marriage." This gives anyone seeking divorce considerable leeway. "Fault" and consent need not enter the picture.

By contrast, New York's "no fault" divorce procedure requires a husband and wife to live apart for at least one year, following a written agreement outlining their proposed divorce settlement. And if no such separation agreement can be reached, divorce is granted only on the following grounds: cruel and inhuman treatment that endangers the plaintiff's physical or mental well-being and renders cohabitation "unsafe or improper"; abandonment for a period of a year or more; confinement of the defendant in prison for three or more consecutive years following the start of the marriage; and adultery.

Given the diverse nature of existing laws, if your marriage cannot be saved, your best first step would be to consult with a lawyer to determine the precise grounds for divorce in your state. If you don't already have a lawyer, your local bar association (which is listed in the telephone book) will provide you with a list of counsel qualified to handle the matter.

Does my ex-husband have any say in where I and my children live?

Q. Three years ago, when my husband and I were divorced, I was granted custody of our two children. Now I'd like to move out of the state, but he's threatening to stop me on the grounds that it would preclude him from seeing the children as often as he'd like. Can he do so?

A. In general, divorced men and women are free to live their lives without interference from their former spouse. However, where children are involved, a parent's rights must sometimes be curtailed in keeping with the best interests of the children and the rights of the other parent.

The first question to be asked in your case is whether your separation agreement or divorce judgment specifically precludes a move of this nature. If so, a court will be reluctant to allow it.

Before reaching any decision, however, a court will consider why you want to move and, more importantly, how it will affect the children. Will it bring them geographically closer to grandparents who love them? Will it allow you to get a higher-paying job, enabling you to better provide for them? Are the children especially close to their father, and would the move deprive them of his love and attention at a time when they need it most, or would extended vacations with him be a satisfactory substitute for more frequent but shorter visits?

If your case goes to court, the judge hearing the matter will decide what he thinks is fair and in the best interests of the children. But it would be better if you and your former husband could accomplish that same end through open discussion and negotiation. Certainly it's worth trying. The worst thing for children is an open battle of this nature between their parents.

Can my new husband legally adopt my daughter?

Q. I am divorced, have a three-year-old daughter, and am planning to remarry. My former husband has not visited or paid a cent for child support in over two years. Can my new husband legally adopt my daughter so that she will have a full-time father?

A. He might be able to, but it won't be easy. Children are considered wards of the state, and, while courts generally decide family matters on the basis of a child's best interests, these same courts are extremely reluctant to deprive a father or mother of legal parenthood, no matter how irresponsible that parent might be.

However, there is a procedure by which your new husband might be able to adopt your daughter. He can serve your former husband with a formal adoption request. If your former husband consents, the court will most likely rule in favor of the change. However, if he objects, the road to success will be fairly bumpy.

The lawyer who handled your divorce is probably familiar with the facts of your case. If for some reason you do not want him to handle the matter, your local bar association will provide you with a list of counsel qualified to help for a reasonable fee.

Reducing child support when he loses his job

Q. My husband, who has two children from a previous marriage, pays $500 a month for their support. Recently he lost his job, and now we simply don't have enough money to make ends meet. Is there any way we can get his child-support payments reduced to see us through this crisis?

A. There might be. All divorce judgments are subject to modification and, given the circumstances, your husband's ex-wife may agree to a temporary reduction in, or deferral of, support payments. If not, your husband can present such a request in court. In essence, he would argue that changed circumstances have rendered the original divorce judgment unfair and impractical. The court would then consider such factors as his ex-wife's present income, whether or not she has remarried, and anything else that might bear on the two parties' overall financial picture.

In the end, the best interests of the children will govern the court's decision. Regardless of financial pressures, children must be fed, clothed, and otherwise cared for. However, if your husband has valid reasons for reducing child-support payments, a court is likely to be sympathetic to his cause. Judges are capable of distinguishing between people who are suffering genuine financial hardship and those merely seeking to evade their responsibilities.

Pensions and divorce

Q. My husband and I are in our late fifties and getting a divorce after almost thirty years of marriage. Our assets are relatively modest, but he has a pension plan that will begin paying benefits when he reaches age sixty-five. If we're no longer married, will I be entitled to a portion of those benefits?

A. In one form or another, most likely yes. Divorce laws differ from state to state but, generally, they may be put in one of three categories. Some states—such as California—have adopted "community property" laws, which hold that all property accumulated during a marriage as a result of the work and efforts of either spouse belongs to both of them. Other states follow the rule of "equitable division," which decrees that, in the event of divorce, all property belonging to either spouse should be fairly divided. In either case, a court will most likely rule that, after thirty years of marriage, you are entitled to an interest in your husband's pension benefits. This leaves a third category—states holding that, in the event of divorce, financial assets and the like belong to the spouse in whose name such property is listed. However, in these states, the court resolving your divorce would most likely take note of your husband's pension benefits and award you increased alimony as a consequence.

Should the marital difficulties faced by you and your husband prove insoluble, your attorney will be able to pursue a fair share of your husband's pension benefits on your behalf.

Overturning a divorce judgment

Q. Several years ago my husband and I were divorced pursuant to an agreement that awarded me custody of our two children and monthly payments for child support. Now he is threatening court action to overturn both the custody and financial arrangements, claiming that he was under "severe emotional stress" at the time we entered into the agreement. Is there a chance the court will set aside the judgment?

A. Divorce judgments can always be modified, but changes of the magnitude suggested by your ex-husband rarely happen.

If your ex-husband actually goes to court, the judge hearing his request will weigh several factors. First, would be the time-honored public policy that there should be an end to litigation. Divorce is unpleasant enough without one side or the other running back to court after an issue has been decided, and this policy would work in your favor. Second, the court would look to conditions as they existed at the time you and your ex-husband entered into the agreement. Was he represented adequately by counsel? Did he understand the nature and ramifications of the agreement he was signing? If so, it is not enough for him to say that he was under severe emotional stress. Chances are the breakup of the marriage was emotionally upsetting for you too. Next, the court will look to the present financial condition of you and your ex-husband. Are child support payments reasonably in line with what the two of you are earning? Has either of you enjoyed a large windfall or inheritance in recent months? And, most important, the judge will look to the best interests of your children. Are you a fit mother? Are your children growing up reasonably happy and well adjusted? If so, it is highly unlikely that, several years after the divorce, a court would alter custody arrangements. One of the worst things imaginable for children is to be placed in an environment where uncertainty and instability with regard to custody govern.

If your ex-husband is truly interested in the welfare of your children, the likelihood is that appropriate adjustments in visitation and child support can be worked out amicably between you. However, if he is simply perpetuating the conflicts that led to the breakup of the marriage, your ex-husband will face a heavy burden of proof in court.

My husband cleaned out our joint bank account before we separated. Is he entitled to the money?

Q. My husband and I separated last month. When the statement for our joint bank account arrived in the mail, I learned that he had completely cleaned out the account. I feel as though I'm entitled to half of that money. Is there any way I can get it?

A. Yes, there is. When a husband and wife separate, the money does not go to whoever grabs it first any more than the furniture would belong to someone who carted it off in a moving van. The joint bank account, like the rest of your assets, must be divided pursuant to a separation agreement reached by you and your husband.

Most likely, the lawyer who represents you in the overall divorce proceeding will negotiate the separation agreement on your behalf. It is to be hoped that you and your husband will be able to reach a fair compromise regarding the division of your assets. However, should agreement prove impossible, the matter will be referred to court, where the judge will weigh relevant state statutes (such as community property laws), the overall financial picture of you and your husband, and the "realities of ownership" with regard to the account.

For example, if most of the money in the account came from an inheritance you received prior to your marriage, the law would weigh heavily in your favor, and most likely you would recover far more than half of the total. By contrast, if the account was built up exclusively from your husband's earnings, a different result would probably be reached. Your lawyer will be able to best advise you on the merits of your particular case.

I earn more than my ex-husband; will I have to pay him alimony?

Q. My husband and I are going to be divorced. One of the problems in our marriage has been his resentment over the fact that I have a better-paying job than he does. Is there any chance that, as a result of the divorce, I'll be forced to pay him alimony?

A. The possibility does exist. Until recently, many states had statutes that allowed courts to impose alimony obligations on husbands but not on wives. These laws were premised on the belief that in most families the husband supports the family while the wife is financially dependent, and that even after a marriage ends these roles will (and should) continue.

However, the rationale for one-way statutes of this nature has been severely undercut by the women's rights movement, and in 1979, the United States Supreme Court handed down a decision that requires courts to award alimony to men where warranted by the circumstances of a particular marriage.

Should your husband seek alimony from you, the court hearing your case will consider several factors:

1. Financial ability—How much money do you and your husband make? Is your salary far in excess of what you need to live on? Does one of you have skills that will guarantee a large salary increase in the future? Do you or your husband have substantial stock holdings or other assets?

2. Financial need—Is your husband's salary so low that he wouldn't be able to live in dignified fashion without financial support? Is he in poor health and in need of extensive medical care? Do foreseeable major expenses lie ahead for either of you?

3. Past economic discrimination—Why is your husband's salary less than yours? Did he give up a better-paying job and move to a particular region of the country so you could practice your trade there? Did he forego graduate school so you could get your degree? In order to further your career, did he make other sacrifices to the detriment of his own advancement and earning potential?

Most likely, the lawyer who represents you in the separation and divorce proceedings will be able to negotiate a settlement agreement that frees you from the burdens of alimony. Moreover, even if your husband insists on such payments, he will have a hard time winning his way in court. Judges are extremely reluctant to grant alimony to men and will do so only under extreme circumstances. Your lawyer will be able to advise you as to whether yours is one of those rare cases in which special circumstances do exist.

Asking an unmarried father for child support

Q. I have an illegitimate child, age nine. At the time my daughter was born, the father had virtually no money and I didn't press him for support. However, he is now making quite a bit of money and is more than capable of offering financial help. After all these years is it too late to file a suit for child support?

A. No, it isn't. Most lawsuits must be brought within a specified period of time, usually considerably less than nine years from the time a cause of action arises. However, statutes of limitation are generally inapplicable when the plaintiff is a minor. Assuming you can prove paternity, it is not too late to file suit against the father for child support on your daughter's behalf.

Your best first step would be to consult a lawyer about your situation. If you do not know an attorney qualified to handle the matter, your local bar association will provide you with a list of qualified counsel. Then, together with your lawyer, you can formulate a strategy to pursue your case. Full-blown litigation might not even be necessary. When faced with a formal request, the father might agree to some form of payment without your having to file suit.

Does my daughter from a previous marriage have the right to change her name to that of her new stepfather?

Q. I am divorced and remarried, with a four-year-old daughter by my previous marriage. My first husband rarely shows any interest in our daughter, but the divorce decree requires that she use his last name until she herself marries. Now she is about to start school, and wants very much to call herself by my present husband's last name. Is there any way she can legally do so?

A. Yes, there is. Technically speaking, children are wards of the state, and a court is empowered to set aside any portion of a separation agreement or divorce decree that runs counter to a child's best interests. Thus, you have the right to petition the court for a name change on your daughter's behalf despite earlier legal proceedings.

The crucial question to be faced by the court will be whether the name change is in your daughter's best interests. Certainly, a child might feel more comfortable with her stepfather if she shares his name, and the same last name might add to her sense of having a full-time father. However, a court might rule that ties to her natural father are an important part of your child's identity and heritage and should be preserved whenever possible. I should add that once your daughter reaches the age of adulthood (which is eighteen in most states), she will be free to change her name legally to anything she wants without need of parental consent.

Can grandparents be granted visitation rights when their children divorce?

Q. My son and daughter-in-law were divorced recently in what became an extremely acrimonious case. The court judgment provided that my daughter-in-law has custody of their two children, ages six and eight, and my son has weekly visitation rights. But no mention was made in court of my relationship with the children, and now their mother refuses to let me visit them at all. My grandchildren and I love each other very much. My son is willing to let me share his time with them, but I do not want to intrude on their limited time together. Is it possible to persuade a court to grant me my own visiting rights?

A. Most likely, yes. Children are wards of the state, and any separation agreement or divorce judgment that runs counter to their best interests can be modified or set aside. From what you have said, modification appears likely in your case. Grandparents can play an extremely important role in a child's development. They give and receive love, add to a child's security, and contribute enormously to his or her sense of belonging—all of which can be particularly important when parents divorce. Indeed, in recent years, many states have enacted statutes which specifically provide for visitation by grandparents in cases of a family break-up.

You should first discuss the matter with your son and his lawyer. The lawyer, in turn, can ask your former daughter-in-law to grant you visiting rights. Ideally, a fair settlement will then be reached. If this proves impossible, your son can file suit for modification of the divorce judgment. It will then be up to the court to decide whether granting you visitation rights would be in your grandchildren's best interests.

Is it legal for a divorcing couple to use the same attorney?

Q. My husband and I are planning a divorce. He has suggested that an attorney who is a mutual friend do the legal work for both of us to cut down on the cost. Would this be proper?

A. The divorce would probably be legal, but I advise against you and your husband being represented by the same attorney. Even in the most amicable of situations, divorce proceedings can pose several potentially explosive problems—child custody, for instance; alimony; the division of property. Divorce lawyers must serve as advocates, not judges. Your lawyer's job is to advise you about all of your potential rights and liabilities and then seek to guarantee that you get everything you are legally entitled to if you want it. It would be virtually impossible for someone representing two sides in a proceeding to perform that task adequately for both sides.

Of course, this does not mean that divorce proceedings must sink to the level of a bitter, mud-slinging feud. Many divorces are marked by good faith and cooperation where legal details are concerned. But good intentions do not negate the time-honored axiom that "no servant can serve two masters."

My ex-husband's mother tells my son bad things about me. Can I make her stop?

Q. I was recently divorced and obtained custody of my five-year-old son. My ex-husband has visitation rights two days a week and shares most visits with his mother (my ex-mother-in-law). Unfortunately, this woman spends most of her time telling my son bad things about me. He is constantly barraged with such comments as, "It's your mother's fault the marriage ended," and, "If you were living with daddy, you'd have more fun." As a result, my child often returns home confused and unhappy. Is there any way I can stop this woman from seeing my son or, at the very least, from conducting such a campaign against me?

A. Quite probably, yes. As you can imagine, it's very hard for the courts (or anyone else) to muzzle an angry relative. But in cases of this nature the child's best interests must be considered paramount, and there are several steps that you can take.

First, and most obvious, you should talk to your former husband about the matter. Perhaps he will recognize that sniping of this nature is not in your son's best interests and will tell his mother to stop.

Should this fail, you'll then have the option of going to court. Most likely the proceeding will take place before the judge who approved your original custody and visitation agreement. You can ask for an order that your ex-mother-in-law be forbidden from making her negative comments in front of your son, with the added proviso that, if she continues, her access to the child will be terminated. The judge will then rule in accord with what he believes to be your child's best interests.

Should litigation prove necessary, the lawyer who handled your divorce will most likely be able to prepare motion papers on your behalf. However, before seeking his help, you should compile a list of incidents as they occur, plus the names of people who witnessed either your ex-mother-in-law's comments or your son's reaction. Also, at some point, you might want to consult a child psychologist, who will be able to gauge more fully the effect of these comments on your son and testify in court on your behalf as an expert witness.

We've been living together for years; do we have a common-law marriage?

Q. My boyfriend and I have been living together for several years. I'd like to get married, but he says it isn't necessary because we already have a common-law marriage. Is he right or not?

A. Probably not. Common-law marriage had its origins in feudal England. Clerics who performed marriage ceremonies were few and far between, and serfs couldn't very well leave the manor to seek them out. Ergo, commoners simply declared themselves husband and wife and began living together until a cleric arrived (sometimes months later) to legitimize the marriage. Later, the tradition carried over to Colonial America, where common-law marriage was widespread.

If and when a common-law marriage is established, the parties have the same property and inheritance rights, potential alimony obligations, and so on, as other married couples. However, relatively few states now recognize common-law marriage, and the requirements are often stringent. First, the couple must live together for a given period of time (the duration varies from state to state). Second, they must publicly identify themselves as husband and wife. And third, they must do so with the intent of establishing a marriage. That is, you cannot "slip" into a common-law marriage against your will. Isolated acts such as registering at a hotel as "Mr. and Mrs." to avoid raised eyebrows will not suffice.

Depending on the circumstances of your relationship and the law of the state in which you live, you and your boyfriend might have a common-law marriage. Also, it's possible that some form of "palimony" obligations between you exist. But the soundest legal advice I can offer is this: If you want to have the legal rights and obligations of marriage, get married.

Getting your ex-husband to pay college costs for your children.

Q. My divorce judgment requires my ex-husband to pay modest child support for my two teenage children. However, it says nothing about his contributing to their college education, and without greater financial help, there's no way I can pay for room, board, and tuition. My ex-husband refuses to discuss the matter, saying I'm entitled to what the court ordered and nothing more. Is this true?

A. Courts have consistently held that, whenever possible, the children of divorced parents should have the same educational opportunities they would have had if their parents had stayed together. Therefore, if your husband refuses to work out a reasonable arrangement for college expenses, you can go back to court for modification of your divorce judgment.

The judge will consider the overall financial picture (including your present salary, your ex-husband's salary, loan opportunities, the cost of college, etc.) and then reevaluate the original court order so that it reflects the best interests of your children. After this process is completed, the judge may order an increase in child support payments to meet the cost of your children's college education.

Visitation rights at Christmas

Q. My husband and I are getting a divorce, and both of us want to spend Christmas with our four-year-old daughter. Which of us has the legal right?

A. Children of divorce are best served when their parents resolve child-care disputes amicably. You and your husband should therefore make every effort—together and through your attorneys—to reach a fair compromise on holiday visitation.

Should this prove impossible, it will be up to the judge assigned to your case to decide who spends Christmas, birthdays, and other holidays with your daughter. In making that decision, the best interests of the child will be the most important consideration. Arguments will be heard from both sides and perhaps from psychiatric experts. The judge will also take into account which parent has custody for most of the year. In all likelihood, the court's decision will be to alternate major holidays between you. But it would be far preferable if you and your husband could make this decision jointly through compromise, rather than leave it to a judicial stranger.

Custody of your young children should you die

Q. Several years ago, my husband and I were divorced and I was awarded custody of our infant daughter. Since then I've remarried, and my daughter has grown quite close to her stepfather, while my ex-husband hardly sees her at all. Is there any way I can insure that my present husband will become my child's legal guardian if I should die before she reaches age 18?

A. This is an instance in which you might succeed, but it won't be easy. Judges are extremely reluctant to deny a father his parental rights, and it's generally felt that children are best off in the care of a blood relative. Children are considered wards of the state, however, and custody matters are decided based on a child's best interests.

Therefore, your first step should be to make a will naming your present husband as your child's guardian in the event of your death. Then, if you die and your ex-husband challenges the will, the court will examine several factors. For example, what did your divorce judgment say about custody in the event of death? How old is your daughter? Does she have a preference as to whom she would live with? Are there children from your new marriage whom your daughter loves and considers family? After evaluating all of these factors—and drawing heavily on the report of a court-appointed therapist—the court will do what it thinks will best guide your daughter through this difficult period in her life.

Divorce settlements: lump sum payments versus alimony

Q. My husband and I are getting a divorce, and I've been offered the choice of alimony payments or one lump-sum settlement. What are the advantages of each?

A. The main difference between these settlements is that a lump-sum arrangement involves just one payment at the time of the divorce, while alimony involves regular payments to an ex-spouse, usually the wife. As a general rule, alimony payments continue for a specific number of years or until the spouse remarries, whichever comes first.

There are several advantages to accepting a lump-sum arrangement. First, you as the recipient, generally don't have to pay income taxes on a lump-sum payment, whereas with alimony you do. Second, you won't have to worry should your husband's financial status worsen at a later date, possibly preventing him from meeting his alimony payments. And finally, should you remarry, the lump-sum settlement is still yours, while the alimony payments would most likely be discontinued.

On the other hand, once a lump-sum payment is used up, there are no periodic payments to replace it. Should you or your ex-husband's financial condition change drastically in the future, a court probably wouldn't increase your award if you had settled on a lump sum, though it is possible to have alimony payments increased.

In the end, it's probably best to take a bottom-line approach. Compare the total amount of money—adjusted for taxes, interest, and inflation—that you're offered under the alimony and lump-sum alternatives. Examine the proposals in light of your husband's financial assets, his earning potential, and your own financial condition. Then, after consulting with the attorney handling your divorce, you'll be able to make the best choice.

Can mediation facilitate a divorce?

Q. My husband and I are getting a divorce after seven years of marriage, and we don't seem to be able to settle things through our lawyers. Recently, I heard about mediation as an alternative to a drawn-out court battle. How does it work?

A. Mediation is a voluntary procedure in which you both present your differences to an impartial third party, usually a lawyer. The mediator is paid an hourly rate, comparable to an attorney's, and this fee is usually split between the two parties.

The mediator will not actually make a decision. Rather, he or she will meet with both parties, together and/or separately, depending on the circumstances. After understanding your respective positions, the mediator will seek to guide you to a fair settlement regarding alimony and child support.

The settlement you reach through mediation will only become binding after it has been approved by the court. However, this approval is usually only a formality. If you and your husband cannot agree through mediation, you'll still have the option of taking your case to court.

Mediation works best when divorcing spouses negotiate with an open mind and are prepared to compromise. Properly conducted, it reduces the bitterness of an extended court battle, as well as the high legal fees that arise with any kind of protracted litigation.

Chapter 5

Consumer Rights

Get it in writing

Q. Last year my husband and I had a fuel bill of $500. Recently a supplier offered us a special deal: For $1,000 he will supply all the fuel we need for three years, and we don't have to pay a cent until the end of each year. The deal seems good, but the supplier says he will not give us a written contract. Since he promises to deliver first and bill us later, do I still need the deal in writing?

A. You sure do! When a supplier refuses to put a "special" offer on paper, things frequently go wrong.

The first pitfall you face is the Uniform Commercial Code. The code is a series of laws governing the sale of goods. It has been adopted by every state and specifically provides that, with certain limited exceptions, a contract for the sale of goods for $500 or more is not enforceable unless signed and in writing.

In addition, many states have laws that preclude the enforcement of any oral agreement that cannot be fully performed within one year. Your contract, which is not in writing, lasts for three years—well beyond the statutory limit. Also keep in mind that at some future date you might have a problem proving what price was agreed upon.

The price of fuel oil may well rise more in the future than it already has. Without a written contract, you could be faced with no fuel at all or a lawsuit demanding payment of more money than you had bargained for concerning the fuel already delivered to you.

Is it legal for a store to have a no refunds/no exchanges policy?

Q. On several occasions I have tried to return merchandise to a store, only to be confronted by a sign that reads "No Refunds/No Exchanges." Is this policy legal?

A. Yes, it is, provided that you are given advance notice. The sale of goods is a contract, and a store can attach almost any condition to the sale that you agree to. Thus, if at the time of your purchase, the store had a prominently displayed sign that read "No Refunds/No Exchanges," you are bound by this policy. On the other hand, if no sign was posted and no warning given, most courts have held that goods may be returned for refund or exchange within a reasonable period of time, as long as there are no health or sanitation regulations to the contrary.

Also, keep in mind that even when a sign is prominently posted, if the product you buy is defective, you have the right to exchange it for one that is in working order. In such an instance, if the identical item is unavailable, the store must offer you a refund. Likewise, if you were tricked into the purchase by means of fraud, a refund or exchange must be offered to you. A clear definition of "fraud" is hard to come by. It can mean anything from false newspaper advertising to an inaccurate sales pitch by a salesperson.

If you feel that you have been treated unfairly, you should telephone your local consumer affairs bureau or your state attorney general's office. They will be able to advise you as to all the relevant state and local regulations. Then, if you wish to pursue the case further, you may file suit for a refund in small claims court. Perhaps your best remedy, though, is simply to take your business elsewhere.

If a hairdresser cuts my hair too short, do I have to pay?

Q. For years I had blond hair reaching down to the middle of my back. Last week I went to have it trimmed. My regular hairdresser was on vacation so I tried a new shop. I told the stylist as clearly as possible that all I wanted was to have two inches cut off. He said fine and, scissors in hand, began to cut away. One snip and he had lopped off ten inches. "It looks better this way," he told me. I was so upset, I paid my $25 and walked out in tears. Only time will grow the hair back, but the fact that I paid him at all annoys me. Do I have any rights under the law?

A. Yes! If you go into a store and order a red couch, you don't have to pay for the delivery of a green one. Your situation is not much different.

In legal terms, the facts of your case may amount to a breach of contract. You went to a person who held himself out as a professional hairdresser. You specifically told him what you wanted, and he was obligated to follow your instructions. In return, you were to pay him $25. The hairdresser apparently did not live up to his end of the bargain. In short, he breached the contract.

Were this only a matter of taste and your complaint limited to, "I don't know why, but I don't like it," then you would have been obligated to pay him. However, when someone hired to perform a service deliberately disobeys his instructions, performing to your detriment and against your will, you owe him nothing. Moreover, a court could reasonably rule that he is obligated to compensate you for all damage unfairly suffered. This could include any direct financial loss to you (such as modeling fees) and, more important in your case, a reasonable amount for "pain and suffering." If you feel strongly enough about the matter, even at this late date, you have the option of filing suit. Small claims court would probably be the best forum for your action.

Staying home to wait for a delivery that never arrives

Q. Last week I stayed home from work for a day so that a rug I had ordered from a local department store could be delivered. Delivery was promised between 10:00 A.M. and 2:00 P.M. When the rug had not arrived by 3:00, I telephoned the store and was told that they were "very sorry" but that, due to a full schedule, the rug would not be delivered for another week.

I'm extremely angry. I took an entire "personal business" day off from work, which has now been wasted, and I would like to know what my legal rights are against the store.

A. You have fallen victim to an infuriating situation that happens far too often. However, the law appears to be on your side. According to the facts you have mentioned, the store is liable for breach of contract. Once it promised to deliver the rug at a specified time, it had an obligation to do so or, at the very least, to notify you of any change in scheduling. By failing to do so, it violated its part of the contract.

Call the rug department manager and see if a new time for delivery can be arranged that would not require your absence from work. If it cannot, and you are forced to take additional time off from your job, ask the store to credit your account with an amount that reflects the additional hours lost from work because of the store's failure to deliver the rug on schedule. If the manager refuses, take your case to small claims court. The instances where claims like this have actually come to trial are relatively few, but your chances for some form of recovery are good.

My film is lost—what can I do?

Q. About a month ago I mailed a roll of film to a well-known photographic supply company for processing, using one of the company's prepaid "mailers." The film has not been returned, and I'm afraid that it's been lost. What can I do?

A. When a package such as yours is properly mailed, the law generally presumes it arrived safely at its destination. Thus, unless the photographic supply company has records showing that your film was never received or can demonstrate that it processed the film and then returned it to you, a small claims court will probably rule in your favor.

However, in all likelihood, your recovery will be minimal. Most "mailers" contain a written warning that the processor's liability is limited to the amount you paid for the film plus processing. In buying and using the mailer, you have in effect agreed to these contractual terms. Thus, no matter what the commercial or sentimental value of the pictures is to you, you will probably be unable to recover more than what you paid for the film and the processing.

The photographic supply company will probably be willing to give you a complimentary roll of film and mailer without your having to file suit. If a post office search falls to locate the film, you would most likely be best off accepting the company's offer.

What are my rights if a jeweler underpaid me for a pin I sold him?

Q. Recently I sold a diamond pin to a jeweler for $1,200—a price he assured me was fair. Last week I learned from a neighbor that the jeweler had resold the pin for $5,000. Obviously, jewelers are entitled to a profit, but I feel as though I was paid far less than the pin's true value. At this late date, is there any way I can receive a fairer price?

A. There might be, but it will not be easy. First, you have to determine whether the price paid to you was equitable. With the price of precious stones fluctuating wildly, it is possible that the jeweler did give you a fair price. You also have to consider the possibility that the pin was really worth only $1,200 and that it was the secondary purchaser who was overcharged.

If, after considering these factors, you still believe you were underpaid, it will be up to you to convince a court that there was some sort of misrepresentation on the jeweler's part. For example, if he lied about the weight or quality of the stone and you made the sale based on his assurance, then you would be entitled to additional payment. Similarly, if he gave you a guarantee that his was the highest price you could get, a judge might decide in your favor. Remember, though, that it is often difficult to distinguish between what is intended as a legitimate sales promise and mere sales "puffery."

In the future, when you sell jewelry you would be well advised to comparison shop before making a final decision.

When cleaners lose expensive clothes

Q. Several weeks ago I took a silk blouse worth $90 to the cleaners for pressing. The following day, when I returned for it, I discovered that the blouse had been lost. The cleaners admit that the loss was their fault, but they refuse to pay me more than $20. Their reason? Their receipt states, "Our liability is limited to $20 per item damaged or lost." What can I do?

A. For a start, you might be able to challenge the $20 limit on the grounds that you didn't have proper notice. Since customers usually don't read the fine print on receipts when they drop clothes off at a laundry, the proprietor is required to do something to draw attention to his policy.

Was there a large sign behind the counter announcing the $20 limit? Was the provision in bold type or otherwise clearly visible on the face of the receipt? Without notice of this nature, a court might consider the limitation unenforceable.

Even if proper notice was given, there could be a second line of attack. In most states, a limitation of liability will be considered void if the proprietor was guilty of "gross negligence"—conduct that is almost scandalously careless. How did the blouse get lost? Are the practices of the establishment unconscionably careless? Does it have a history of past thefts without action to track down the culprit? If you could prove that the proprietor took next-to-no steps to safeguard his customers' property, your case would be relatively strong.

If you cannot reach a satisfactory settlement with the cleaners, the most sensible course of action would be for you to file suit in small claims court, where you will be able to proceed without the aid of a lawyer. To bolster your case in court, you should bring the laundry receipt and, if you can, some proof of the price you paid for the blouse. You might also check with your local consumer affairs bureau to see if similar complaints against the cleaning establishment have been filed.

How to get out of a long-term contract

Q. Recently I signed a long-term contract with a local health club. Now I want out. Is there any way that I can break the contract?

A. There might be. If you were induced to enter the contract by promises that turned out to be false, the agreement would be unenforceable. Did club officials misrepresent the club's size, location, or facilities? Did they mislead you with regard to the quality of courses of instruction or the qualifications of club employees? If so, they are guilty of fraud, and you are entitled to break the contract.

Even if the contract was honestly negotiated, it is also possible that a court would rule that it runs for a period of time that is so long as to be "unconscionable" or "against public policy." In such a case, the contract would be considered null and void. In some states the length of time that renders a contract unenforceable is left to the judge's discretion. But other states have enacted laws that place specific time limits on contracts for health club services. In New York, for example, no such contract can bind a member for a period of more than thirty-six months.

In addition, the New York statute includes other provisions for getting out of health club contracts. Members have an absolute right to cancel within three days of receiving the written contract (this is something that the contract must state clearly and conspicuously). Buyers may also cancel if they become physically disabled for over six months or move to a location more than twenty-five miles from a health club operated by the club owner. In New York you also can cancel if the services you have contracted for decline in quality or become unavailable. And, except for contracts for the use of tennis and racquetball facilities, a health club contract requiring payment in excess of $3,600 by the person using club facilities is unenforceable.

Your best first step would be to send a letter to club officials requesting that your membership be terminated. If they refuse, contact the attorney general's office in your state for more information on local statutes that may support your case. Then you will know how best to proceed.

A new blouse is torn—who's responsible?

Q. Recently I bought a blouse at a local department store. When I got home and tried the blouse on, I noticed that it was torn under one arm. The manager refused to refund my money, saying that he had no proof that I wasn't responsible for the damage. I'd like to sue for a refund in small claims court, but how can I prove my case?

A. Your case might be stronger than you seem to think it is. In essence, this incident boils down to your word against nobody's. You can testify to the fact that, as soon as you tried to put on the blouse, you noticed that it was torn. The store manager is in no position to make a credible claim to the contrary unless he or a salesperson carefully examined the blouse immediately before selling it to you. Obviously, if you had a record of frequent similar lawsuits, a court might look askance at your claim. But, in the absence of some mitigating circumstance, there should be no reason for a court to doubt your credibility.

Ask the store manager for a full refund of your money or an appropriate exchange of merchandise. Then, if the store still refuses to satisfy you, take your case to small claims court. When you appear in court, bring the blouse and a copy of your receipt, as well as any available witnesses.

How "implied warranties" can save you money

Q. About a year ago my husband and I had new linoleum installed in our kitchen. At first it looked great, but after a few months the edges began to curl. Now the entire floor needs to be done over. Are we legally entitled to a free replacement?

A. Quite possibly. If the linoleum came with an express guarantee of any kind and the problems began before the warranty period expired, then you're clearly entitled to free repair or replacement. But even without such a guarantee, your chances for getting free repair or replacement are good.

In recent years every state in the country has adopted the Uniform Commercial Code, which provides that virtually all products have an automatic "implied warranty" that they be "fit for the ordinary purposes for which such goods are used." Accordingly, if the premature curling of your kitchen floor resulted from a defect in the linoleum itself, both the manufacturer and retailer will have violated the code. If the problem was poor installation rather than defective manufacture—for example, the contractor may not have used enough glue around the edges—then the installer will have failed to perform his services in a professional manner. In either case, you're entitled to a refund or free replacement.

Your best first step would be to send a letter to the contractor, explaining your position. Then, if you don't get a satisfactory response, you can take the matter to small claims court, where you will be able to proceed without the aid of a lawyer. It would also be helpful if you had cancelled checks relating to the transaction, as well as a photograph of the floor (showing the curling linoleum), for use as evidence in court.

When a repairman promises but doesn't deliver

Q. Several months ago I had my automobile transmission repaired by a mechanic who promised to make any future repairs or adjustments "free of charge." Now I'm having more trouble with the transmission, and he "doesn't remember" the promise—and I never got it in writing. Is there any way I can force him to live up to his promise?

A. There might be. Your first step should be to review whatever contract, if any, you do have in writing. What does it say about guarantees? Are there any provisions on future repairs or adjustments that seem to support your position? If so, the matter should be straightforward; the mechanic will have to abide by the written contract.

If not, there are two lines of attack you could try. First, you could argue that the mechanic gave you an "express oral warranty" and that his promise to make future adjustments or repairs "free of charge" became part of your contract. Now it is your word against his, and it is not enough for him to simply say he "doesn't remember." Unless he can swear that he never made the promise, the judge will probably decide in your favor.

There is also another route you can follow. Every repair job is a service that comes with an "implied warranty," meaning that the person who does the repair must perform in a professional manner. For example, a plumber who charges a fee to fix a leaking faucet must, in fact, stop the leak. And if you can show that your mechanic's work was shoddy and led to the new breakdown, you'll be entitled to a free repair or refund.

The best forum for your case will be small claims court. Present whatever records you have of the repair. If possible, ask another mechanic or someone familiar with automobile transmissions to testify on your behalf. Also, since most states and municipalities have consumer protection agencies that license automobile mechanics and repair centers, check with the appropriate agency in your area to see whether similar complaints have been lodged against the mechanic or whether there's anything the agency can do on your behalf.

When professional photos don't measure up

Q. Last week I took my daughter to a photographer's studio to have her picture taken. But the proofs I received several days later were all terrible. The photographer now refuses to take additional proofs and is unwilling to refund my deposit. What are my legal rights?

A. Not every child photographs like a professional model, but professional photographers have a contractual obligation to perform like professionals. Thus, the key issue in your case is whether the photographer lived up to the standards of his trade. Was his studio lighting bad? Were the photos blurred? Was your daughter photographed with her eyes inadvertently shut? If so, the photographer didn't do his job properly and you're entitled to either a refund or additional proofs.

On the other hand, if he performed in a professional manner and produced several reasonably flattering likenesses of your daughter, he will have lived up to his end of the bargain and it wouldn't be fair to penalize him.

To see if the photos really are as uncomplimentary as you think, ask friends and family members for their opinion. If after that you still think you have a valid complaint, you can take the matter to small claims court. Should you go to court, take your daughter with you, along with several recent complimentary photographs of her, to use as evidence. This way, the judge hearing the case will be better able to determine whether the photographer performed properly under the contract.

When your utility bills seem too high

Q. Our gas and electric bills are much higher than those of neighbors with comparable homes, and my husband and I suspect that someone else's utility use is being recorded on our meter. However, the utility company says that appliance use varies and we're obligated to pay the requested amount. What are our legal rights?

A. Every state has a commission that regulates utilities, sets rates, monitors billing procedures to ensure that consumers are properly charged, and investigates billing disputes. Before taking your case to this commission, however, try this test. Locate the electric meter for your home. Then turn off all lights and electrical appliances, including the refrigerator and any electric clocks. If the meter disk is still turning, it will lend credibility to your belief that you are being overcharged. And, more important, it will entitle you to a meter inspection—not just a reading—by the utility.

If, after inspection, the problem still isn't solved, you can demand a hearing before the Public Service Commission (check the headings under "State Government" in your local telephone directory).

When a store charges more than the price tag

Q. Last week at the supermarket I picked up a container of orange juice marked 89 cents. When I got to the cash register, however, I was told that the container had been incorrectly marked, and I was charged $1.89. Should I have been sold the juice at the price marked?

A. Not necessarily. When you purchase an item from a supermarket, in effect you enter into a contract. But before a sale is made, a store has the right to withdraw its offer if it was made in error. Certainly, if the juice had been labeled with too high a price, you'd expect the store to correct its error and sell the juice for the proper amount. What follows for one side follows for the other. If the store made an honest error in marking the juice, your best step would be to pay the requested amount or not buy it. There are, however, some exceptions to this rule. If you can show that the store's "error" was intentional—that the juice was falsely advertised or mislabeled as a form of "bait and switch"—you'd be entitled to buy it at the price marked. Also, if the store had been notified of the mistake by other customers but had done nothing to correct it, you'd again be entitled to the lower price.

When a used car is a lemon

Q. Recently, I bought a used car—"as is"—for $1,200. The dealer assured me that the car was in working order, but specified that there was no warranty. Now, only four weeks later, the transmission is broken. What, if any, are my legal rights?

A. Contrary to what the dealer said, there was a warranty: He himself gave you one in assuring you that the car was "in working order." Also, every state in the country has laws that afford used-car buyers additional protection. In New York, for example, car dealers have long been required to give buyers of secondhand vehicles a written statement guaranteeing that the car complies with state automobile safety requirements and will provide satisfactory transportation on public highways. A dealer's failure to deliver this statement is punishable by a fine of $50, or up to thirty days imprisonment, or both. And a subsequently enacted New York "lemon law" offers even greater protection.

Regardless of the state in which you live, a dealer can also be found guilty of fraud if he deliberately covers up a major defect. An example of this would be a makeshift transmission repair designed to last only long enough for the car to survive your test run.

Whatever the particular circumstances of your case, the best first step would be to send a letter to the dealer demanding an immediate repair or refund. Then, if you don't get a satisfactory response, file suit in small claims court. You might also check with your local consumer affairs bureau to see if similar complaints have been lodged against the dealer. If so, the bureau might pressure the dealer to settle—or could even cancel his license to do business.

Appliance warranties—who's responsible for fulfillment?

Q. Recently I purchased a kitchen appliance that broke within the warranty period. Am I entitled to repairs from the local store where I bought it, or must I carry the burden of dealing by parcel post with an out-of-state manufacturer?

A. Quite possibly you'll be able to demand repairs or a free replacement from the local merchant. Under the Uniform Commercial Code (which has been adopted by every state in the country) most goods carry an "implied warranty" that they will be "merchantable." This warranty is the responsibility of both the manufacturer and seller. Among other requirements, goods, to be merchantable, must be "of fair average quality" and "fit for the ordinary purposes for which such goods are used." A defectively manufactured kitchen appliance does not meet this standard.

There are ways in which a seller or manufacturer can put restrictive conditions on an implied warranty. For example, many manufacturers offer conspicuously worded "limited warranties" of their own, stating that repairs will be made only at authorized service centers. However, merchants cannot escape their own responsibilities under the Uniform Commercial Code by relying on a manufacturer's restrictions. And so, unless the store specifically indicated otherwise to you at the time of sale, it will be obligated to make good on its own "implied warranty."

Your best first step will probably be to ask the merchant for a free repair or replacement. Then, if this proves futile and you don't want to deal by parcel post or United Parcel Service with the manufacturer, you can file suit in small claims court.

Preplanned funeral arrangements

Q. My father is considering entering into a contract for preplanned funeral arrangements. To what extent will the agreement—which calls for an elaborate funeral—be binding should my father change his mind, or should the family feel after his death that the arrangements are inappropriate?

A. This will depend on several factors. First, there is the issue of the contract itself. Does it have a cancellation clause? If so, how can that clause be exercised? It might be that the so-called contract is little more than a paper record of your father's wishes at a particular point in time without legal effect.

Moreover, every state in the country has legislation that regulates funeral homes, and this legislation often provides an escape clause from preplanned funeral arrangements. In New York, for example, such arrangements can be cancelled by the subject person during his lifetime, or by his next of kin (or executor) at any time after his death until the goods and services contracted for are provided. Moreover, any money paid in advance to a funeral director, undertaker, or cemetery for preplanned arrangements must be deposited in a special trust fund and, if the arrangements change, must be returned on demand with interest to the payer or his estate. Violation of this statute is a misdemeanor, subjecting the guilty party to loss of license to do business, a fine, and/or imprisonment. The law does not apply to the sale of lots or graves by a cemetery.

Funeral regulations are administered by varying agencies from state to state. In New York, for example, the State Department of Health has primary oversight capacity. To determine the law in your particular area, contact your state attorney general (listed in the telephone directory). That office will provide you with detailed information or refer you to the appropriate governing body.

I think the mileage on a used car I bought was turned back. Can I do anything about this now?

Q. Six months ago I bought a used car from a local dealer. According to the odometer, the car had been driven 12,000 miles at the time of my purchase. Since then I have added an additional 5,000 miles in local use. Last month the transmission broke down. When I took the car to our service station for repairs, the mechanic told me he was "certain" that the car had been driven at least 50,000 miles and possibly more. I now think that the odometer was reset before my purchase. Is there anything I can do about this now?

A. Under the Federal Motor Vehicle Information And Cost Savings Act, it is against the law for any person to disconnect or reset the odometer of a car. This same act also provides that, any time a dealer buys or sells a motor vehicle, the cumulative mileage registered on the odometer must be disclosed in writing. Violation of the act is a criminal offense, subjecting the guilty party to a fine of up to $50,000 and/or one year's imprisonment. Moreover, under this act you can file a civil suit and, if you are successful, you will be entitled to recover three times the amount of your loss or $1,500 (whichever is greater), plus the costs of your lawsuit and reasonable attorney's fees.

The Motor Vehicle Information And Cost Savings Act is administered by the United States Department of Transportation, Washington, D.C. 20590. If you wish to pursue the matter, send a letter to the department. It will investigate your complaint, and try to determine whether the odometer was reset and whether it is the car dealer or an earlier owner who is responsible. Also, very often, a buyer such as yourself can locate the original owner on his or her own by sending the car's serial number to the manufacturer or, in the case of a foreign-made car, to the distributor.

In addition, if you so desire, you can contact your state attorney general and the district attorney in the area where you live. They will advise you with regard to possible civil and criminal proceedings against the seller provided for under state law.

Whatever the outcome of your case, though, you should remember that an odometer reading is only a partial indication of a car's condition and value. The next time you purchase a used motor vehicle, have it examined by an independent automobile mechanic as an added precaution.

Warranty cards—must you mail them?

Q. Several months ago I bought a tape deck with a one-year warranty. However, when it broke, the manufacturer refused to repair it, saying I had never mailed in the warranty registration card. What are my legal rights?

A. Contrary to what the manufacturer says, there are several ways you might get the warranty enforced.

First, it's possible that you did mail in the warranty registration card, and it was simply misplaced by the manufacturer. If you can testify in court with certainty that you mailed the card, the manufacturer will be hard pressed to prove you wrong.

A court might also rule that mailing the card is not essential to validate the warranty. Such a ruling would depend, to some degree, on the wording of the printed material that came with the tape deck when you bought it. If you can verify the purchase date with a sales receipt or other supporting evidence, the court may consider the registration card irrelevant.

Last, under the Uniform Commercial Code, virtually all goods, unless otherwise stated, come with an "implied warranty" that they are "fit for the ordinary purposes for which such goods are used." If the tape deck you purchased was of such shoddy quality that it malfunctioned after minimum usage, a court might find that the implied warranty had been violated—in which case you would be entitled to free repair, a refund, or replacement.

When returning goods, how large a credit am I entitled to?

Q. Last month I purchased a sweater for $29.95. Unfortunately, it was too small, so several days later I took it back to the store with my receipt and asked for a credit. The manager then told me that all similar sweaters had been marked down to $22.95 after my purchase, and he would only give me a credit for the lesser amount. Was I entitled to a full credit?

A. Most likely, yes. Most courts have held that goods may be returned for a refund, credit, or exchange within a reasonable period of time unless there are sanitary regulations to the contrary, a clearly displayed sign reading "No Refunds/No Exchanges," or other special circumstances.

Had the price of the sweater gone up by $7 after your purchase, the manager would hardly have credited your account for $7 more than you paid. And, conversely, the fact that the price went down does not entitle you to less.

If you wish to pursue the matter, your best first step would be to send a letter to the store outlining the circumstances of your case and requesting the credit. Then, if a satisfactory response is not forthcoming, you can file suit in small claims court.

Apartment referral services

Q. Recently I paid $50 to an apartment referral agency for a list of "available" apartments suited to my needs. However, when I went to look at the apartments it referred me to, they had either been "just rented" or were broken-down junk heaps. The agency now says that it has discharged its obligation. Am I entitled to my money back?

A. Quite possibly. You and the referral service entered into a contract by which you agreed to pay $50 in exchange for a service that the agency agreed to deliver. By failing to provide that service, the referral agency breached the contract. And while the agency could conceivably argue that the apartments it offered were in fact "suited to your needs," a court is likely to be sympathetic to your cause. After all, if the apartments shown to you were suitable, you would have rented one.

In addition, a growing number of states have enacted laws that specifically regulate apartment referral services. In New York, for example, apartment "information vendors" are allowed to charge an advance fee. But, aside from apartment sharing or roommate referral services, that fee is refundable. All a customer need do is notify the referral service in writing that he or she has not leased an apartment through information supplied by the vendor and has no intention of doing so. The referral service must then refund the entire amount paid, minus $15 for administrative costs. The New York law also says that the fee cannot exceed one month's rent. If it does—for instance, you lease an apartment for less rent than anticipated—the excess must be refunded to you. Violation of this statute can subject the guilty party to both civil proceedings and criminal misdemeanor charges. An apartment referral service can also lose its license to do business.

The attorney general's office in the state where you live should be well versed in this area of the law. Call it for further advice.

My TV set broke down the day after I bought it; am I entitled to a replacement?

Q. Recently I purchased a new television set. On the day after I got it home, the sound failed. The store says it will make repairs, but refuses to give me a new set. Meanwhile, I'm now afraid that the set is a lemon and will give me trouble for as long as I own it. Am I legally entitled to a new one?

A. Quite possibly, yes. The Uniform Commercial Code provides that sales by a merchant of his product carry with them an "implied warranty" that the item sold is "merchantable." The same law also states that in order to be merchantable, goods must meet the following minimum standards:

1. They must be of average quality and acceptable to the trade.

2. They must be fit for ordinary and reasonable use.

3. They must be adequately packaged and labeled, and must conform to any promises made on the package and label.

If your set is a "lemon," then the above requirements have not been met and you are entitled to a new television. On the other hand, if a relatively minor adjustment will solve the problem once and for all, the store will probably be within its rights in refusing an exchange if it repairs the set free of charge.

My advice would be for you to let the store make an effort to repair the set on the understanding that your TV warranty will run from the date of repair, not the date of purchase. Then, if the set fails again within the warranty period, you should demand a new one from the store.

Must I return unordered merchandise that I received in the mail?

Q. Last week I received a religious medallion in the mail. I had never heard of the organization that sent it, nor did I ask for it. Also enclosed in the package was a letter stating that I was to pay $9.95 or return the medallion to the sender. I don't want the medallion, and I'm annoyed at the prospect of making a special trip to the post office and paying for postage to return it. What are my legal obligations and rights?

A. Only two kinds of merchandise can be mailed to someone without his or her consent—free samples clearly marked as such and goods from charitable organizations seeking contributions. In each instance, the recipient may regard the merchandise as a gift and do whatever he or she wants with it. In all other cases, it is illegal even to send unordered merchandise.

If you signed an agreement of some sort to receive and pay for a given number of religious medallions each year, you would be required to live up to your end of the contract. However, based on the facts as you describe them, that is clearly not what happened in your case. Thus, you do not have to return the medallion to the sender. You can keep it, throw it out, or do whatever you wish with it. Then, if the sender in any way harasses you for payment, the matter should be reported to your local post office or the Chief Postal Inspector of the United States, Washington, D.C. 20260. They will then proceed against the sender on your behalf.

I won a suit against a local store; can they refuse to pay because of a technical difference in business names?

Q. Last month I sued a local store in small claims court and won a $30 judgment when the proprietor failed to appear in court. Initially, I was pleased with the result. However, when I sought to collect the $30, the proprietor told me that his store's formal incorporated name is different from the one used for business purposes and that the judgment was thus invalid. Is he right?

A. Yours is an all-too-familiar problem, and in recent years many states have enacted "sue them as you see them" laws to counteract it.

For example, under a New York statute, any person, partnership, or corporation that is sued in small claims court for any conduct arising from its business activities must pay any judgment rendered against its "true name" or any other name in which it conducts business. This latter category includes, but is not limited to, the name maintained on signs at the business premises, sales slips, advertising, checks, telephone-directory listings, and the like. If such a judgment remains unpaid thirty-five days after the creditor seeks payment, he or she is entitled to return to small claims court and commence a new action for the sum of the original judgment plus reasonable attorney's fees, court costs, and a $100 penalty. In one New York case, a judgment against a shoe repair shop concerning a $5.50 pair of heels was ignored by the repair shop owner, which resulted in a second judgment of $122.98 for the plaintiff.

The office of the clerk at the small claims court where you won your original judgment will be able to advise you regarding the existence of "sue them as you see them" laws in your state. The same court officials will tell you how best to pursue your claim and collect your judgment in this or any other small claims court suit. However, in any future action, before filing suit, it might be wise if you checked the defendant's formal name of incorporation, which should be on file at the county clerk's office where the defendant does business. This will make it easier to collect whatever judgment you are eventually awarded.

Can I get my money back if the contact lenses I bought are too painful to wear?

Q. Six months ago I bought my first pair of contact lenses for $200 (which included diagnosis, the lenses themselves, and lessons on how to wear them). At first I was excited about the prospect of never wearing glasses again, but the lenses have been a total failure. I cannot wear them for even a few hours a day without pain. Is there any way I can get my money back?

A. If the lenses were misfitted, you would be entitled to either a new pair or your money back, based on a claim of breach of contract. However, if you are simply "one of those people who can't wear contact lenses," the success or failure of your claim would rest on the reasons for your inability to wear them.

For example, some people cannot be properly fitted for contact lenses due to the curvature of their eyeballs. This is a condition that can be diagnosed before lenses are prescribed and, if you have it, you would probably be entitled to a refund. Other possible reasons for the inability to wear lenses successfully (such as tear ducts failing to produce enough tears or tight eyelids that rub against the lenses each time you blink) can sometimes, but not always, be diagnosed in advance. If your disability could have been diagnosed before you were fitted for lenses, you would probably be entitled to a refund.

But if there is no physical reason for your lack of success, and the only problem is that you are incurably squeamish about putting the lenses in your eye or wearing them, it would be unfair to hold the seller responsible (unless the seller made a false representation of some sort, such as, "It won't hurt a bit; not even the first time you put the lenses in").

If you continue to have problems with the lenses, feel that the seller is at fault, and are unable to reach a satisfactory settlement, you can file suit for a refund. Should you sue, the best forum for your case would probably be small claims court.

What are my rights if my stereo was damaged while being fixed?

Q. Recently I took my stereo to a local repair shop for a minor adjustment of the tone arm. When I brought it home one week later, the turntable was damaged. The store, of course, disclaims any responsibility for this new damage and refuses to repair it without an additional charge. What are my legal rights?

A. This is a case where the burden of proof rests with you. You will have to convince a court that the turntable was in working order when you took the stereo in for repair and damaged when the store returned it. To do so, it will first be necessary for you to testify in court about the working condition of the machine. To bolster your claim, you should have one or more friends on hand as witnesses to confirm your testimony. Obviously, your case will be stronger if you can cite other patrons who had similar incidents with the repair shop, and you might check with your local consumer affairs bureau to see if there is a record of similar complaints. Also, the clerk's office in local courts should be able to tell you whether similar lawsuits have been brought against the shop.

Take your case to small claims court. Should you prevail, the court will be empowered to award you the cost of repairs for the damaged turntable plus the direct cost of bringing your case to court.

Must I pay the caterer for a party I cancelled in advance?

Q. After hiring a caterer for my husband's fiftieth birthday party, I had to cancel the affair due to family illness one week before the scheduled date. Now the caterer insists on being paid in full even though no services were provided. Is he entitled to full payment?

A. Probably not, although most likely he will be entitled to some compensation. Your case boils down to controversy over a breach of contract. The caterer agreed to provide certain services; you agreed to pay for them. Thus, if your agreement was put in writing, the first thing you should do is read the contract. What does it say about cancellation? The caterer will not be entitled to more than the contract allows, and he might even have to accept less.

All parties involved with a breach of contract have a duty to "mitigate their damages"—that is, to limit as best they can any financial loss once they know that the contract will be broken. For example, when the caterer received your notice of cancellation, he had an obligation to try to cut his own losses by cancelling his food orders from wholesalers. Similarly, if he was able to recoup any losses by rebooking an orchestra previously reserved for you, you would be spared that cost.

Also, some states and municipalities have laws that specifically limit the amount of damages a caterer may claim in connection with a cancelled contract. In New York City, for example, if a consumer cancels a catering contract and the caterer is able to rebook the date, the cancellation fee may not exceed either 5 percent of the total contract price or $100, whichever is less, plus actual expenses he has reasonably incurred. And even if the caterer is unable to rebook, the cancellation fee may not exceed the combined total of his lost profit and expenses.

Your best first step would be to try to work out a fair settlement with the caterer. If this cannot be done, he will have the burden of suing and trying to prove his case.

Late furniture delivery

Q. Three months ago I ordered a sofa from a department store and was promised delivery "within six weeks." Now, twelve weeks later, the sofa hasn't been delivered and I want to cancel the order but the store won't refund my money. What are my legal rights?

A. When you ordered the sofa, you entered into a contract which obligated the store to deliver the furniture by a certain date. Some stores seek to water down this contractual requirement by inserting a phrase in their written contracts to the effect that "time of delivery is not of the essence." This phrase, where it exists, is entitled to some weight and often results in the store being granted additional time to deliver furniture by the courts but, even then, delivery must be by a "reasonable" date. If not, you can refuse delivery and sue in small claims court for a refund of your deposit.

Also, some states and municipalities have enacted specific laws that go even further in regulating the sale of furniture. In New York City, for example, the furniture store must give you an estimated delivery date in writing at the time of purchase and notify you in writing if there is a delay. Then, if the furniture isn't delivered within thirty business days of the specified date, you have the option of cancelling your order and receiving a full refund or giving the store more time to deliver. Certain pieces of custom-made furniture are exempt from this law, and the store may be granted additional time if an event beyond its control (such as a trucking strike) causes the delay. But even here, general contract principles will usually require delivery on or reasonably near the agreed-upon date.

Your best first step would be to send a letter to the store asking why there has been a delay and when the furniture will be delivered. Quite possibly, the store will then agree to a price reduction in order to settle the matter, or allow you to cancel the order. If its response is unsatisfactory, you can sue for a refund in small claims court.

Vocational training school refunds

Q. Two years ago my son enrolled in a vocational training school that advertised the promise of steady work at a good salary. Since completing his courses, however, he has been unable to find a job, and the school has done nothing to help him. Is there anything he can do to get his tuition back?

A. There might be. In 1972, to combat misrepresentation and other abuses, the Federal Trade Commission (FTC) enacted a series of regulations that apply to virtually all vocational and home-study schools.

In essence, these regulations provide that a school may not misrepresent its accreditation, facilities, programs of instruction, or teaching methods; issue a diploma or other certificate of completion that misrepresents the accomplishments of its students; use promotional material that implies it is offering employment; or mislead prospective students with respect to the cost of its courses or related books or equipment. In addition, the school must disclose to prospective students, clearly and conspicuously in writing, all relevant facts that would be likely to affect a student's decision to enroll in the training course. Among these facts are an honest appraisal of students' earning potential and the demand for their services upon graduation, and whether post-graduation training will be required in order to make them employable.

A free copy of these regulations, titled *Guides for Private Vocational and Home Study Schools,* can be obtained by writing to the Bureau of Consumer Protection, Federal Trade Commission, Washington, D.C. 20580.

If the school refuses to refund your son's tuition, he can write a letter to the FTC explaining the facts concerning his case. The FTC is empowered to investigate any complaints it receives, and will offer further guidance to your son.

In addition to the federal guidelines, many states and municipalities have laws of their own that regulate the conduct of vocational training schools. Thus, your son might also contact your state attorney general's office and local consumer-affairs authorities for advice.

Paying more than "list price"

Q. I just bought a camera for $200. Now I'm dismayed to learn from a camera-supply catalogue that I paid $50 more than the manufacturer's suggested list price. Is there any way I can get back the extra amount of money I paid?

A. Possibly. As a general rule, retailers are allowed to charge more than the manufacturer's suggested list price, but this does not relieve them of the obligation to be honest. Thus, if the salesperson told you, "This is the lowest price around," or gave some other dishonest sales pitch, you would be entitled to a partial refund on grounds of fraud.

Also, it is possible that the sale violated local law. In New York City, for example, it is unlawful for any business to sell a consumer product for more than the manufacturer's suggested retail price unless that price is "clearly and conspicuously printed" next to the price actually being charged.

Your best first step will probably be to contact local consumer affairs authorities or the attorney general's office in your state to find out if the sale violated any local laws. Then, if it has, you can sue for a refund in small claims court, where you will be able to proceed quickly and without the aid of a lawyer.

What can I do when an item advertised on sale is "no longer in stock"?

Q. Last week I went to a local department store to buy a washing machine advertised as being on sale at a large discount. However, when I got there, I was told that only a limited quantity of that particular model had been available and they were now sold out. Was the store legally obligated to sell me the machine I wanted at the advertised price?

A. The resolution of your case depends primarily on the wording of the advertisement. If the ad was clearly worded and explicit, leaving nothing essential open to negotiation, it constituted an offer; and the acceptance of that offer created a contract. The key is whether upon reading the ad you reasonably believed that you were entitled to purchase a washing machine at the specified price. If so, then the law will lean in your favor, particularly if the store engaged in the deceptive practice of "bait and switch"—advertising one product with the intention of substituting another for it.

Extenuating circumstances, however, might exist. For example, if the advertisement stated that only twelve washing machines were available, to be sold on a first-come-first-served basis, the store would not be required to provide customers with more machines at the sale price. Also, if demand for the machines exceeded any reasonable expectation, a court might rule in the store's favor.

Most states and municipalities have extensive regulations concerning retail advertising. You should first send a letter outlining your problem to the consumer affairs bureau in your area. The bureau will then call or write the store about your complaint. This action may prompt the store to make a fair-settlement offer, either in the form of a cash payment or the sale of the machine at the advertised discount price.

If a satisfactory resolution is not reached, you can file suit against the store in small claims court. Should you prevail, the court will be empowered to award you an amount equal to the advertised sale discount.

A jeweler sold me fake earrings—what can I do?

Q. Several months ago I bought a pair of gold pierced earrings with "14k" clearly marked on them. After wearing the earrings for several weeks, my ears became infected, and I went to our family doctor for treatment. Afterward, he suggested that I have the earrings chemically tested to see whether they really were 14k gold. Sure enough, the test results showed that they were not. What action can I take against the jeweler who sold me the earrings?

A. The jeweler is clearly guilty of breach of contract, and possibly also negligence and fraud. In any event, you should be able to recover several types of damages from him.

First, you are entitled to return the earrings for a full refund. You bought them with the understanding that they were 14k gold, and you should not settle for anything less.

More important, you are also entitled to recover damages for any injury suffered as a natural result of the true chemical makeup of the earrings. In other words, if you can prove that your ears became infected because the earrings were not 14k gold, you will be entitled to reimbursement for your doctor bills and also a reasonable amount for "pain and suffering."

Assuming the jeweler is unwilling to make a fair settlement offer, small claims court is your best bet. Your family doctor and whoever conducted the chemical analysis should be available as witnesses and should bring all records relating to your case. In addition, if you think the jeweler was guilty of deliberate fraud, I would advise reporting him to the district attorney and your local consumer affairs agency in order to spare other customers an experience similar to your own.

Do I have the right to cancel an order given to a door-to-door salesman?

Q. Recently I ordered an encyclopedia from a door-to-door salesman who came to my home. One day later I began to regret the decision and called to cancel my order. I was then told that the papers had already been processed and that my call was "too late." Did I have a legal right to cancel the order?

A. Yes, you did. Since high-pressure sales tactics are too often used by door-to-door salesmen, the Federal Trade Commission has enacted a series of regulations designed to protect consumers such as yourself. These regulations apply to the sale, lease, or rental of virtually all consumer goods and services where the purchase price is $25 or more and the sale is solicited by the seller at a location other than his store, office, or other place of business.

Under these regulations, door-to-door salespeople must furnish buyers with a statement that 1) lists the name and address of the seller, 2) bears the transaction date, and 3) contains words to the effect that "You, the buyer, may cancel this transaction without penalty at any time prior to midnight of the third business day after the date of this transaction." Also, at the time of the sale, the seller must furnish the buyer with two copies of a cancellation form that the buyer may deliver or mail to the seller. (If the cancellation form is mailed, it need only be postmarked before midnight of the third business day following the initial transaction.)

Should you cancel your order, the seller must, within ten business days of receiving your cancellation notice, return any downpayment or deposit. Also, if any goods were delivered under the contract, you can simply make them available at your residence for repossession by the seller (or, if you and the seller agree, you can return them in some other way at the seller's expense). Then, if the goods are not picked up or their return is not arranged for within twenty days of your cancellation notice, you may dispose of them as you wish without further obligation. That means you can keep them, give them away, or throw them out.

Most door-to-door salesmen are aware of the FTC regulations and will abide by them. If the salesman you dealt with insists on violating the law, you should file a complaint with the Federal Trade Commission, Washington, D.C. 20580. Since you were not given the lawfully required "cooling off" period to reconsider your purchase, the commission will see to it that you are not forced to pay for it.

Unnecessary funeral costs

Q. My father died several months ago. The cost of his funeral came to $3,000, including several hundred dollars for embalming (which the funeral home director told me was mandatory under state law). Recently I learned that embalming is not required, and I am beginning to doubt the propriety of several other "required" charges that surfaced after the funeral. In short, I feel as though I was exploited at a time when I was particularly vulnerable. Is there anything I can do to get my money back and, more important, keep other people from being similarly exploited?

A. Yes, there is. Every state in the country has legislation that regulates funeral homes and their conduct of business. In New York, for example, no person can engage in the business of funeral directing unless licensed by the state, and this license may be suspended or revoked if the director violates any law relating to funerals or is in any way guilty of deceit. The same statute also requires the funeral director to furnish a written statement at the time the arrangements are made, listing the services and merchandise to be provided and their price.

Moreover, in 1984, a series of federal regulations went into effect requiring funeral homes to provide itemized lists of goods and services and forbidding misrepresentation with regard to state cremation and embalming requirements.

Like the law itself, the office responsible for enforcement differs from state to state. In New York, the Department of Health is charged with investigating alleged funeral violations. My advice is for you to telephone the state attorney general's office in the area where you live. It will tell you how best to pursue your case and, if warranted, will take action against the funeral home to prevent the recurrence of similar incidents in the future. A free copy of the federal regulations may be obtained by calling the Federal Trade Commission, at (202) 326-2222.

How can I get a moving company to reimburse me for the china it broke?

Q. When my husband and I moved from Chicago to New York, the moving company broke several pieces of valuable china. Now the movers refuse to reimburse us. What are our legal rights?

A. Whenever someone moves, the possibility exists that personal belongings will be damaged or lost. However, unless you signed a contract that specifically limits the mover's liability, you will be protected under rules adopted by the Interstate Commerce Commission (ICC), which regulates all movers engaged in interstate operations. (Moves within a state are governed by local laws, which are similar in principle.)

Under ICC regulations, movers are responsible for the "actual value"—the market value at the time of shipment—of any loss or damage to goods that they pack or are properly packed by the consumer. For example, if you purchased a mattress five years ago for $200, inflation might make today's replacement cost $300. But considering its depreciation over the years, the mattress's actual value would be $150, and that would be all you could expect to collect if the moving company lost it during the move.

Although sentimental value is not weighed in determining actual value, a genuine antique will appreciate with age. It is also important in your case to know that a mover who damages one item from a set is usually liable only for that item—not the entire set—even if the damaged item cannot be repaired or replaced. However, if you can prove that the loss has reduced the value of the remaining items in the set, the mover will be liable accordingly.

To file a claim for lost or damaged goods, you should call or write the mover immediately and request a copy of the company's claim form. Complete the form, and return it by mail. Under ICC regulations, the company must acknowledge your claim within 30 days of receipt, and either pay, deny your claim, or make a firm settlement offer within 120 days. In the event that you do not receive a satisfactory response, you should write the Deputy Director, Office of Consumer Protection, Interstate Commerce Commission, 12th and Constitution Avenue, N.W., Washington, D.C. 20423. This office will assist you in understanding your rights and, if warranted, contact the carrier on your behalf. While the ICC itself cannot file suit, it can explain how you can do so if all else fails.

Free pamphlets, *Lost or Damaged Household Goods* and *Loss and Damage Claims,* are available from all moving companies engaged in interstate commerce.

Can I get a refund if a new swimsuit starts to fade soon after I buy it?

Q. Last month I bought a new swimsuit to take on vacation. It looked great at first, but the colors began to fade after three times in the water. The store where I bought it refuses to give me a refund, claiming that the suit was damaged by a pool that contained too much chlorine. Am I entitled to a refund?

A. You probably will be entitled to either a refund or a new suit. The Uniform Commercial Code provides that goods must be fit for the purpose for which they are purchased, as long as the seller knows what that purpose is and has reason to believe the buyer is relying on the seller's judgment about the goods' suitability. This "implied warranty" will protect you unless at the time of sale 1) the seller specifically stated in writing that no such warranty existed, 2) the goods were clearly marked as defective, or 3) the buyer was or should have been aware of defects after examining the goods.

In your particular case, anyone selling a swimsuit knows that the purchaser is planning to swim in it. And, since it is perfectly reasonable to swim in a chlorinated pool, the suit must be manufactured so that it is resistant to chlorine. Obviously, some fading of color must be expected over the years. And if the pool where you swam contained such a high level of chlorine that it was dangerous for human use, then some damage to the swimsuit in such a short period of time might be allowable. As these circumstances apparently do not apply to your case, the Uniform Commercial Code's "implied warranty of fitness for purpose" will work to your benefit.

Poor wedding photos: is the photographer liable?

Q. My husband and I hired a photographer for our daughter's wedding on the basis of his portfolio and the promise that he himself would take the pictures. On the wedding day, however, he sent an assistant instead, and the photographs turned out to be mediocre. We feel we've been taken advantage of, and wonder if there are any legal steps we can take to be compensated for the assistant's less-than- professional photographs.

A. First, review any written contract you have with the photographer. If it specified that he himself would take the photographs—or if a judge accepts your testimony that there was an oral promise—then there has been a breach of contract. Likewise, if the photographs are poor enough to be considered unprofessional, the photographer will be held liable, whether he or an assistant took them.

Regarding the damages you may be awarded, you can argue that this was a once-in-a-lifetime event, and your daughter's wedding memories will be forever diminished because of the poor photographs. The photographer, on the other hand, could claim that the contract was substantially fulfilled, and the photographs were professional enough for you to keep—therefore, your damages are minimal.

Most likely, the judge will consider both of your arguments, examine the quality of the photos, and determine whether the photographer's failure to appear himself was unavoidable (due, for example, to illness or car trouble) or whether it was an act of bad faith (such as deliberately double-booking the date). If the latter is true, you could be awarded considerable damages.

What to do when mail-order merchandise is late

Q. Early in November I ordered several Christmas gifts from a mail-order catalog, and they haven't arrived yet. With Christmas approaching, I'm getting nervous. Am I legally entitled to cancel the order and purchase my gifts some place else?

A. You might be. Under the Federal Trade Commission Act, mail-order houses have an obligation to notify prospective buyers "clearly and conspicuously" at the time of solicitation how long it will take to ship the items. If no such notification is given, FTC rules require the seller to ship the items within 30 days of receipt of a properly completed order.

If the shipping date can't be met, the seller is obligated to advise you promptly of the delay and give you the option of either agreeing to a later shipping date or receiving a full refund. The seller is also required to provide you with a postage-paid envelope or similar cost-free means of replying. Should you opt for a refund, it must be sent to you by first-class mail within seven days of the time the seller receives your notice of cancellation.

Keep in mind, though, that the time allowed for processing an order doesn't start until after the seller receives your order. And merchandise is considered "shipped" when the seller brings it to the post office or other delivery service—not when you receive it. Moreover, receiving mail-order items in December may take longer than you expect because of the enormous volume of Christmas mail, which makes delivery service slower than usual. Your best first step would be to call the mail-order house (many have toll-free numbers) or send a letter asking if the merchandise you ordered has been shipped. For more information on your rights or to file a complaint, write to the Federal Trade Commission, Pennsylvania Avenue at Sixth Street, N.W., Washington, D.C. 20580.

Is the laundry liable for garment shrinkage?

Q. Recently I took a coat to be dry-cleaned, and, when I went to pick it up, it had shrunk considerably. The dry-cleaners claim it wasn't their fault, that this type of material shrinks and "most people know it;" but I didn't. Can I be compensated for the damage?

A. Most likely, you can. Dry cleaners are supposed to be experts at their trade. As such, they have a contractual obligation to use professional care in cleaning. If they warned you that there was a possibility of shrinkage and you chose to risk it, then they might not be liable for the end result. But unless the risk was explained to you beforehand, they can't assume that you'll be aware of and accept the possible consequences.

If a fair settlement with the cleaner is impossible to reach, your next step would be to file suit in small claims court. Should you prevail, the court will award you damages based on the original cost of the coat, minus its present value after shrinkage, taking into consideration normal wear and tear.

Who pays for undelivered goods?

Q. Last month I signed a receipt when some sheets were delivered to my home. When I opened the box later, I realized that one of the sheets I'd paid for wasn't included. The store now refuses to send a replacement, saying that by signing the receipt I lost my grounds for a claim. Is this true?

A. The store can use the signed receipt as evidence in court that you accepted the order, but that doesn't mean you forfeit your legal rights.

First, write the store a letter, asking them to check their records. Be sure to include your account number and date of the order's delivery. Their records may reveal that the missing sheet was never sent, in which case the store will probably decide to send another one to you.

If this does not resolve the problem, your next step would be to take the matter to small-claims court. The judge will weigh your sworn testimony that you never received the merchandise against the written receipt, and may well rule in your favor—particularly if you explain to the judge that, when you signed the receipt, you did not inspect the package to make sure it contained all the merchandise you ordered. Also, if the store cannot produce a witness who can testify that the missing item was actually delivered, this would weigh in your favor.

Chapter 6

Children Yours and Other People s

When your child is threatened with suspension

Q. Our son is being threatened with suspension from school for disciplinary reasons, and, having heard his side of the story, we believe the threat to be unjust. What legal steps can we take to remedy the situation?

A. The course of action open to you will depend on whether your son's school is public or private. Private schools are allowed considerable leeway in disciplining students, and, if your son is suspended by a private institution, your only alternative may be to sue for breach of contract. Courts have long recognized that suspension is an extreme measure that undermines a school's basic function—to educate. When absent by virtue of suspension, a student obviously is not being educated. Thus, if you sued a private school, you could argue that, though you paid the tuition, the school broke its part of the bargain.

In the case of public schools, a far wider range of remedies is available. The United States Supreme Court has set down minimum guidelines for public school suspensions as follows:

1. Before any suspension, a student must be notified of the charges against him and, if he denies them, given a chance to tell his side of the story.

2. Except in emergency situations, a hearing before an impartial official must precede the suspension.

3. If a presuspension hearing is impractical, a hearing must be held as soon after the suspension as possible.

4. Both the student and his parents must be advised of their right to attend any hearing.

In addition, many states have enacted laws of their own. In New York, for example, a student threatened with a suspension of more than five days has the right to be represented by an attorney at any hearing. In Connecticut, students cannot be suspended until after a hearing. In most states, only a principal, superintendent of schools, or school board can suspend a student. But grounds for suspension vary widely—from "refusal to conform to the reasonable rules of the school" in New Hampshire, to "temper tantrums which disrupt a class" in Iowa.

I would recommend discussing your son's case with school officials to get their side of the story. Quite possibly, with discussion, the matter can be resolved to the satisfaction of both parties. If not, ask for a copy of the state education law and the school district's bylaws to learn local suspension procedures. Ideally, you will be able to resolve the matter without suspension and without a permanent blot on your son's school record.

Putting your baby up for adoption

Q. I am an unwed mother about to give up my baby for adoption. How much will I be allowed to know about the adopting parents? Will it be possible for me to monitor my child's development at some time in the future?

A. Adoption laws vary from state to state, but the chances are that you will be told virtually nothing about the people who adopt your baby and will be unable to follow your child's progress.

Adoption proceedings have one major purpose—to promote the best interests of the child. Before the proceeding, a natural parent is sometimes given information about the adopting family, such as its religion and educational background. However, the law is based on the belief that the child benefits from a close-knit relationship with his or her new parents and nothing that might interfere with this relationship is allowed.

Thus, most states forbid disclosure of the names of natural and adoptive parents to one another. Adoption records are generally sealed by court order, and any person who violates their confidentiality can be held liable for contempt of court. These procedures have been relaxed in several states in recent years, but, for the most part, they still apply. Of course, this can be a bitter blow to people like yourself. Giving up a child always involves pain. Feelings of guilt are common, and there is an inevitable urge to make sure that your child is "all right." These emotions are understandable, but an adopted child's future rests with his or her new family, and the law generally provides that this future be free from any intrusions, even from his or her natural mother.

If a neighbor's child is hurt while playing in my yard, am I liable?

Q. Recently several neighborhood children started playing on a large rock formation in our backyard. I don't mind their playing in the yard, but I am afraid that one of them will fall and injure himself. If that happens, will my husband and I be liable?

A. Probably not. Landowners are required to exercise "reasonable care" regarding the safety of persons whom they permit to enter their property. However, with this in mind, most courts have ruled that homeowners have no obligation to remedy conditions that are purely natural in origin, such as fast-moving streams, large trees, and alluring rock formations. The law presumes that even children are capable of understanding the danger involved in dealing with these objects. Thus, if an injury occurs, you probably will not be held liable.

Also, in order for a child to recover damages for an injury sustained on someone else's property, it is generally held that at least two additional requirements be met: 1) The owner must have known that the condition causing the injury involved an unreasonable risk of harm to children, and 2) that it would cost relatively little to remove the potential danger, and the risk of serious injury is comparatively great. Furthermore, for a child to recover damages in a case like this, it must be shown that he or she was too young to recognize the danger involved. Nonetheless, it is obvious that you don't want the children who play in your yard to be injured—in part, because you don't want to risk being sued, and also because you are concerned about their welfare. Thus, I suggest that you send a letter to your neighbors stating that you have observed their children climbing on the rock and are worried about their safety. Ask them to warn their children about the danger involved, however minimal it might be. For your own protection, keep a copy of the letter.

Are we liable if a child climbs over the fence around our swimming pool and is injured?

Q. My husband and I have a swimming pool in our backyard. We put up a chain-link fence because there are so many children in our neighborhood. If a child climbs over the fence and is injured in the pool, will we be held liable?

A. It will depend to a large degree on the fence. Under the "attractive nuisance doctrine," a person who maintains a potentially dangerous artificial condition (such as a swimming pool) on his or her property must exercise reasonable care to protect children who might be attracted to it but are too young to appreciate the danger involved. Thus, should a child be injured in your pool while trespassing, a court would weigh the precautions you took to prevent any harm to the neighborhood children.

How high is the fence? Is it kept in good repair? Is the gate locked when the pool is not in use? Each of these questions (and others like them) bear on the issue of liability.

If you have taken every reasonable precaution to guard against the possibility of a child's being injured, then it is highly unlikely a court will rule against you. However, if your safety efforts have been slipshod or half-hearted, you and your husband might be held liable.

I should also note that many municipalities have ordinances that require pools to be enclosed in accordance with certain specifications. Obviously, if such an ordinance exists in your neighborhood, you must comply with it.

Perhaps your best first step would be to contact local authorities to determine the minimum safety standards imposed by local law. Then, in addition to meeting these requirements, you should take all other reasonable steps to make your pool as safe as possible.

Our home was vandalized by two boys. Can we force their parents to pay for the damage?

Q. Not long ago my husband and I returned from a vacation to find our home vandalized. Eventually, two fourteen-year-old boys were apprehended. They pleaded guilty to minor charges and were given suspended sentences by the judge because of their "relatively young age." The boys have virtually no money. Is there any way we can sue their parents and force them to pay us for the damage?

A. There might be. As a general rule, parents are liable for the intentional misdeeds of their children if they encouraged the improper conduct. Likewise, a parent who knows that his or her child has a propensity to do wrong and makes no attempt to control the situation may be held responsible for the resulting damage.

If you cannot cite any examples of parental negligence, the success or failure of your case will probably hinge on the will of your state legislature. In recent years, more than half the states in the union have passed laws that hold parents liable for damage caused by the intentional misdeeds of their children, regardless of parental fault. Some of these states place a limit on the amount of money that can be recovered from a parent. Others allow for recovery in cases of personal injury but not property damage. For example, in California a parent can be held liable for up to $10,000 in personal or property damage caused by the willful misconduct of a child up to the age of eighteen. In New York, the maximum liability is $1,500 for damage to privately owned property and slightly higher for municipally owned property.

Opponents of these laws have argued that it is unfair for a parent to suffer financial losses as a consequence of his or her child's behavior. But, as people such as yourself have learned from firsthand experience, it is even more unjust for an innocent victim to bear the burden.

If you wish to pursue the matter, contact your local police. They should be able to tell you whether or not your state has a statute regarding parental liability for a child's misconduct. Then, depending on the extent of the damages sustained, you can file suit in small claims court or a court with the power to award a greater amount in damages.

Fighting college rejection

Q.. For as long as I can remember, our daughter wanted to attend college at our state university. This past month, her application for admission was rejected. Her high school grades are just a shade below ninety, her college board scores are excellent, and her overall record is far better than the records of half a dozen other students who were accepted from her high school. She wants to attend college there very much. Is there any way she can sue to make them take her?

A. You have a tough road ahead, but there are several steps that can be taken. The first move calls for the use of common sense rather than legal expertise. Ask your daughter's guidance counselor to telephone the Dean of Admissions at the college and inquire about the reasons for the rejection. It is possible, albeit unlikely, that her application was misfiled or some important information, such as grades or college board scores, was erroneously recorded. If in fact this did occur, the school will probably volunteer to reconsider the application.

Should the reasons for her rejection satisfy the college but not you, you do have the option of filing a suit. State universities are subject to the Fourteenth Amendment to the United States Constitution, which guarantees certain procedural safeguards and equal protection under law. However, such a lawsuit will be an uphill battle. You will have the burden of proving that, in its deliberations, the admissions committee violated these rights. If it could be shown, for example, that the college was flooded with applications and, in order to lighten the admissions committee's work load, summarily rejected 20 percent of them without any evaluation whatsoever, a court would probably order reconsideration of your daughter's record. Similarly, decisions made on the basis of race, wealth, or other unconstitutionally discriminatory criteria would be cause for a court-ordered reevaluation.

Keep in mind, though, that the college admissions process is highly subjective. No court will be anxious to overrule the judgment of trained administrators, and whether or not your case succeeds, the litigation is likely to be long and expensive. Also, you should remember that those students from your daughter's high school who were accepted might have positive qualities or plus marks on their records that you don't know about. Maybe one of them is an outstanding pianist, or another had grades slightly below your daughter's only because he or she held a part-time job. College admissions are based on more than grades, and rightfully so.

When a toy hurts a child

Q. Our two-year-old daughter needed emergency hospital care after being injured while playing with a birthday toy. Are my husband and I entitled to reimbursement for her medical costs?

A. Your medical insurance may very well cover the incident, but, if not, you still might be entitled to reimbursement (as well as other compensation) from either the manufacturer or the seller of the toy.

While the law varies from state to state, damages are almost always awarded if the product was defective in any way or there was negligence in its labeling, packaging, or marketing. Toys sold for children must be safe for them to use, and any necessary precautions must be clearly stated. Play ovens, for instance, should be made as "child-proof" as possible, with clear instructions on how to use them and conspicuous warnings on any dangers, such as overheating and short circuiting. Toys aimed at two-year-olds should not have removable parts small enough to go down a child's throat. Young children tend to put anything they can get their hands on into their mouths, and, if a stuffed animal intended for infants has a loose eye that falls off and can be swallowed, that product is defective. Similarly, if a toy with sharp metal edges is labeled "appropriate for children of all ages" and a child cuts himself badly while playing with it, both seller and manufacturer are liable for negligence.

Where "product liability" is determined to exist, the injured party can collect reimbursement for medical expenses, plus other damages. The amount of this compensation will depend on the nature of the injuries, and, if your daughter's were particularly severe, I would recommend consulting an attorney before taking any action. But if all you and your husband want is medical reimbursement, you should start by sending separate letters to the seller and manufacturer of the product, stating your case. Then, if a satisfactory settlement cannot be reached, you can sue for damages. It will strengthen your case if you have copies of sales receipts, medical bills, and any other documents relating to the incident.

Can schools tell kids how to cut their hair and dress?

Q. My teen-age son was recently ordered by officials at his high school to "get a haircut or face the consequences." Is such a requirement lawful?

A. It might be. In general, private schools are allowed to regulate students' personal appearance as they see fit. But where public schools are concerned, the courts have left it up to each state to determine whether its schools can enforce such standards. Half the states in the country permit schools wide latitude in regulating student appearance, but this doesn't mean that such regulation is required. The remaining states allow regulation only where such rules can be said to foster some legitimate educational purpose. A see-through blouse, for instance, would probably be forbidden as too disruptive. Long hair might be considered a hazard in shop class if not pinned up.

To determine your son's legal rights, contact the local board of education and request a copy of all legal guidelines governing student hairstyle and dress.

What action can we take to protect our daughter from harassment by another child?

Q. Our neighbors have a twelve-year-old boy who constantly bullies our seven-year-old daughter. He swears at her, throws things at her, and has harassed her to the point that she's afraid to play outdoors on her own. I've complained to his parents on several occasions, but they always just smile and say, "Boys will be boys." Are there any legal steps we can take to protect our daughter?

A. Yes, there are, but obviously there are limits to the law's protection. Children do call each other names and taunt one another, and no child can or should be totally sheltered. However, this does not give any child the right to terrorize another, and your neighbor's child should be dealt with.

Perhaps the best first step would be to send a letter to the child's parents, formally warning them of the situation. As a general rule, parents are liable for the misdeeds of their children if they encouraged the improper conduct or knew that their child had a propensity to do wrong and made no attempt to control the situation. A warning that they will be held financially responsible for any injury to your daughter might encourage them to exert more control.

Then, if the child's bad conduct continues, you can seek a court order against his harassment of your daughter. Such an order would require him to refrain from belligerent behavior, and his parents would then be responsible for its enforcement.

And, last, it's quite possible that the boy's actions constitute a criminal offense. Use of obscene language, harassment, threats of physical harm, and the like are all violations of penal law, and the child could be liable to criminal prosecution as a juvenile offender. Thus, if his parents refuse to cooperate, you do have the option of reporting the matter to the police for further action.

Minors and contracts

Q. Our fourteen-year-old daughter joined a book club recently without fully considering her purchase obligations under the club contract. Now, after receiving several selections by mail, she wants to end her membership before fulfilling the club's purchase requirements. What are her legal responsibilities and rights?

A. Most likely, she will not be bound by the contract. Young people are particularly susceptible to the lure of advertising and are often the ones least able to meet the payments. Thus, in virtually all states, contracts are considered unenforceable if they have been entered into by someone under the age of eighteen without parental consent. Because your daughter is a minor, she will be spared the obligation to buy more books, despite the club's contract. Most book clubs are aware of the law and will not seek to enforce a contract against a minor. Your best first step would be to send a letter to the club explaining your daughter's plight. Then, if a satisfactory response is not forthcoming, you can refer the matter to your state attorney general's office or simply refuse to accept further shipments.

I should add that no book-club contract is binding, regardless of the participant's age, if the contract fails to spell out clearly the consumer's obligations and rights. For example, if you were to respond to an advertisement that failed to mention additional charges for postage and handling, or that neglected to advise you of the club's requirement that a minimum number of books had to be purchased each year, the contract would be invalid.

School gym class injuries

Q. My son broke his leg during a required gym class at school. Is there any way we can collect medical compensation?

A. There might be. In the past, lawsuits involving school athletic programs were generally brought against the manufacturers of defective equipment. However, in recent years, the tendency has been to hold schools responsible. The contention may be that the school was negligent because it hired a gym teacher with inadequate training, or that the injured student was not given proper instruction. No absolute standard for evaluating such allegations exists, but there are certain guidelines which might prove helpful.

The questions to ask are: Was your son being supervised at the time of his injury? Did he receive proper instruction regarding equipment use and the manner in which the game or activity in question should be played? Was he warned of the dangers inherent in what he was being asked to do? Was the gym instructor properly certified, and familiar with both safety rules and the latest teaching techniques?

If the answer to any of the above questions is "no," and if that failure was the proximate cause of your son's injury, then the school (and possibly the gym instructor) can be held liable.

Given the seriousness of your son's injury, your best first step would be to consult an attorney. If you should file suit and win, you and your son will be entitled to reimbursement for his medical expenses as well as reasonable compensation for pain and suffering and any permanent disability.

Are baby-sitters liable for injuries?

Q. I baby-sit for extra income. How can I protect myself against a lawsuit in the unhappy event that a child is injured while in my care?

A. People who provide services often seek to protect themselves against liability by asking clients to sign a written waiver. It is unlikely that a parent would want to use a baby-sitter who made such a request, however, and in some instances even written waivers are not binding.

You can purchase insurance that will safeguard your financial interests, and, if you baby-sit for children in your home on a regular basis, you might want to do this. You should know, too, that even if a child is injured while in your care, it does not necessarily mean that you are liable. To be held legally responsible, the child's parents would have to prove that you failed to exercise a reasonable standard of care in performing your duties.

If you are conscientious and careful, the law should be in your favor.

Getting a refund on summer camp

Q. Several months ago, my husband and I signed up our son for a summer camp program. Now, due to illness, he is unable to attend, but the camp refuses to return our money. What are our legal rights?

A. First, look at the wording of the contract you and your husband signed with the camp. What does it say about cancellation in the event of illness? If there is a specific clause on the subject, that clause will govern. If not, a court will infer a "reasonable" cancellation clause.

Needless to say, people can differ as to what is "reasonable." However, in situations involving summer camps, classes, music lessons, and the like, several standards could work in your favor. For example, the court will ask if the camp had adequate notice to fill your son's spot with another camper. If so, it might rule that a full refund is warranted. It's possible a court will void the contract on grounds of "impossibility"—that is, rule that your son's illness rendered the contract unenforceable because it was understood by everyone that your son's good health was prerequisite to the agreement being carried out.

If the camp continues to refuse to refund your money, small-claims court would appear to be your best forum. Make sure that, when you appear in court, you bring a letter from your doctor outlining your son's health problems.

When can children work?

Q. My 14-year-old son would like to get a full-time job during his summer vacation. Will he need work papers? And what limitations, if any, will there be on the type of employment he can accept?

A. The federal Fair Labor Standards Act prohibits the employment of children under the age of 18 in jobs that might be detrimental to their health and wellbeing. Under this law, children ages 16 and 17 are barred from "hazardous" employment but can hold nonhazardous jobs for unlimited hours. (Federal regulations list 17 types of hazardous employment—for example, roofing and jobs that involve exposure to radioactive substances.) Children ages 14 and 15 can work in nonmanufacturing, nonmining, nonhazardous jobs outside of school hours if their employment is limited to three hours on a school day, 18 hours in a school week, eight hours on a nonschool day and 40 hours in a nonschool week. Their jobs may not begin before seven A.M. or end after seven P.M., except from June first through Labor Day, when evening hours are extended to nine P.M. Employment for children under age 14 is largely limited to delivering newspapers, performing in radio, television, movie, or theatrical productions, and working for their parents in a family-owned business (unless that business qualifies as hazardous employment). Also, all of the federal restrictions are relaxed somewhat for agricultural employment.

Work papers are not required under federal law. Every state, however, has its own child-labor laws, which frequently require work papers and, in some cases, impose restrictions more severe than the Fair Labor Standards Act. For example, under New York law, newspaper-carrier permits are issued to boys and girls ages 11 to 18 and must be carried by the child while working. Children under 16 cannot work for a public messenger service, and children under 18 cannot work as window cleaners. Also, an employment certificate is required for all children under age 18 before they can begin any kind of work.

Contact your state department of labor for specifics regarding the requirements in your area.

When you disagree with your child's school

Q. Our son has been placed in a special class for slow learners in school, and both my husband and I feel that the assessment is wrong and that he is being educated poorly as a result. What can we do?

A. First, call for an appointment at your son's school, and discuss the matter with those responsible for his classification. They will either acknowledge that an error has been made or try to persuade you that the classification is correct. If you're still not satisfied, your next move will depend on whether your son's school is public or private.

With public schools, it is easier to challenge the classification. Ask to see your son's entire school file. Under the federal Family Educational Rights and Privacy Act, upon oral or written request, the school must make virtually the entire file available within a reasonable period of time. Forty-five days is the limit. If you still disagree with the assessment once you've reviewed the file, you can sue the school board to change your child's classification. The board will have to prove in court that your son's ability and performance are such that special education is warranted.

Private schools, on the other hand, are given greater leeway in dealing with their students and may respond to your dissatisfaction by simply telling you to find another school for your son.

Chapter 7

Banks, Finance, Credit, and Taxes

How can I stop a collection agency from harassing me?

Q. My husband recently lost his job, and we are saddled with several large debts that we are unable to pay right now. Most of our creditors have agreed to defer payment, but one store has turned our case over to a debt-collection agency that has been harassing us endlessly. What can we do?

A. You can't make the collection agency "disappear," but you can put an end to its harassment.

In 1977, Congress passed the Fair Debt Collection Practices Act—a law designed to protect consumers such as yourself from harassment as well as deceptive or otherwise unfair collection practices. The law applies to all debts incurred for personal use, where collection is sought by a debt-collection agency. The act provides the following:

1. The debt-collection agency is forbidden to disclose information about your personal finances to your friends, neighbors, or employers.

2. Its representatives may not telephone you before 8:00 A.M. or after 9:00 P.M., make repeated calls, or telephone you at work if your employer prohibits such calls.

3. Obscene language and threats of violence are forbidden.

4. The collection agency may not obtain information about you from anyone by means of false pretenses. It also can't misinform you about your legal rights—such as telling you that it has the right to arrest you.

5. No employee of the agency may impersonate a public official or serve false legal papers on you.

6. If you notify the debt-collection agency in writing that you wish it to refrain from any further contacts, the agency must do so, except that it can then take lawful court action against you and your husband.

The Fair Debt Collection Practices Act allows for lawsuits against debt-collection agencies in both the state and federal courts. Any consumer who wins his or her suit is entitled to fair compensation for the harassment suffered, punitive damages, and reimbursement for all litigation costs including reasonable attorney's fees.

Correcting your credit record

Q. My request for a student loan was recently turned down by a local bank. When I asked why, I was shown a credit company report that inaccurately stated I was in default on payments to a local department store. I always pay my bills on time. What steps can I take to correct the record and get my loan?

A. Your first step should be to ask the reporting agency to disclose all information about you that exists in its files. This request may be made by letter or in person, and the agency must comply without delay either orally or, if you and the agency agree, in writing.

If, after looking over the information, you still dispute the accuracy of the agency's report, you may request either orally or in writing that the report be corrected. The agency must then reinvestigate, correct its records, and notify the bank of its error "within a reasonable period of time." Once the bank receives the corrected report, it may be expected to reconsider your application for the loan. Should the agency continue to insist that you defaulted on payments to the local department store, any future report it issues must include a notation that the item is disputed by you. This will put potential lenders on notice that there is another side to the story and that this side is in your favor.

Credit reporting agencies are subject to regulation by the Federal Trade Commission, which also administers the Fair Credit Reporting Act. If for any reason your problem continues, you should contact the Commission for assistance.

However, in all likelihood, the agency will do its best to treat you fairly. After all, its business depends on providing accurate credit information to its customers. If the bank loses out on an opportunity to do business because of an inaccurate credit report, it will be just as angry with the agency as you are.

Am I liable for a check that has been stolen and forged?

Q. Last month my checkbook was stolen. I reported the theft to the police and called the bank to stop payment on the blank checks, but now I'm being threatened with a lawsuit by a local merchant who accepted one of the checks. Will I have to pay for the thief's purchase?

A. This is a case where the law is on your side. When the store accepted the check, it assumed the risk of forgery and theft. Indeed, incidents of this nature are a primary reason why many businesses will not accept checks from someone who is not a regular customer.

If you were guilty of a grossly negligent act—such as giving your checkbook and identification to a total stranger to hold while you went swimming—a court might rule that your conduct amounted to "constructed compliance" with the check forger's scheme. Under such circumstances, you could conceivably be held responsible. Otherwise, you will not be obligated to reimburse the store for its loss. Rather, it is the store that must bear the cost of accepting the forged check as an unfortunate part of doing business.

At this stage, the burden of action lies with the store owner. Unless he takes further steps and files suit, you are not obligated to do anything. However, to safeguard your position, you should ask the police to send you a copy of your theft report for your records. Also, make sure you keep copies of all related correspondence with the bank, since they may prove helpful in the future.

If I return merchandise paid for with a credit card, must I pay the bill first and then collect my refund from the store?

Q. Last month I used a nationally recognized credit card to purchase some furniture at a local department store. As soon as it was delivered, I realized I had made a mistake. The workmanship is extremely poor and, quite frankly, I think the store sent me a different set of furniture. They say that because it was a sale, the merchandise is not returnable. Can I simply return it anyway and refuse to pay the credit-card company, or must I pay the bill and then sue the store for a refund?

A. Most likely, you will be able to return the furniture and not pay the bill.

Cases such as yours are governed by the Federal Truth in Lending Act. Under this law, if you have a problem with goods purchased with a credit card, you must first try to return them (as you have tried to do) or give the seller a chance to correct the matter. Then, if the seller is unwilling to take the goods back or rectify the error (and the choice of which the seller must do is generally yours), you can refuse to pay the credit-card company's bill provided that 1) your grievance is legitimate, 2) you bought the merchandise in your home state or within one hundred miles of your current mailing address, and 3) the purchase price was more than $50.

If your case meets these requirements, send a letter to the credit-card company, stating your account number and fully outlining your complaint. The company will handle the matter from that point on. Also, you should send the credit-card company a check for whatever portion of your bill is not in dispute.

Can I correct a two-year-old tax return and get back the money I overpaid?

Q. In completing my federal income tax return this past month, I realized that I neglected to take several substantial deductions two years ago. Is there any way I can correct my error and get back the amount I overpaid?

A. Yes, there is. Each year millions of Americans make errors in filling out their federal income tax returns. Thus, the Internal Revenue Service has devised a procedure that will enable you to amend your return and receive a full refund of the overpayment.

The first step you should take is to write or telephone your local IRS office and ask for a copy of Amendment Form 1040X and the accompanying instruction sheet. These will be provided to you free of charge. Then fill out the form, and return it to the appropriate IRS center. Your refund will be mailed to you.

An amended federal income tax return generally must be filed within three years of the date the original return was due (April 15 for most taxpayers) or within two years of the time the tax was paid, whichever date is later. Also, keep in mind that if you overpaid your federal taxes, you might also be entitled to a state refund. Here, your best course of action would be to review your state income tax return for the year in question, and, if you made a similar error, contact local tax authorities about the refund process. In any event, your present experience should serve as an added reminder to keep copies of past returns and supporting records on file for possible future use.

Do we have to report our cleaning woman's wages to the government?

Q. My husband and I employ a cleaning woman who comes in once a week and is paid $20 per half-day. We pay her in cash and do not report her earnings to the government. Are we breaking any law by doing this, and, if so, what are the possible consequences?

A. Few areas of the law are as complex as the Internal Revenue Code. It confuses even the best intentioned of taxpayers, and, like many others, you and your husband appear to have run afoul of this law.

The most common federal income reporting and withholding requirements relate to income tax withholding, the federal unemployment tax, and Social Security.

In your particular case, the wages paid to your cleaning woman are modest enough so that you appear to be exempt from federal income tax withholding requirements and federal unemployment tax. However, Social Security taxes will be levied on you and your employee, and you as the employer are responsible for the collection and payment of both portions. This means that you must withhold Social Security from your cleaning woman on a weekly basis and furnish her with a W-2 form at the end of the year. Even an inadvertent failure to obey this law could subject you to penalty and interest payments as well as liability for all back Social Security taxes, whether or not you collected any portion of them from your employee. Also, if your failure to comply with the law is deemed intentional, you could be criminally prosecuted. This might seem silly to you, since the amount of money in question is small and there are probably tens of thousands of people who are doing exactly the same thing as you. But "the law is the law."

Also keep in mind that each state has its own requirements with regard to state income tax withholding, workers' compensation, and the like. If you want to properly resolve the matter of taxes once and for all, telephone the Internal Revenue Service and your state tax bureau for assistance.

My credit card was stolen—do I have to pay for the thief's purchases?

Q. My wallet was stolen last week and one of my credit cards was taken. I notified the card company within hours, but by the time I did, the thief had already purchased two television sets, an air conditioner, and a stereo system. Am I legally obligated to pay for the merchandise?

A. No, you aren't. Under the Consumer Credit Protection Act, a card holder is liable for the unauthorized use of his or her credit card only up to $50. Thus, you are not responsible for anything the thief charged over that amount.

Moreover, you are not even required to pay the $50 unless the credit-card company can prove each of the following:

1. It warned you prior to the theft that you would be held liable for unauthorized use of the card.

2. It provided you with a self-addressed prestamped notification to be mailed by you to the company in the event of either loss or theft. And

3. The unauthorized use of the card occurred before you notified the company that it had been lost or stolen.

Reputable credit-card companies are well aware of these provisions and will not act in violation of them. Should you receive a bill for an amount in excess of that which is lawfully owed, you may simply refuse to pay it. Under such circumstances, all you need to do is send a short letter to the credit-card company reminding it of the Consumer Credit Protection Act's provisions.

When a stockbroker gambles with your money

Q. When my father died, I received a modest inheritance, which I turned over to a brokerage house for investment. I made it quite clear that I was only interested in secure, long-term investments—"blue chip" stocks or U.S. Treasury bills—but, contrary to my instructions, the representative I dealt with put the money into speculative ventures that have dropped in value. Can I recover my losses?

A. Brokerage houses are required to use "due diligence" to meet customer needs and wishes. If your broker ignored instructions, there are several steps you can take.

For a start, you can file a complaint with the Securities and Exchange Commission (450 Fifth Street, N.W., Washington D.C. 20549) or any of its regional offices. This agency supervises the enforcement of federal laws regarding the sale of securities and investigates possible wrongdoing. Usually, however, it will mount an investigation only when it has received several complaints against a brokerage firm or when a particularly flagrant violation has been reported.

If the agency won't investigate, your best alternative may be a procedure known as arbitration. In arbitration, disputes are resolved out of court by an impartial expert. Virtually every brokerage house in the country is a member of at least one trading exchange that requires it to submit to arbitration. (The name of the trading exchange to which your house belongs will be noted on the information it has sent you regarding sales and purchases of securities.)

Be aware, however, that if you submit to arbitration, you will probably forfeit your right to pursue the case in court. An arbitrator's award is generally considered final.

If you decide on arbitration, you can get information on how to proceed from either the Securities and Exchange Commission or the trading exchange on which the stock was purchased. Essentially, you will have to: 1) prepare a written statement of your claim, 2) sign an agreement submitting your dispute to arbitration, and 3) mail these papers to the director of arbitration at the appropriate exchange, along with a check to cover arbitration costs. For claims under $2,500, the cost is $15. For disputes involving larger amounts, a sliding scale is followed.

When your claim is received, a copy will be sent to the brokerage firm, and it will have twenty days in which to respond. If the arbitrator considers it necessary, or if you request it, he will arrange a hearing. Otherwise, he will decide the matter solely on the basis of the papers submitted. He is expected to render a decision within thirty business days of receiving all the papers, and, if he decides in your favor, he will award you compensation for the money you have lost and perhaps also for the income you would have earned if the money had been invested as you originally requested.

Credit discrimination against women

Q. When my husband and I got married, we agreed that I would keep my maiden name. However, in buying automobiles and other big items for our home, we've found that a number of companies refuse to do business with us on a separate-name basis, insisting that all contracts for credit be signed with his last name only. Is this requirement lawful?

A. Generally, it is not. Over the years women have been subjected to discrimination in the extension of credit. To remedy this type of abuse, in 1974 Congress passed the Equal Credit Opportunity Act. In simple language, the statute states, "It shall be unlawful for any creditor to discriminate against any applicant with respect to any aspect of a credit transaction on the basis of sex or marital status." The Act applies to any person or organization that regularly extends or arranges for the extension of credit, including banks, loan companies, department stores, credit-card companies, and credit unions. Charge accounts, loans, mortgages, and all other kinds of financial credit are covered.

Enforcement of the Equal Credit Opportunity Act is divided among several federal agencies. For example, if a stockbroker refuses to extend credit to you on the same basis as he would a man, the Securities and Exchange Commission will handle the matter. If you are denied a bank loan by a member of the Federal Reserve System because of sex or marital status, turn to the Federal Reserve Board.

To find out where to file other complaints, contact the Federal Trade Commission, Washington, D.C. 20580, which has general jurisdiction over the Equal Credit Opportunity Act. It will investigate any complaint you make or refer you to the appropriate agency.

A former friend refuses to pay back a loan—is there anything I can do?

Q. Several months ago I lent $300 to the man I was dating on the promise that he would pay me back within thirty days. Now we've broken up. I have asked him repeatedly to repay me, but he denies having borrowed the money at all. Is there any way I can sue him and prove my case in court?

A. Yes, there is. Essentially, your case boils down to a question of credibility. It's your word against his and, while you are the plaintiff and will have to shoulder the burden of proof, the judge just might decide that you're more believable than he is.

Your first step should be to file suit in small claims court, where you can, if you wish, proceed without hiring a lawyer. Quite possibly, the threat of a lawsuit alone will encourage your former friend to pay up. If he does not and the case actually goes before the judge, you should tell your story in a simple, straightforward fashion. Obviously, it will be helpful if there is some paper record of the transaction (such as a cancelled check or letter asking for a loan), but such evidence is not absolutely essential. Also, if your former friend has cheated other people out of money in the past, it would be to your advantage if they testified as witnesses. This would show the judge a pattern of conduct on your adversary's part that could be weighed by the court in making its final decision.

Remember, the essential ingredient in your case is credibility. So, when you testify, don't exaggerate or assume an air of vindictiveness. Just try your best to come across to the judge as being honest.

When husbands keep money secrets

Q. To this day I don't know whether my husband has $500 or $50,000 in the bank. Whenever I ask, he won't tell me a thing. Do I have a legal right to full knowledge of our family finances?

A. You might, depending on where you live. Many states now have "equitable division" laws, which hold that both husband and wife are entitled to a "fair share" of the property accumulated by them during the course of their marriage. Also, a growing number of states have followed California's lead and enacted "community property" laws, under which a wife is entitled to half of her husband's earnings after expenses (and vice versa), unless there is a written agreement to the contrary. If you live in a community property state, you could most likely get a court-ordered accounting of your husband's finances.

But, obviously, taking a spouse to court should be considered only as a last resort. And, for the sake of marital harmony, I would mention these laws only if your other efforts to persuade your husband fail. Rather than talk about the law, you might first suggest to your husband that he tell you everything possible about the family finances, so that you won't be unprepared should he unexpectedly die. You might also point out that, with your knowledge of current prices, product durability, and the like, you could help him plan the family finances if you knew more about your financial situation.

Someone has been using my telephone credit card. Am I legally obligated to pay for their calls?

Q. My most recent telephone bill included charges for several long-distance calls to a number that I don't recognize. Apparently someone has learned my telephone credit-card number and is using it to make calls that are then billed to me. Since I requested the credit card, am I legally obligated to pay for the calls in question?

A. No, you aren't. The federal Consumer Credit Protection Act provides that you, as a credit-card holder, cannot be held liable for unauthorized use of your card unless the card issuer has provided a method for determining whether or not the user is authorized. Generally, when a person uses a credit card, her signature is checked to ensure that she is the authorized card holder. However, when someone uses a telephone credit card, there is no way to compare signatures or otherwise find out whether the user is authorized. Thus, the statutory requirement for holding you liable for payment has not been met.

The phone company is well aware of the Consumer Credit Protection Act and will not seek payment in violation of it. If you tell your local telephone company business office about the problem, a company representative will correct your bill and contact the parties who received the disputed calls in an attempt to learn who is using your credit-card number.

We were just audited by the IRS on a false tip from an "unidentified informant." Can we find out who it was and sue?

Q. My husband and I have just been subjected to an extensive audit by the Internal Revenue Service because an "unidentified informant" reported that we had cheated on our income tax return. After an investigation, the IRS ruled that we had, in fact, fully paid our taxes, but the incident cost us quite a bit in terms of lost time, accountant's fees, and annoyance. Is there any way we can find out who the informant was and sue him?

A. Probably not. The Internal Revenue Code requires that all tax returns and information regarding them be kept confidential. And while certain exceptions (such as requests for data by congressional committees) do exist, your situation, I'm afraid, is highly unlikely to be among them.

Unfortunately, the secrecy accorded informants does allow for some abuse. Individuals with grudges can file false "tips," and their targets may be subjected to inconvenience and expense. However, the IRS does try to keep this to a minimum. Only tips with apparent substance are investigated, and these are disposed of by the IRS as quickly as possible.

For example, an anonymous tip that you were claiming two nonexistent children as false deductions might be resolved by the IRS's simply checking local school records. Indeed, the IRS Office of Public Affairs reports that, in the overwhelming majority of cases, tips are disposed of without the taxpayer even being notified that his or her return is under scrutiny.

What can you do about an error after you step away from a bank teller's window?

Q. Last week I cashed a check for $100 at the bank where I regularly do business. I stepped away from the teller's window, and a few minutes later realized that the teller had given me $20 too little. When I returned to point out the error, the bank manager told me that I had lost my right to rectify the error once I stepped away from the teller's window. Was the manager right?

A. No, he wasn't. You didn't "lose your right" when you stepped away from the window, but you did make your claim harder to prove.

Essentially, your case boils down to one of credibility. Unless the teller had $20 too much at the end of the day or has been the target of similar complaints, a court will have little to rely on except your word that you were shortchanged by $20. Still, that could be enough to sustain a judgment in your favor if the judge feels that you are honest.

If you feet strongly enough about the matter, file suit against the bank in small claims court. In effect, the case will boil down to your word against the teller's, and you as plaintiff will bear the burden of proof. However, the judge might rule in your favor and, quite possibly, your filing a complaint will lead to an offer of settlement by the bank.

Should you win in court, the judge will be empowered to award you the original $20 plus reasonable court costs and expenses. But this will not include attorney's fees, so, given the nature of small claims court and the small amount of your claim, it would be advisable for you to handle the case without the assistance of a lawyer.

How can I protect my father's interests now that he can't manage his own finances?

Q. My father handled all of his financial affairs until recently, when he was incapacitated by a stroke. Since then, he has made a fairly good recovery, but his judgment is not as reliable as it once was, and I question whether he is really capable of managing his own finances. Is there anything I can do to ensure that he doesn't waste the money he has worked so hard to save?

A. There are several steps you can take, depending on the severity of your father's condition and the state in which he lives.

The first, and simplest, step would be to have your father execute a "power of attorney" in favor of you or another trusted person with good business sense. By signing a statement to that effect and having it notarized, your father would enable the recipient of the power of attorney to handle certain financial transactions on his behalf. A power of attorney can be cancelled at any time, and the designate's specific responsibilities can be as broad or narrow as your father wishes. Powers of attorney are recognized in every state.

Should your father's condition warrant greater supervision, it will be necessary to go to court. Some states provide for the court appointment of a "conservator" when a person is competent but not fully able to manage his own affairs. All states provide for the appointment of a "guardian" if a person is incapacitated to the point that he can no longer care for his own financial well-being.

A guardian is someone legally responsible for managing the person and property of another who is unable to act on his own behalf. As a general rule, anyone with a legitimate interest in the ailing person's welfare (such as a close relative, prospective heir, or officer of the bank where he does business) can petition the court to appoint a guardian. Then, if the court does find that the person in question is unable to manage his affairs properly, it will name a guardian—most often someone agreed upon by the next of kin.

Initially, you should discuss your father's condition honestly with him and other family members. Then, if your concern persists, get in touch with your family lawyer and ask what course of action he or she recommends.

Am I allowed to deduct a bad debt from my income taxes?

Q. Several years ago I loaned $1,000 to a friend on the understanding that it would be repaid at the end of two years. Our agreement was in writing and my friend acknowledges the debt, but she is unable to pay it. Can I deduct the amount of my loss from my income taxes? And if I do, does that mean the friend will no longer be legally obligated to repay me?

A. A bad debt can be deducted from income on your tax return without wiping out the obligation. However, the debt must really be uncollectible, not just forgiven because you feel sorry for your friend. If you simply forgive the debt without making a genuine effort to collect, then it will be considered a gift and you will not be allowed to deduct it from your taxes at all.

Should you be audited, the surest way to prove uncollectibility would be to get a court judgment that your friend owes you the money, and turn the judgment over to the sheriff's office. If the sheriff examines your friend's finances and reports back that she is unable to pay, your proof will be evident. However, this method is extreme for a transaction between friends, and tax authorities may be satisfied with lesser proof, such as signed statements from you and your friend attesting to her plight.

I should add that, if you deduct the amount of the debt from income on your present tax return and your friend later repays it, future payment must then be reported as income for the year in which it is received.

Can a store ask you to pay a finance charge on an overdue bill without telling you about it beforehand?

Q. Last month I neglected to pay a small bill from a local store. This month, in addition to the amount I admittedly owe, I was billed $3 as a "finance charge." No previous notice of "finance charges" was ever given to me. Is this extra charge legal?

A. No! Charges such as the one you have described are regulated by the federal Truth In Lending Act, which provides that, before a finance charge can be levied, the credit terms must be "clearly and conspicuously" disclosed to the consumer. Among the terms that must be disclosed are: 1) the conditions under which a charge may be imposed, 2) the amount of the charge, and 3) the timing of the charge.

Since you were not notified of these terms, the finance charge is unlawful and you are not obliged to pay it. A simple letter to the store informing it of the Truth In Lending Act's provisions should suffice to terminate the matter.

Tax-return errors: Who pays the penalty—you or your accountant?

Q. I've just received a notice from the Internal Revenue Service stating that there was an error in my previous federal income tax return and that, in addition to the tax, I've been assessed a penalty and interest charge. My records indicate, however, that I gave all necessary information to my accountant and the mistake was his fault. Shouldn't he pay?

A. You might be entitled to partial reimbursement from your accountant. Like other professionals paid to provide a service, accountants must perform in a responsible manner and exercise a reasonable standard of care. Should they fail to do so, they can be held liable for negligence and breach of contract.

To determine who's at fault, review your tax return with your accountant. It may turn out that you failed to provide certain relevant information or that the IRS made a mistake. In the latter event, the accountant can prepare a response to the IRS notice.

If your accountant was at fault, however, he will be obligated to reimburse you for any penalty assessed by the government. You will be required to pay the tax itself because, had the initial computation been correct, you would have been obligated to pay it anyway. As for the interest charge, your accountant could argue that you benefited by using the money before your tax bill was corrected and so you should pay it. But your accountant might be liable for that portion of the interest charge that exceeds the actual return you made on your financial investments.

When a bankrupt person owes you money

Q. My husband and I are owed several thousand dollars by a man who just declared bankruptcy. What can we do about it?

A. Bankruptcy occurs when a person's financial liabilities outweigh his or her assets and a court chooses to wipe the slate clean by applying those assets to pay off debts. An individual cannot simply declare himself or herself bankrupt, however. Only a federal bankruptcy judge can do that, at the request of the debtor or one of the creditors. Then a court-appointed trustee will notify all creditors listed by the debtor, gather the debtor's assets, pay the tax obligations and employees of the debtor, and distribute leftover funds to other creditors on a pro-rata basis.

As for your particular situation, several options exist. It's possible that the trustee will be able to award you partial compensation from the debtor's assets. Also, in some instances, someone else might be obligated to make good on the debt. (For example, if another person cosigned a loan agreement between you and the debtor, that person would be liable to pay it off.)

In some cases, as in unpaid loans, you'll be able to cut your losses further by deducting the amount lost from your total income when you file your income-tax return next April—although a deduction will not be allowed if the debt was an unpaid bill for personal services. Also, if the money owed you is the consequence of a court judgment involving moral turpitude or fraud on the part of the debtor, it must be paid in full. The debt will not be wiped out by a bankruptcy proceeding.

The court-appointed trustee involved in this particular bankruptcy should be familiar with the facts of your case. Once you are given formal notice of the proceedings, contact him or her for advice.

Recovering your losses if someone gives you a bad check

Q. Recently, someone gave me a check for several hundred dollars. I deposited it in my bank account and wrote several checks against it. Then the original check I had been given bounced, and, as a result, my own checks were returned for insufficient funds, and several penalty charges were levied against me. What legal steps can I take against the person who gave me the bad check?

A. This is a case in which the law leans in your favor. Based on the facts as you describe them, the person who gave you the bad check is liable for breach of contract. And, if he or she knew the check was bad, you can sue for fraud as well. In either case, you are entitled to the full amount of the check plus bank penalty charges and lost interest. In the case of fraud, you might also be awarded compensation for damage to your reputation and any business problems you had as a natural result of being passed the bad check.

Your first step should be to write the person who gave you the check and ask for a good-faith replacement, plus compensation for your losses. Then, if a fair settlement cannot be reached, you can file suit in small claims court.

Are you liable for your husband's premarital debts?

Q. My husband had credit problems before we were married, and now his creditors want me to use my savings to pay off his debts. Am I legally obligated to do so?

A. Definitely not. His creditors are not entitled to your assets. However, I suggest you take the precautionary step of maintaining clearly separate assets now and in the future. Whenever possible, all bank accounts, stock, property deeds, and the like should be registered in your name alone, not held jointly with your husband. This is perfectly proper, provided you purchase them with your own money, and it will protect you from creditors with whom your husband did business before you were married. It is also advisable to avoid joint financial undertakings with your husband, such as cosigning loans, until all his financial problems are resolved.

The best way to pay—credit card versus installment buying

Q. I want to buy some furniture for my new apartment, but I'm short on cash. Is it better to buy on an installment plan or to pay with a credit card?

A. First, make sure you are not overextending your finances and will be able to pay back this debt. Next, compare interest rates. Sometimes, rates charged on installment contracts are lower than those charged on money owed to credit card companies. Obviously, the lower the rate, the better it is for you. When paying in installments, however, you'll be required to sign a contract agreeing to the store's individual payment schedule, and you may have to pay a substantial service charge.

Also, under most installment contracts, the purchaser doesn't actually own the item until the last payment has been made. This means that, if you miss a payment, the seller has the right to repossess your furniture quickly. By contrast, if you buy your furniture with a credit card, you'll own it in full immediately. If you fail to pay your bill, the only recourse your creditor has is a full-blown lawsuit.

When your brokerage firm is in financial trouble

Q. I have an account with a brokerage firm that is experiencing financial difficulties. What steps can I take to protect my legal rights?

A. The most obvious step is to switch your account to another brokerage house. However, if you want to stay with your present broker, there are several steps you can take. Ask that all stock certificates and other proof of ownership regarding financial transactions be registered in your name and sent to you, rather than held by the firm for your account. Request that all dividends and other payments (such as proceeds from the sale of stock) be sent to you, not held by the company.

Should the brokerage firm's financial problems grow worse, it might be necessary to "liquidate" the company. In such an event, most likely you'll be protected by the Securities Investor Protection Corporation.

SIPC is a nonprofit corporation designed to protect customers who invest in United States securities markets. Virtually all broker-dealers whose principal business is within the United States are members. SIPC will not guard against losses from the rise or fall in market value of your investments. However, it will protect you against certain other losses that occur when a brokerage firm becomes insolvent. Under SIPC's regulations, all securities and cash held by a firm that fails financially are distributed among the firm's customers. After that, SIPC funds are made available to satisfy the remaining claims of each customer up to a maximum of $500,000 per customer (including up to $100,000 on claims for cash, as distinct from claims for securities). Most types of securities (such as stock, bonds, notes, warrants, and certificates of deposit) are covered by SIPC. However, no protection is provided for unregistered investment contracts or for gold, silver, or other commodity interests. Cash is protected if the money was left in an account for the purpose of purchasing securities, whether or not the broker paid interest on the cash balance. For a free pamphlet entitled How SIPC Protects You, write to Securities Investor Protection Corporation, 805 Fifteenth Street, N.W., Suite 800, Washington, D.C. 20005.

When your bank debit card is stolen

Q. I recently lost my wallet, and someone used my bank debit card to withdraw several hundred dollars from the automatic teller machine at my local bank. Now the bank refuses to restore the money to my account. What are my legal rights?

A. As a general rule, a cardholder's liability for the unauthorized use of a lost or stolen credit card is limited to $50—and the penalty applies only to purchases made before the loss or theft is reported.

However, a different standard applies to automated teller machine cards. Under the federal Electronic Fund Transfer Act, your liability for an unauthorized withdrawal is limited to $50 if you notify the bank that issued the card within two business days after learning of the loss or theft. Thereafter, your potential liability jumps to $500. And if you fail to report an unauthorized transfer that appears on your bank statement within 60 days after the statement is mailed to you, you risk unlimited loss on withdrawals. This includes all the money in your account, plus whatever credit line the bank has extended.

You should report any lost or stolen credit card to the bank immediately—by telephone and in writing. The bank will then have ten business days to investigate your complaint, and thereafter must restore the disputed amount to your account pending completion of its investigation. If the bank's final decision fails to resolve the matter to your satisfaction, you may file a complaint with the Division of Consumer and Community Affairs, Board of Governors of the Federal Reserve System, Constitution Avenue and 20th Street, Washington, D.C. 20551. Also, under the Electronic Fund Transfer Act, you may sue the bank for three times the amount improperly withheld from your account, plus $1,000 in punitive damages.

If your name is misspelled, is a check still valid?

Q. The other day I received a check made out to me, but my name was misspelled. Is the check valid, and if so, how should I endorse it?

A. The check is valid. Endorse it on the back by writing your name as it was misspelled on the check, followed by the word "sic" in parentheses. Then, directly beneath this, sign your name correctly. This procedure will ensure that the check is properly deposited to your account.

Here are some other check-writing guidelines to remember when the validity of a check is in doubt:

- Checks written in pencil are valid, but for your own protection, you should always use ink; anyone can erase a penciled-in amount and substitute a larger one.

- Many banks refuse to honor a check with an entry that has been crossed out or written over, even if the change has been initialed by the payer.

- A check is technically valid for six years, unless a time limitation is printed on the front. But most banks are reluctant to honor a check more than 90 days old.

Claiming dependents as tax deductions

Q. Since my divorce, my parents have provided the primary financial support for me and my daughter. Can they claim her as a dependent for a deduction on their federal income-tax return next year?

A. They might be able to claim both you and your daughter, as long as both dependents meet the following requirements:

- The dependent must be a citizen or resident of the United States (or a resident of Canada or Mexico) or an adopted alien child who has lived the entire year with a U.S. citizen in a foreign country.

- The dependent must be related to the taxpayer as a parent, child, or sibling. You will be qualified to take the deduction whether this is a step or blood relation. The dependent may also be claimed if he or she is a grandparent, grandchild, or in-law or—if related by blood—an aunt, uncle, niece, or nephew. Any other person who lived in the taxpayer's home as a member of his or her household for the whole year is eligible to be claimed as a dependent, too.

- The dependent, if married, must not file a joint return with his or her spouse—except where a return wasn't required and they filed jointly to obtain a tax refund.

- The dependent must have received less than $1,040 in gross income for the year. Children under age 19 and full-time students, however, are exempt from this limitation.

- The dependent must have received more than half of his or her support from the taxpayer.

From what you have written, unless some intervening circumstance exists (such as a provision in your divorce judgment specifically allowing your ex-husband to claim your daughter as an exemption), you and your daughter meet these requirements and can be claimed as dependents by your parents.

Am I responsible for my roommate's debts?

Q. I've lived with a friend for several years, and I'm worried because she owes people money. Can I be held legally responsible for her debts?

A. No, not unless you've agreed to be liable. Someone who consigns a lease, loan agreement, or another type of financial document can be held responsible under the terms of the signed contract. Likewise, if you and your friend have entered into a joint business venture, you may be obligated to pay the business's debts. And, if you jointly purchased furniture or other household items that haven't been fully paid for, you might be held responsible for the unpaid balance or find the property subject to repossession. Aside from such situations, however, you're responsible only for your own debts.

Keep in mind, though, that when two friends live together, their finances can become intertwined. So, if you're concerned about your roommate's debts, you might want to keep detailed records documenting who owns what. That way, if her creditors ever seek payment through court action, your financial assets and personal belongings will be safe.

Age discrimination and credit

Q. My father, who is in his mid-60s, has been denied a credit card and car loan by a local bank on the grounds that his age makes him a poor credit risk. Is this lawful, and, if not, what can he do about it?

A. In 1968 Congress passed the Consumer Credit Protection Act, which provides in part that "it shall be unlawful for any creditor to discriminate against any applicant... on the basis of age." This applies to all banks and most other lending institutions.

There are, however, some ways in which a bank can lawfully consider age in connection with a credit transaction. For example, a borrower must be old enough to enter into a contract legally (age 18 in most states, but up to 21 in others). Also, creditors can inquire about an applicant's age to determine credit history, find out how long an income level will continue, and learn pertinent facts about credit worthiness. But a bank cannot turn down credit card or loan applications solely because of age, nor can it close a credit account or require reapplication simply because a customer reaches a certain age.

If your father feels he has been unlawfully discriminated against, he should write the Board of Governors of the Federal Reserve System, Constitution Avenue and 20th Street, N.W., Washington, D.C. 20551. Complaints regarding credit institutions other than banks should be addressed to the Federal Trade Commission, Pennsylvania Avenue and Sixth Street, N.W., Room 496, Washington, D.C. 20580. These agencies will investigate your father's complaint, and may refer the matter to the Attorney General of the United States for further prosecution.

Your father can also hire his own attorney and bring suit against the bank, if he does so within two years of the alleged discrimination. If he wins the suit, under the Consumer Credit Protection Act, he would be entitled to recover any financial loss suffered as a result of the bank's unlawful conduct, punitive damages up to $10,000, court costs, and reasonable attorneys' fees.

Chapter 8

Accidents Large and Small

What should I do to protect my rights if I'm involved in a car accident?

Q. Several months ago I was involved in an automobile accident. It was not my fault, and the other driver's car sustained only minor damage, but I wound up losing a $300 judgment in small claims court. What steps can I take to protect my legal rights if I am involved in an accident again?

A. Perhaps the most important thing you should do is notify your insurance company immediately after the accident. Then, if you are sued and lose a court judgment within the terms of your policy, the company will be responsible for paying the judgment up to the amount specified in your insurance contract. Also, in virtually all cases, the insurance company will furnish a lawyer for your defense, provided you notify it promptly of any accident or lawsuit.

In addition, there are a number of steps you can take at the accident site. Get the name, address, and telephone number of each witness and the other driver. Make a note of the latter's driver's license, car model, and license-plate number. Also, jot down the time of day, weather conditions, and your version of the accident. In order to guard against a phony damage claim, ask one of the witnesses to make a note of the damage sustained by each car.

In the event of injury, call for an ambulance, or make certain that the injured party is otherwise properly treated. And don't leave the scene of the accident without stopping to identify yourself. "Hit-and-run" driving is a criminal offense.

Do you have to report every car accident, no matter how minor?

Q. I was recently involved in a minor accident when another driver collided with my car. He acknowledged that the accident was his fault and was extremely apologetic. There was no damage to my car and his bumper was only slightly dented. We exchanged license numbers and the man told me, "You don't have to report this to your insurance company. It was my fault. I won't file a claim against you."

I suffered no damage of my own and am inclined to follow his suggestion. The accident wasn't my fault, and I don't want it on my insurance record. If I don't report the incident, could it affect me later?

A. Yes—and very adversely. An automobile insurance policy is a contract, and you have to live up to certain contractual obligations spelled out in the policy. If you read your policy carefully, I suspect you will find a clause requiring you to report all accidents to the insurance company as soon as possible. If you fail to do so, the company may well contend that it is not obligated to defend you in any suit arising out of this particular accident.

You might be right in thinking that the other driver accepts full responsibility for the incident and will not sue. However, people involved in automobile accidents sometimes develop injuries which lead to a later "change of heart." Also, a number of states have enacted "no-fault" legislation requiring damage payments regardless of blame.

Report the accident to your insurance company as soon as possible.

My car hit a huge pothole—can I make the state or city pay for the repairs?

Q. Last week I was driving to work when my car hit a huge pothole in the center of the road. Fortunately, I was only going twenty-five miles an hour so I wasn't injured, but it will cost $500 to repair the damage to my car. Am I entitled to a reimbursement from the city or state government?

A. You might be. But first you must prove that one of these governments was negligent. Potholes are an inevitable result of heavy traffic and poor weather, and the mere fact that one exists does not prove that the city or state is at fault. You must show either that the road was poorly constructed or that the authorities responsible for road repair and maintenance had been warned of the condition prior to your accident and had failed to correct it.

This, of course, leads to a second question: Which authority is responsible for the upkeep of this particular road? In the area where you live, the state might be responsible for highway maintenance, and the town government for the maintenance of local streets. Possibly, your local county government also has some responsibility. If you are going to file suit, you must be sure that it is against the proper party.

And then you must find out whether the responsible government entity is immune from a lawsuit. One of the quirks in American law is that no state can be sued unless it "consents" to the suit. And while every state has legislation that allows it to be sued in certain types of cases, these statutes vary in scope. Local municipalities are usually granted similar protection. Also, even when a state or municipality consents by statute to be sued, it sometimes sets up unusual procedural requirements. For example, an individual planning to sue the City of New York must serve a notice of his or her intention to sue within ninety days of the incident complained of.

As you can see, your case involves several complex questions of law, and the modest amount of money involved makes it unlikely that you will want to spend much on a lawyer. My advice is to contact your local bar association and ask for the names of several attorneys who can explain the local law to you in a single sitting for a minimal fee. Then, with their counsel, you will know how best to proceed.

I broke my tooth in a restaurant—can I sue?

Q. I broke a tooth on a sliver of metal when I bit into a piece of pie in a restaurant. When I complained to the restaurant manager, he said, "Don't blame me, I bought the pie from a bakery. Sue them if you want."

My dentist says it will cost several hundred dollars to cap the tooth. When I asked the restaurant manager for the name of the bakery where he bought the pie, he said he did business with several bakeries and did not remember which one had sold him the pie in question. Do I have grounds for suing the restaurant?

A. Yes. The problem of injuries caused by restaurant food has been a subject of controversy in the courts for many years. There once was a time when a patron could only recover damages if the restaurant had been negligent in preparing the harmful meal. However, virtually every state in the country now follows a doctrine known as "strict liability" with regard to the sale of food. Under this rule, a restaurant may be held liable for the sale of defective food that causes harm in some way, even though the restaurant was not negligent and exercised all reasonable care in preparation.

The principle of strict liability is involved when the food causing the injury is "defective." Some courts have held that the inclusion in food of a substance natural to the product (such as a cherry pit in a piece of pie) does not constitute a defect. However, food that is contaminated or contains a foreign substance such as wire or glass is defective by any standard. The inclusion of a sliver of metal in a piece of pie places that pie squarely in the category of "defective" products.

If you have not already done so, write out a list of details surrounding your accident, including such items as the date of the incident and the names of witnesses. Keep a careful record of all dental bills and, if you still have the offending sliver of metal, hold on to it. When your dental work is finished, you will then be in a position to pursue your claim against the restaurant in small claims court or some other forum of your choosing.

When a worker is injured in your home

Q. Several weeks ago a television repairman hurt himself when he fell in my apartment. Now he's threatening to sue me for damages. Under what circumstances can I be held liable?

A. When the repairman slipped and fell in your home, it gave him a potential claim against you for negligence. But you will not be held responsible unless you can be shown to have caused the fall in some way. To be liable, you must have allowed a dangerous condition to exist in your apartment—for instance, wet floors—and this condition must have been the cause of the repairman's fall. If he fell simply because he was clumsy or for some other reason beyond your control, you're not liable.

Many homeowners and apartment dwellers have liability insurance that covers incidents of this type. If you have a policy, you should report the accident to your insurance company at once. And to guard against similar incidents in the future, make certain that your home is free of potential hazards, such as area rugs that slide around and ceiling lamps that are hung too low.

I was injured while skiing. Can I sue?

Q. Last month I dislocated my knee in a skiing accident. Even though the resort had signs warning "Patrons Ski At Own Risk," I feel that the resort was at fault. Am I entitled to compensation for my injury?

A. You might be, depending upon a number of factors. First, you will have to establish who was at fault and how you can prove it. What exactly caused your injury? Was it a badly maintained trail? Did you rent defective equipment from the resort? You'll have to demonstrate through your testimony and, if possible, that of others that the resort failed to adhere to reasonable safety standards—and that this failure led to your injury.

The next issue to consider is the warning signs. A sign saying "Patrons Ski At Own Risk" does not absolve the resort of all liability. However, it does mean that the resort is not responsible for skiing accidents beyond its control simply because they occur on its premises. And in some states there are laws that go even further in limiting the liability of such resorts. In Utah, for example, a recently enacted statute holds that certain risks are inherent in skiing and that no compensation from a ski-resort operator is necessary for injuries to a skier resulting from those risks. The "inherent risks of skiing," according to this statute, are the following: "those dangers or conditions which are an integral part of the sport, including changing weather conditions, variations or steepness in terrain, snow or ice conditions, surface or subsurface conditions such as bare spots, forest growth, rocks, stumps, impact with lift towers and other structures and their components, collisions with other skiers, and a skier's failure to ski within his own ability."

Regardless of warning signs and statutes, you'll have a fairly good chance of recovering damages if you can prove that the resort was guilty of "gross negligence"—that is, unconscionable carelessness. An example of this would be a resort allowing a ski lift it knew to be defective to remain in operation. However, establishing gross negligence is not an easy matter, and it's best left to a lawyer. If you don't have one, your local bar association (which is listed in the telephone directory) will provide you with a list of attorneys qualified to handle the matter at a reasonable rate.

Your car, with someone else driving, is involved in an accident

Q. Last month a friend borrowed my car and was involved in an automobile accident. Am I liable to the other driver if my friend was negligent?

A. You might be. In most states, the owner of a motor vehicle is liable only for his or her own negligence or, if a household head, the negligence of a family member. However, a growing number of state legislatures (including those of California and New York) have adopted a different standard. These states have enacted laws that hold a car owner responsible for the operation of an automobile whenever the vehicle is driven with the consent of its owner.

Moreover, courts have shown a marked tendency in recent years to expand upon owners' liability. Thus, even in states where liability can be predicated only on negligence rather than ownership, owners have been found legally responsible to injured persons if they: 1) loaned their car to someone who they knew was a reckless driver; 2) loaned their car to someone who was under the influence of liquor or drugs; 3) failed to ascertain whether or not the borrower had a valid driver's license; or, in a few cases 4) carelessly left their keys in the car, which led to its being stolen, after which an accident resulted.

Whenever an accident involving you or your automobile occurs, it should be reported to your insurance company at the first available opportunity. Then, with the aid of the insurance company and (if you wish) your own attorney, your rights and obligations can be fully assessed.

I broke a vase in a store. Must I pay for it?

Q. Last week, while shopping, I picked up a vase on display to admire it. Then, much to my distress, I dropped it. At the sound of the crash, the store's owner appeared, pointed to the price tag lying on the floor, and told me I owed him $60. 1 did not intend to buy the vase, broken or otherwise, and the incident was clearly an accident. Still, the store's owner continues to insist that I pay him the $60. Am I legally obligated to do so?

A. Unfortunately, this sounds like a case where the legal merits weigh against you. Vases don't usually fall to the floor without someone being at fault and, as the person holding it, you are the one most likely to blame.

Basically, the store's case boils down to the charge that you were negligent in handling the vase. It is possible that you will be able to present evidence to contradict this contention. For example, if you could prove that someone with greasy fingers handled the vase before you and, as a result, it slipped from your firm grasp, you would not be responsible for the damage. Likewise, if someone bumped into you from behind at the moment you picked up the vase, that person rather than you might be held liable.

Should you be sued by the store, even without these mitigating factors, it is conceivable that an understanding judge will rule in your favor. One could well argue that public display of the vase invited handling, and handling makes some breakage inevitable. But, considering the case from the store's point of view, you must admit that a businessman can hardly stay in business if he can do nothing about the destruction of his property, whether accidental or not. It is not necessary for him to post a sign saying "If you break it, you've bought it," for you to be held liable.

One step you might take to avoid a lawsuit is to suggest to the store owner that he see whether his insurance policy covers the loss. If it does not and he continues to insist on payment, the decision as to whether to reach a compromise settlement or let the case be taken to court is up to you. However, keep in mind that the store's loss is less than the retail price of the vase. Like any other retail outlet, it bought the vase from another source for resale at a profit. Thus, you shouldn't pay more than the wholesale price of the vase.

A car accident—and both drivers are at fault

Q. Recently, while driving to work, I was involved in an automobile accident when another driver went through a red light and struck the side of my car. Now his insurance company is refusing to pay me a penny, saying I was partially to blame for the accident. In truth, I was going five miles over the speed limit and there are witnesses to that fact, but the accident was primarily his fault. What are my legal rights?

A. That will depend to a large degree on where you live, where your car was insured, and where the accident occurred. About half the states in the country have adopted "no-fault" automobile insurance. Under these laws, a party who suffers personal injury or property damage can be reimbursed by his or her own insurance company regardless of who was at fault in the accident. The maximum reimbursement varies from state to state, from as low as $2,000 to as high as $50,000. Further damages can be sought from the other driver if circumstances warrant.

Also, over two-thirds of the states employ the rule of "comparative negligence" in resolving automobile accident claims. Under this standard, an injured party can recover damages even if he or she was guilty of contributory negligence. However, the amount of damages recovered will be reduced in proportion to the claimant's own negligence as determined by the court. For example, if your car repair bill was $500 and you were found to have been 20 percent responsible for the accident, your recovery would be $400.

If the other driver's insurance company continues to maintain its hardline position on settlement, your best step would probably be to consult with an attorney to determine the law in your state.

What can I recover after an automobile accident?

Q. Last month my car was badly damaged in an accident. The other driver's insurance company is willing to pay for the repairs (which totaled $800), but it refuses to reimburse me for towing charges or the amount I had to pay a car rental agency while I was waiting for my own car to be fixed. Am I legally entitled to reimbursement for these extra expenses?

A. If the accident was the other driver's fault, you are entitled to reimbursement for all damages directly caused by his negligent conduct. This includes: 1) damage to your car; 2) any personal injuries suffered by you; and 3) all other expenses reasonably incurred by you as a result of the accident. Towing charges and car rental payments fall within the last of these three categories. If the other driver's insurance company is unwilling to reimburse you for them, you have the option of refusing their settlement offer and filing suit for the full amount.

Keep in mind, though, that lawsuits can be slow and expensive, and their end result is never guaranteed. Thus, you should carefully consider accepting a reasonable settlement offer. Also, you would be well advised to review your own automobile insurance policy and the membership plan of any automobile club to which you belong, as they might provide reimbursement for your towing and car rental payments.

If someone is injured while using one of our tools, are we liable?

Q. On several occasions neighbors have borrowed power saws, electric drills, and other tools from my husband. If someone is injured while using them, will we be held liable?

A. In most instances, no—but there are certain circumstances where a court might hold you responsible. Therefore, several precautionary measures should be taken:

1. Warn any neighbor who borrows your tools about the hazards inherent in handling them.

2. Make sure the borrower is fully versed in the tool's operation.

3. Do not lend a tool that is defective in any way.

4. Make certain that any person borrowing a tool has the capacity to use it safely. (For example, power equipment should never be lent to a child or someone who is intoxicated.)

In essence, these rules amount to little more than the exercise of common sense. But if you violate them, you may be called on to pay for the consequences. The care you show for your neighbor's safety should be equal to that you would exercise on behalf of your family and yourself.

The "Dram Shop Doctrine"

Q. Last month my husband was seriously injured when he was struck by a car. The driver was so intoxicated that the police could barely understand his speech, and a blood test revealed three times the level of alcohol required for a finding of drunk driving. But the driver is penniless and the car is not covered by any insurance. Is there any way we can recover for my husband's injuries?

A. There might be. Some states have set up insurance pools designed to compensate victims of uninsured drivers. Others allocate funds to the victims of certain types of criminal conduct (and, keep in mind, driving while intoxicated is a criminal offense). However, recovery from these pools is generally limited to a relatively small amount. Thus, your best chance for success will probably lie within a still-developing area of the law known as the "Dram Shop Doctrine."

The Dram Shop Doctrine holds that the seller of an intoxicating beverage can himself be held liable when he serves someone up to or past the point of intoxication and the sale results in harm to another person, such as your husband. About one-third of the states in the country have adopted this rule. Moreover, some courts have extended it to cover liquor served at private parties in addition to that offered for sale.

Your best first step would be to consult with a lawyer regarding the existence and applicability of uninsured driver pools, crime compensation boards, and the Dram Shop Doctrine in your state. Then, if the Dram Shop Doctrine does apply, you should find out from police records where the driver did his drinking. It might be that those who share the responsibility for the driver's condition are both able and legally obligated to compensate your husband for his injuries.

Jagged edges and minor mishaps

Q. Last week, I tore an expensive skirt when my knee brushed against a bolt on the underside of my table at a local restaurant. Is the restaurant obligated to pay for a new skirt?

A. The owners of a restaurant, store, or any other establishment open to the general public have a duty to provide safe surroundings for their customers. This does not mean that a commercial establishment must be accident-proof, but operators of a business are required to exercise reasonable care in avoiding hazardous conditions. In your case, as you describe it, the restaurant failed to meet this burden.

Your first step should be to notify the restaurant of the mishap. Quite possibly, it has an insurance policy that will pay for a new skirt. If not—and if the management fails to make a reasonable settlement offer—you can file suit in small-claims court. Your case will be strengthened if you bring the skirt as well as proof of its purchase price to the hearing.

If it's your husband who's at fault, can you recover damages for a car accident?

Q. Recently my husband and I were in a car accident. He was driving, the accident was his fault, and I was the only one injured. Our insurance company has refused to pay for my medical expenses. Are they correct?

A. Traditionally, a wife could not sue her husband to recover damages for personal injuries, regardless of how they were sustained. In recent years, however, the law of spousal immunity has changed, and most states now allow lawsuits between a husband and wife for bodily injury. This right is limited in a few states by "guest statutes" that prevent a passenger from recovering damages from the driver unless the driver was guilty of wanton misconduct or intoxication. If your state does not have such laws, you should be able to collect for medical expenses and personal injuries.

Carefully review the wording of your insurance policy to see what it says about accidents of this nature. Then, if a satisfactory settlement cannot be reached with the company, you should consider filing suit against your husband. Such a move would not mean that you are angry with him. Rather, it is a technical necessity to force the insurance company to make good on its policy obligations.

Consult your family lawyer regarding the law of spousal immunity and automobile guest statutes in your state. If you do not have a lawyer, your local bar association can give you the names of several qualified attorneys. Then, if the law permits, you can proceed with your claim. Your lawyer should also find out if your state has "no fault" insurance laws that will allow you to recover your medical expenses regardless of the circumstances of the accident.

If your seatbelt was unbuckled, will you be unable to collect damages after an accident?

Q. Last month, I suffered minor injuries in an automobile accident. The accident wasn't my fault, but the other driver's insurance company is refusing to pay me a penny because my seatbelt was unbuckled at the time of the accident. What are my legal rights?

A. This will depend on several factors. In recent years, a growing number of states, such as New York, have enacted laws requiring drivers and front-seat passengers to wear seatbelts. Also, some courts have ruled that, even without these statutes, a person can be found "contributorily negligent" if his or her seatbelt is unbuckled and injuries are suffered during an accident. To exercise this defense, however, the other driver's insurance company must prove that your unbuckled seatbelt contributed to your injuries. And, in any event, the fact that your seatbelt was unbuckled is unlikely to be judged relevant in regard to any damage to your car. Furthermore, over two-thirds of the states now follow the rule of "comparative negligence" in resolving automobile-accident claims. This means that you can recover some damages even if you were partially responsible for the accident. In such an instance, however, the amount recovered will be reduced in proportion to your own negligence as determined by the court. If you were 50 percent to blame, for example, you can recover only 50 percent of your losses. Also, if your state has "no fault" automobile insurance, the issue of blame becomes irrelevant.

Your first action should always be to report any accident to the police and to your insurance agent, who will be able to give you a good idea of your rights in this matter. And, in the future, use your seat belt for safety reasons as well as legal ones.

9

Wills and Inheritances

Is it really necessary for me to have a will?

Q. My husband flatly refuses to make a will. He says that, under the law of our state, husbands and wives inherit everything from each other anyway, so a will won't make any difference. Is he right?

A. Probably not. In most states, when a husband dies without a will, his estate is divided between his wife and children. In some instances, parents and siblings also partake. But even if your husband is right about the law of your particular state and you would inherit everything upon his death, there are still several valid reasons for him to have a will.

A well-drawn will might provide tax benefits that would increase the amount of your inheritance. It would name the person or persons responsible for serving as executor of your husband's estate and guarantee that his wishes were properly carried out after his death. Also, you might die before your husband; or you could both be killed in the same accident. A will would provide for these and other contingencies, guaranteeing that your husband's property is disposed of in a way he would have wanted, regardless of events.

Every adult with even modest assets or family responsibilities should have a will. And this includes you as well as your husband. Regardless of his final decision, you should have a will of your own.

Writing your own will

Q. I am young and in good health, but would like to have a will in case of accidental death. I have a modest bank account, a car, and the normal number of personal belongings. Is it necessary for me to pay a lawyer to draw up a will, or can I do it myself and have it be legally binding?

A. It is possible for you to draw up your own will, but for several reasons I recommend against it.

First, you want to be certain that your will is valid. Each state has its own minimum requirements for what constitutes a valid will. Generally, it must be in writing, dated, witnessed, signed, and acknowledged by you to be your "Last Will and Testament." However, some states impose additional requirements, and it would be foolish to risk invalidating your bequest on a technicality.

Second, even if you have a guidebook which purports to outline the minimum requirements for a will in your particular state, a lawyer can be helpful in assuring that your will covers all contingencies and will be interpreted the way you want after your death. For example, you might plan to leave your entire estate to your nieces and nephews. But what happens if, after you write the will, one of them dies or you have a child of your own? A carefully drafted will provides for these and other less expected occurrences in the event you die before a revised will is drafted.

Third, wills are occasionally challenged by disgruntled people who claim that the will resulted from undue influence upon the deceased, was obtained through fraud, or was the product of a person with an unstable mind. Such challenges are more easily rebutted if the will has been drawn by an impartial attorney.

Wills are relatively inexpensive. It is not uncommon for a lawyer to charge as little as $100 or $200 for a well-drafted piece of work. This is a small price to pay if you consider the consequences of an inadequately drafted will.

If I die without a will, what will happen to my estate?

Q. I have a small bank account and a nicely furnished apartment. What will happen to my money and personal belongings should I die without having drawn up a will?

A. It is a commonly held misconception that, when a person dies without a will, the estate of the deceased "goes to the government." However, this generally does not occur.

Every state has a law specifying how a person's assets should be divided if he or she dies without a will. While the law varies from state to state, in each instance it calls first for the payment of funeral expenses, taxes, and other debts. Then the remaining estate is usually divided among the dead person's surviving spouse and children. If none exist, parents, brothers, sisters, grandchildren, and grandparents are generally next in line in varying order, followed by aunts, uncles, nieces, nephews, and cousins. The purpose of these laws is to distribute a dead person's assets in a manner that he or she would have approved had a will been drawn. But the law is an admittedly imperfect substitute for a written will. You and everyone else with modest assets should have a will.

My father died—am I responsible for his debts?

Q. My father died recently after a long illness. Am I legally responsible for his debts?

A. Probably not. As a general rule, when a person dies, his debts are paid out of his estate. Thus, if your father left cash, stocks, Treasury bills, or other liquid assets, the executor of his estate would be required to use them to pay back your father's creditors. Then, if the debts were still not covered, the executor might be required to sell your father's personal property or real-estate holdings to make good on obligations incurred before his death.

However, once the assets of an estate have been exhausted, creditors usually have to absorb any additional loss themselves. Certain exceptions to this rule do exist. If you and your father cosigned a loan agreement, for example, you could be held liable for the unpaid balance. Or, if the two of you entered into a joint business venture, you might be held responsible for the business's debts. However, excluding such special circumstances, most courts have ruled that it is unfair to saddle one person with the debts of another, and this principle should operate in your favor. However, unless one of your father's creditors actually makes a claim against you, it is unlikely that you will need legal counsel. Thus, your best course of action at this point will probably be to wait and see what claims, if any, are forthcoming against you.

Can you spend a child's inheritance?

Q. Our two children recently inherited several thousand dollars each from their grandfather. Can we use this money to help pay for their college education, or must it be kept in trust until the children are adults?

A. Most likely you will be able to use the money for your children's education, but first you should take precautions to clarify your right to do so.

Generally, when a child inherits money, it is held in safekeeping until he or she reaches the "age of majority"—eighteen in most states, twenty-one in others. Until then, a "custodian—usually one of the child's parents—is given responsibility for managing the funds and seeing that they are prudently invested.

The custodian can be sued for mismanaging the child's assets, but it's highly unlikely that money spent for a college education would be considered "mismanagement." To be on the safe side, however, you should consider applying for a court order authorizing you to use the funds for college costs. (Depending on your family's financial situation, this simple proceeding can be broadened to include expenses for other nonessentials, such as piano lessons or orthodontics.) If you don't already have an attorney, your local bar association will be able to provide you with a list of counsel qualified to handle the case at a reasonable rate.

Can I challenge a provision in my mother's will that seems unreasonable?

Q. My mother died recently and left a provision in her will stipulating that I was to receive a substantial monthly income unless I marry someone who is not of our religious faith. Are restrictions such as this legal?

A. That depends on the law of the state where your mother lived. The law of wills is based on the belief that a person should have the most freedom possible in disposing of his or her property and that a deceased person's wishes should be carried out after death whether they are wise or foolish.

However, there are instances where the strings attached to a bequest run so counter to public policy that they will not be upheld by the courts. For example, if your mother left money to a state university for a scholarship fund with the proviso that it be awarded to "whites only," a court would not allow the university to fulfill her wish. Instead, depending on the wording of the will and the law of the particular state, the bequest would be divided among your mother's other beneficiaries or given to the university on a nondiscriminatory basis. Similarly, a provision requiring you to remain unmarried for your entire life would most likely be ruled invalid, while a provision that you receive a substantial monthly income as long as you attended classes as a full-time student would probably be upheld.

Your case falls somewhere in the middle. It is not completely inimical to public policy to suggest that religion is a significant determinant in the success of a marriage. Yet the law generally bridles at the notion that there should be a penalty for marrying outside of one's faith. Thus, the outcome of your case will rest on where your state draws its particular public policy line. My advice would be for you to retain a lawyer who can pursue the matter on your behalf. You should not rely on the lawyer who prepared your mother's will to represent you, since his responsibility will be to defend the will's validity, should the matter come to court.

How can you have an entire will invalidated?

Q. My father just died, and in his will he left almost everything to his second wife. As a result, my sister and I will inherit virtually nothing. We're not "money grubbers," but it strikes us as being extremely unfair. The marriage was less than two years old, and we were loving daughters for almost four decades. Is there any way we can have the will set aside?

A. There might be, but your case will be difficult to win. The "law of wills" is designed to carry out the wishes of the deceased. This means that a court cannot set aside a will simply because it is "unfair." In order to succeed, you and your sister will have to prove a great deal more.

The most common grounds for invalidating a will are a court finding that the deceased lacked what is known as "testamentary capacity"—that is, the mental competence necessary to make a will. If you can show that your father failed to understand the value and character of his estate or the disposition he was making, then the will might be overturned. Similarly, if he was suffering from a strange delusion (such as the idea that you and your sister were plotting to kill him) and acted accordingly, the will could be ruled invalid.

A will procured by fraud will also not be allowed to stand. If, for example, your father's second wife falsely told him that you and your sister had specifically asked that he leave you nothing, the will would be set aside. The same would be true if the will was the result of extreme "undue influence"—persistent and unremitting pressure that came to dominate your father's thoughts completely and, in effect, robbed him of free choice. (If, for example, your stepmother continually threatened to commit your father to a nursing home unless he made a will to her liking, the will might be ruled invalid.)

It's also possible that the will could be set aside on a technicality. Some states have very strict laws regarding the manner in which a will must be witnessed. Others have similar statutes that might pertain to your situation in another way. I should add that, if the will is declared invalid, the last previous will made by your father would then go into effect.

Leaving your child tax-free money

Q. I have a certificate of deposit at a local bank with my daughter as co-owner. If I die before the certificate comes due, will she be entitled to keep the full amount without paying an inheritance tax?

A. Probably not, unless you adjust your financial affairs now in her favor.

Most certificates of deposit with co-owners are written by banks as "joint tenancies"—that is, if one party dies, the survivor is entitled to the full amount. However, for inheritance tax purposes, the Internal Revenue Service takes a different view. It holds that in cases of a joint tenancy the property is presumed to have belonged entirely to the deceased—except insofar as the survivor can prove that he or she put the money in originally. Thus, if you paid for the certificate, your daughter will be required to pay an inheritance tax, which, with state and federal taxes combined, could amount to a substantial sum.

However, several perfectly legal tax loopholes exist. For instance, you could give your stake in the certificate to your daughter now, and so avoid an inheritance tax. More complex techniques, such as establishing a trust fund, might also be available. Your best first step would be to consult a bank official, lawyer, or accountant for advice.

Do you need to draw up a new will when you move to a different state?

Q. My husband and I have just moved to a new state and have gone through the troublesome and time-consuming process of changing our automobile registration, homeowner's insurance, and so forth. Must we also change the wills our lawyer drew up several years ago?

A. It might be advisable for you to do so. If your wills were properly executed under the laws of the state where you used to live, they will most likely be recognized by the courts in your new home. However, complications could arise. For example, it is frequently difficult and more expensive to probate a will after a person's death if the witnesses and executor live far away from the deceased. Moreover, a revised will might enable you to take advantage of certain tax benefits offered by your new home.

Generally speaking, it makes sense for people to review (although not necessarily change) their wills every few years, thereby making certain that the provisions are clear and up-to-date. Given the advisability of this review and your own change in circumstances, I would recommend getting in touch with a lawyer to determine whether your own wills should be redrafted.

If I remarry, what can I do to make sure that my children will inherit all of my money?

Q. I am a widow with three children. This summer I plan to marry a man I have known for several years. Both of us are financially well off, and should I predecease him, I would like my children to inherit all of my money. However, I am told that some states require a wife to leave at least part of her estate to her husband. Is this true, and, if so, what can I do about it?

A. You are correct in believing that some states require a wife to leave a "minimum share" of her estate to her husband (and vice versa). However, each of these states provides that a husband can waive his statutory inheritance. Thus, you and your fiancée can sign a contract that will ensure that your children inherit all of your financial assets.

Contracts of this nature can be drawn up either before or after your wedding, although writing up one now will safeguard your children against any second thoughts your husband might have later. The contract should include a full and fair revelation of your financial condition, and specifically state that your husband agrees to forfeit his statutory share in your estate in the event you die before him. You might also decide that the contract should govern the disposition of any jointly held real estate, bank accounts, and major personal property items. In order for your children to be fully protected, it would be best if the contract were drawn up by a lawyer who has the confidence of the entire family.

When someone dies, who keeps items of sentimental value?

Q. My grandmother recently died, leaving a will that divides her estate equally among her four grandchildren. A dispute has arisen among us regarding ownership of some items that have sentimental value. What legal guidelines exist to help resolve this?

A. This is a common problem. First, you should try to work things out among you, perhaps with help from the attorney handling the estate. Then, if an amicable solution cannot be reached, the estate's executor will be forced to take charge.

An executor is responsible for making sure that the deceased's assets are distributed according to the provisions of the will and state law. In this case, without an agreement among the grandchildren, the executor might have to sell the disputed items to the highest bidder (in or out of the family) or obtain a court order to resolve the matter. However, neither of these steps is desirable. A sale may result in the sentimental items being lost to the family, and taking the matter to court can be costly. Thus, compromise among family members is the best policy. This sort of problem can be avoided if the person making the will states who is to inherit specific items.

How can you prove that a lost will existed?

Q. My father died recently, and, although he told several family members that he had made a will, none of us can find it. What legal steps should we take?

A. Initially, you should make every effort to locate the will. Search your father's financial files and safe-deposit boxes; telephone any attorney listed in his address book. If you still can't locate the will, you'll have two options.

First, every state in the country has a "lost-will proceeding," whereby a lost or destroyed will can be probated. However, the courts require a high standard of proof in this type of case. For example, in New York, the person claiming that a will exists must first present proof that the will was not deliberately destroyed by the deceased in order to revoke it. Next, it must be shown that the will was executed according to the requirements of state law. Finally, at least two witnesses who saw the will and can testify to its substance must be available. These witnesses aren't required to remember the exact language of the will, but each must know the will's entire content and agree on its provisions. If an unexecuted copy of the will is available, one witness is sufficient.

If you do not have an attorney to advise you in regard to your father's estate, contact your local bar association (listed in the telephone directory) for a list of attorneys capable of handling the matter for a reasonable fee. Also, this case should serve as a reminder to keep your own will in your safe-deposit box (or your lawyer's) and to tell family members where it can be found in the event of death.

Chapter 10

Doctors, Hospitals, and Related Medical Issues

What can I do about a doctor who set my broken arm improperly?

Q. Two years ago I broke my arm in a car accident. Since then, I have suffered continual pain and have never regained full use of the arm. Now I've been told by a second doctor that the bone was set improperly and will have to be surgically broken and reset. Is there any legal action that I can take against my first doctor?

A. Yes. Not every operation can be a success. Sometimes, even though a surgeon performs with the utmost care, unforeseeable complications arise or an injury defies healing. If a doctor fails to live up to professional standards, however, the patient can seek a remedy for medical malpractice.

Malpractice occurs when a professional fails to exercise reasonable care in the performance of his or her duties and the client suffers as a result. In instances of medical malpractice, the doctor in question can be held responsible for the patient's additional medical bills and partial loss of livelihood, as well as for the pain and suffering experienced as a result of the doctor's actions.

Keep in mind, though, that medical malpractice suits are usually extremely complex. They require a detailed knowledge of medical procedures and should never be handled by a novice. If you continue to feel that your first doctor did not do a proper job, you should discuss your case with an attorney who specializes in medical malpractice. Often, the lawyer will then consult medical specialists to determine whether grounds exist for filing suit.

To spare your being burdened with unreimbursed legal expenses, most attorneys will handle this type of case on a contingency-fee basis—that is, their legal fee will consist of a percentage of the total amount you eventually recover. If you lose, their fee is nothing.

Must I pay for a cancelled doctor's appointment?

Q. Several weeks ago I cancelled a doctor's appointment on the morning of the day for which my visit was scheduled. Now the doctor is insisting I pay for the appointment anyway. What are my legal obligations and rights?

A. This is a case involving contract law. The doctor agreed to perform certain services for which you agreed to pay, and a time was set aside for the agreement to be carried out. The doctor now claims that you breached the contract by not appearing at his office. However, should the matter go to court, you stand a good chance of winning.

Unless there's a specific understanding to the contrary, most courts will assume that a reasonable cancellation clause should be read into contracts for doctors' appointments. Under such a clause, the doctor would most likely be entitled to some reimbursement if you failed to cancel and simply didn't show up. But if you advised him ahead of time—the sooner the better—you're on fairly solid ground.

Another thing to take into consideration is the nature of the doctor's practice. Does he schedule patients one per hour, and was he unable to fill your time slot? Or does he usually have several patients waiting to see him? If the latter is the case, the court will be more likely to rule in your favor.

Also, you won't find many doctors who will deduct an amount from their bills because of the time patients lose in waiting for them. And if a doctor fails to reimburse patients for their lost time, he will be on shaky footing in demanding reimbursement for his own.

This is a matter that you should be able to resolve amicably with the doctor. If not, your best course of action will be to do nothing. The burden of suing and proving the case will rest on the doctor's shoulders, and it's unlikely that he'll embark on litigation that would be a highly unprofitable nuisance for him.

Who controls my medical records?

Q. Recently our family doctor of twenty years died. When I wrote to the administrator of his estate and asked that our family records be sent to me, the man refused, saying that they were the property of the estate. Are we legally entitled to our medical records?

A. As a general rule, records made by a doctor in the examination and treatment of a patient are considered the property of the doctor. The rationale for this rule is twofold. First, the records might contain confidential references to the patient's relatives or friends. And second, since they contain medical terminology, they could easily be misinterpreted or misunderstood by a layperson.

However, it is equally clear that full knowledge of a patient's medical history is very often essential to proper medical treatment. Thus, the Principles of Professional Conduct of the American Medical Association require that a doctor (or his estate) make all relevant medical records concerning a given patient available to the doctor who is presently treating that patient. This canon has been adopted by most courts that have considered the issue and should govern your situation.

The best course of action for you to follow is to have your new doctor request that your family's medical records be forwarded to him. In all likelihood, the administrator of your former doctor's estate will comply with the request.

"Required" hospital release forms

Q. I just underwent surgery at our local hospital and before the operation was required to sign a form agreeing to any procedures the hospital staff might apply. Without signing the form, I would have been refused treatment. Are requirements like this lawful?

A. As a general rule, yes—but with certain qualifications. Medical malpractice litigation has skyrocketed in recent years, and many hospitals have sought to limit their liability by requiring waivers such as the one you describe. Suppose, for example, you were having an appendectomy and the surgeon discovered an unrelated malignant growth. Without the release, he might be reluctant to follow good medical practice and remove the growth for fear of being sued for unauthorized surgery. However, with the waiver, he could properly tend to your health.

Thus, the waiver can be an instrument for good medical care. Furthermore, it does not absolve hospital officials from being held responsible for all of their actions. In the first place, there are instances where the waiver itself might be considered void. If, for example, the form was thrust upon you moments before the operation, a court would probably rule that it had been signed under duress, and was thus invalid. Similarly, a judge could declare the waiver invalid if, before signing it, you were misled about possible surgical procedures that might be followed, or the risks that they might involve.

Also, even if the waiver is valid, it does not excuse the hospital from liability for malpractice; it applies only to sound medical procedures.

Must I pay a doctor's bill that I think is exorbitant?

Q. Last month I went to a dermatologist, who examined a wart on my foot and gave me a prescription. The entire procedure took less than five minutes. Two days later, I received a bill for $150. 1 realize that medical care can be expensive and I rarely complain about the size of a bill, but this one seems exorbitant. Am I legally obligated to pay it?

A. Possibly not. In essence, you and the doctor entered into a contract. He agreed to provide certain services, and you agreed to pay for them. But since price was not discussed, you are only obligated to pay a reasonable amount for his services.

Thus, as with other cases, if the bill is outrageous, you do not have to pay it. For example, no one would try to justify a charge of $1,000 for the treatment you describe. If such a bill were received, it would be considered ludicrous. Taking into account such factors as the going rate for dermatologists in your area, as well as the doctor's expertise and the amount of time spent with you, a court might well find that $150, while not nearly as absurd, is also excessive.

You might first ask your doctor to reconsider the amount charged. If he refuses, send him a check for whatever you think is fair. Write "payment in full for services rendered" on the face of the check, and enclose a letter explaining that the doctor can accept your check as full payment or return it and sue you for the full amount charged. In all likelihood, if your settlement offer is fair, he will accept it. If he does not, he will have the burden of suing and proving his case. He might argue that you should have asked about his fee in advance, but it can also be argued that he should have taken it upon himself to tell you.

Should the matter proceed to small claims court, it will be up to the judge to determine what is fair and reasonable.

The statute of limitations and medical malpractice

Q. My eight-year-old daughter was born deaf. Recently I have come to believe that her disability was the fault of the doctor who cared for me during pregnancy and administered the birth. After all these years, is it too late to file a suit for medical malpractice?

A. In all probability, you will be able to file suit as your daughter's guardian on her behalf.

As a general rule, legal proceedings must be brought within clearly specified periods of time. For example, most states require that lawsuits for libel be brought within one year of the offending remarks. Actions for breach of contract have a longer "statute of limitations," although here again the time period differs from state to state. Claims for medical malpractice, like other causes of action, must be initiated within a given period of time. But when the injured party is under eighteen years of age, extra time will normally be granted.

For example, the rule in New York is that, in the absence of qualifying circumstances, a medical malpractice suit must be commenced within thirty months of the act complained of. However, where the injured party is under eighteen and the act occurred before July 1, 1975, the period is extended until thirty months after the victim's eighteenth birthday. (For injuries to minors arising from acts of medical malpractice committed after July 1, 1975, New York law provides that the right to file suit exists until thirty months after the victim's eighteenth birthday or until ten years from the date of the act, whichever comes first.)

As you can see, the deadlines for filing a lawsuit are extremely complex. My advice would be for you to ask your local bar association for the name of an attorney who will be able to tell you exactly what the relevant time period is in your own state.

Can a hospital refuse to treat a child unless it has parental consent?

Q. Several weeks ago a neighbor's child, who was staying at our house while her parents were out of town, fell and broke her leg. My husband and I rushed her to the hospital, but when we got there, officials told us they would not reset the leg unless they had parental approval. Fortunately, we were able to get in touch with the parents, but what if we had been unable to? Can a hospital legally refuse to provide treatment in a case like this?

A. The law on this type of case varies from state to state and, in some instances, may even depend on whether the hospital is a public or private one.

As a general rule, parental consent is necessary for surgery on a minor, and the increase in malpractice suits filed against hospitals in recent years has left administrators reluctant to perform surgery without it. However, in many states an exception to this rule does exist.

For example, a New York law provides that "medical services may be rendered to persons of any age without the consent of a parent or legal guardian when, in the physician's judgment, an emergency exists and an attempt to secure consent would result in delay of treatment which would increase the risk to the person's life or health." Moreover, that same statute, like the law in many other states, requires most hospitals to provide emergency medical treatment to those persons who need such care and apply for it.

Thus, the crucial question faced by the hospital regarding your neighbor's child was probably whether delay in setting her leg would simply result in discomfort or genuinely endanger her health. Were the latter true, hospital administrators could have applied for a court order to operate or, in some states, would have been obligated to go ahead on their own. However, given the nature of the child's injury, it is likely that the attending physician felt delay would not cause further harm. If this was the case, the hospital was probably within its rights in refusing treatment until the child's parents could be consulted.

To protect your own children in instances such as this, you should consider giving a trusted friend or family doctor the right in writing to authorize surgical procedures for your children in the event you are away and cannot be reached. Many hospitals will provide a copy of an authorization form upon request, but if such a form is not available, your family lawyer can prepare one for you.

Living wills, and the right to die

Q. One of my fears is that someday I might be kept alive in a "vegetative" condition. What steps can I take now to prevent this from happening?

A. It is now the law of most states that "competent" adults may refuse medical care necessary to keep them alive. For the purposes of these laws, a person is considered competent if he or she understands both the nature of the proposed treatment and the consequences of its being withheld or withdrawn and is capable of exercising choice. But many incurably ill patients are not competent. They are comatose or otherwise suffering from significant brain damage or major organ failure, and they are incapable of making decisions. Vigorous medical treatment simply prolongs their dying. In such situations, "living wills" are crucial.

A living will is a written directive to family, friends, and health-care professionals made while a person is in full command of his or her faculties. It says simply that the person signing the document does not want to be subjected to life-prolonging medical measures should the signer's physical condition become hopeless with no chance of recovery. The key to a living will is that it expresses the desire of the patient. The patient's wishes, not those of the family members, govern.

The law draws a distinction, however, between allowing and causing a patient's death. Passive steps, such as withholding medical treatment or disconnecting a respirator, are legal. Active steps, such as administering poison to a patient, are not—not even if the patient requests it.

A decade ago, only a handful of states had living will statutes. Today, the number has grown to 38, plus the District of Columbia, and 11 more are actively considering such legislation. Also, in many states where legislation doesn't exist, courts have upheld the provisions of a living will under general legal principles. And in 1991, Congress enacted the Patient Self-Determination Act, which requires that all patients admitted to any hospital for any reason be asked if they want to plan for their death by filling out a living will.

It is *not* necessary that a living will be drawn up by an attorney. It is important, though, that the will follow the form prescribed by the law of the state where you live. It's also important to give copies of the signed document to people who might be called upon to produce it on your behalf. These would include a relative, perhaps a friend, and your personal physician. You should also keep a copy among your papers at home so it can be easily located.

Many organizations support the right of terminally ill patients to die with dignity. One such group with a particularly good record is Choice In Dying, 250 West 57th Street, Room 323, New York, NY 10102. At your request, the society will send you, free of charge, the appropriate living will form for your state. Enclose a self-addressed, business-size, stamped envelope with your request.

Chapter *11*

Travel

Is it legal for an airline to "bump" me from a flight?

Q. When I arrived at the airport to check in for a flight, I was told that the airline had overbooked and my seat was no longer available. What are my legal rights?

A. "Bumping" is legal. It is the inevitable consequence of passengers who make advance reservations for several flights at once and then fly without cancelling their unused reservations. Faced with this practice, most airlines overbook to protect themselves against empty seats. Unfortunately, if everyone with a reservation shows up, someone has to be bumped. However, an airline can deny boarding only within strict guidelines, and knowing these rules will make it easier for you to enforce your rights.

The regulations are applicable to all domestic airlines as well as flights by foreign carriers that originate in the United States. Any passenger who has a confirmed reservation and arrives at the terminal before the required check-in time is protected.

In the event that a flight is oversold, the airline must first ask for volunteers who are willing to relinquish their seats in return for a negotiated cash payment or airline-ticket vouchers usable for another flight.

Then, if not enough volunteers come forward, the airline may deny boarding to other passengers.

Under the rules, bumped passengers are entitled to retain their ticket vouchers and receive compensation equal to the face value of their ticket through their next stopover (with a maximum of $200). If the airline cannot arrange for alternative transportation that will get you to your destination within two hours of your originally scheduled arrival (within four hours on international flights), the compensation is doubled, with a $400 maximum. Payment must be made by a check, delivered or mailed to you on the day the incident occurs.

Several exceptions to these rules do exist. An airline may bump passengers without penalty if seats are requisitioned by the United States government or because a plane smaller than the one originally scheduled has been substituted for safety reasons. Also, if an airline overbooks one class of customers, it can reassign passengers to another section of the plane. Should a passenger be switched from first class to tourist, he or she is entitled to a refund for the difference in price, but an airline may not charge extra if it upgrades a passenger's ticket to remedy overbooking.

Does a car rental agency have a legal obligation to deliver a car on schedule?

Q. Last week my husband and I reserved a car from a well-known rental agency and were promised it would be available at nine o'clock on Saturday morning. We arrived on time but the car did not. Due to overbooking, the agency did not have a car for us until eleven o'clock and our day in the country was ruined. Is there any legal action we can take against the car rental agency?

A. Yes, there is. Like airlines, car rental agencies sometimes overbook to guard against last-minute "no shows," but this does not relieve them of the obligation to live up to their contracts. According to the facts as you describe them, the agency had a contractual obligation to have the car ready for you at nine o'clock. And, when it failed to do so, the contract was breached, entitling you to an award of damages.

Many car rental agencies will make on-the-spot adjustments to compensate customers for late delivery. If you were not offered what you thought was an equitable adjustment and the bill has now been paid, your simplest remedy will probably be to write the agency a letter asking for a fair settlement of your grievance. Then, if an appropriate response is not forthcoming, you can sue in small claims court without the aid of a lawyer.

Should you sue, the court will be empowered to award a reasonable amount for lost time, plus any direct financial loss you suffered. For example, if you had tickets for a concert in the country and missed the performance because of the delay, an amount equal to the face value of the tickets might be awarded. The value of your time will be harder to calculate and will be left largely to the judge's discretion. In a few states, there are statutes which place a limit on the amount you can recover.

Also, a number of state attorneys general have begun to investigate car rental agencies and their practices. If the agency does not respond satisfactorily to your claim letter, you should consider filing a complaint with the attorney general's office in the area where you live.

What are my rights if an airline misplaces my luggage for several days?

Q. I recently returned from a vacation in Florida that was all but ruined the day it began. The airline lost my luggage, and by the time it was recovered six days had gone by. Am I entitled to recover damages from the airline?

A. Yes, you are. When you purchased your airplane ticket, you entered into a contract under which part of the airline's obligation was to deliver your luggage on time.

When luggage is lost and not recovered, most airlines will pay for its replacement. However, the issue of luggage that is temporarily misplaced and then returned to the owner is more difficult to resolve. Standard airline policy calls for reimbursement to the passenger for "reasonable" costs incurred as a result of the snafu. For example, if in order to enjoy your vacation you had to buy a new bathing suit to replace the one you had packed, the airline would pay for it. But the question of what constitutes a "reasonable" cost is sometimes difficult to resolve, and many airlines fail to consider the hardship caused by temporarily misplaced luggage. In fact, some airlines even require the passenger to return or pay for replaced items if the original luggage is located.

The end result is, airlines are required by law to compensate passengers on domestic flights for all direct and consequential damages incurred from the mishandling of luggage up to $1,250. "Consequential damages" include, among other things, the purchase of items which are needed for immediate use, the additional transportation expenses involved in bringing duplicates to the passenger, or loss of compensation where a business purpose is frustrated by baggage mishandling.

We lost a day of our vacation because our travel agent forgot to book a flight. Can we demand a refund?

Q. My husband and I have just returned from a vacation in Europe, where we had a rather unpleasant experience. Our travel agent forgot to make reservations for a connecting flight that she had assured us had been provided for, and, as a result, we spent fourteen hours sitting in an airport until seats on a later flight became available. Our entire trip was only ten days, and one of them was completely wasted. Can we take any legal action against the travel agent?

A. According to the facts as you describe them, your travel agent appears to be liable for breach of contract. You paid for certain services, and she failed to provide them. So she must reimburse you for the damage suffered.

The first step you should take is to send the agent a letter asking for a partial refund. Then, if you don't receive a satisfactory response, you have the option of suing. Small claims court, where a plaintiff may proceed without the aid of a lawyer, is probably the best place for you to take your case.

At the time of trial, you should bring all the evidence that supports your claim, such as the written itinerary prepared in advance by your travel agent. If possible, also bring documents (such as a letter from the travel agent or airline) showing that the agent did in fact forget to arrange the connecting flight. This is important because, if reservations were properly made and it was the airline that was at fault, then it is the airline rather than the agent that will be liable.

Assuming that you are entitled to a refund, the next question is "how much?" You will probably want to recover at least one tenth the total cost of your trip. On the other hand, the travel agent may argue that one tenth of the commission is a fairer standard. Because there is no set yardstick for measuring damages in cases like this, the court has great leeway in making a decision. It can award damages on the basis of land costs or land costs plus air transportation. It can choose to weigh only the number of days you were scheduled to spend sight-seeing, or also include time traveling to and from your destination. The court will probably also consider the "good faith" efforts of your travel agent to make the appropriate reservations. Because of the arbitrary nature of this decision-making process, you would be well advised to accept what you feel is a reasonable settlement offer.

Is a hotel liable when a guest's property is stolen?

Q. Last month my husband and I stayed in a hotel for several nights. One evening, while we were out for dinner, someone broke into our room and stole over $1,000 worth of jewelry from my suitcase. The jewelry was not insured, and the hotel claims it is not liable for the loss. Is there any way we can be compensated?

A. There might be, but it won't be easy. Under common law (that is, the law as it was interpreted by courts before the passage of relevant statutes), hotels were generally held liable for the theft of property belonging to their guests. However, most states have enacted laws that limit liability of hotels for property (and, in particular, jewelry) stolen from guests' rooms, provided that notice of the law is given the customers and a safe-deposit box is available on the premises for the safekeeping of customers' valuables. Without such a statute, in order to recover from the hotel all you would have to do is show that it failed to exercise "reasonable care" in guarding against the theft. But if such a statute exists in the state where you were robbed, you will have to show that the hotel was guilty of "gross negligence," and even this might not suffice if the hotel complied with the provisions of the law. In New York, for example, whenever a hotel provides a safe for money or jewelry belonging to its guests and conspicuously posts a notice thereof, it cannot be held liable for the theft of such items except in the most extreme circumstances (such as ignoring a report of a robbery in progress).

Local police in the area where the theft occurred should be able to outline the state's particular law on theft for you. Then, if it is not in your favor, you should consider ways to minimize your loss. Some states have crime-compensation programs that would offer partial relief. Some of the loss can probably be written off as a deduction from income when you pay your taxes. It is also possible that your insurance policy covers more than you think it does. However, your best first step is to contact local authorities to find out what the law is regarding hotel liability and whether or not the hotel complied with it.

Can the price of a charter flight be increased after you sign up for it?

Q. I've signed up for a charter flight to Europe but am told by friends that the cost of these flights is sometimes increased prior to departure. This strikes me as extremely unfair. A dollar amount is clearly written on the company's brochure, and it seems to me that I'm entitled to the flight at the price I agreed to. What does the law say?

A. If the company brochure states that the dollar price will not be changed, then you are entitled to a flight to Europe at "the price agreed to." However, virtually all charter-flight organizations include qualifying statements in their promotional literature.

Charter flights are arranged by independent companies that reserve space on planes operated by major airlines. If the airline raises its rates, it is only natural for the chartering company to pass this increase on to the customer rather than bear the loss itself. Thus, most charter-flight brochures warn that the cost of airfare is "subject to change" in the event that higher rates are set.

Fare increases can also result from booking what is known as a "pro rata affinity charter." These are flights where a group of people, such as an alumni association or labor union, are brought together by a charter company for the purpose of obtaining a lower fare. However, if all seats on the flight are not sold, participants may be required to pay for the empty seats as well as their own. This is frequently indicated by brochure language to the effect that "air-fare is subject to change depending on the number of participants."

Read your promotional material carefully to determine what your rights and obligations are. Then, if you still have questions, contact a travel agent who will be able to help you sort out the pitfalls and advantages of charter flights.

Remember, the purchase of an airplane ticket is the making of a contract and, as with all contracts, you must read the fine print. If there is any language in the agreement that you do not understand, it is important to have it explained before you sign on the dotted line.

Can a car rental agency charge for "extras" after quoting a set price?

Q. I rented a car from a well-known car rental agency after being quoted a certain price over the telephone. However, when I went to pick up the car I found that the price did not include several "extras," which raised the total bill to far more than I had expected. Are hidden charges like this legal?

A. No, they are not. When you made your reservation by telephone, you and the car rental agency entered into a contract, and one of the terms agreed upon was price. Thereafter, you could not require the agency to charge you less, and it could not charge you more. Everything required for normal vehicular use should have been provided without additional charge.

Keep in mind, though, that there are a few exceptions to this rule. For example, if a sales tax exists in your state, its addition to the bill would be lawful. Also, if certain items (such as added insurance or a larger car) were optional and you voluntarily chose them at the time you picked up the car, you would be required to pay the price.

Most car rental agencies obey the law, but a growing number of abuses have been found to exist. To correct this matter, you should first write the agency's main office and ask for an appropriate refund. Then, if you do not get your money back, one of your options will be to file suit for a refund in small claims court.

What the travel agent must tell you about costs

Q. Last month my husband and I took a vacation that was arranged by a local travel agency. They booked our flight, made hotel reservations, and took care of other details. Before our departure, we paid them a lump sum that they assured us would cover all basic expenses. However, when we got to our hotel, we were advised of a $50 service charge that we were obligated to pay before being given a room key. The agency had not told us about this charge beforehand and now refuses to reimburse us for it. What are our legal rights?

A. The law requires that travel promotional material be quite explicit regarding which items are covered by the basic charge and which aren't. Thus, brochures frequently carry wording to the effect that "visa fees and airport departure taxes are extra" or "laundry and alcoholic beverages are not included." The general rule is that a traveler has the right to expect that all items necessary to the trip will be included in the basic charge, unless the brochure specifically spells out some exceptions. As you were not told of any such exceptions, you have a right to reimbursement of the $50.

First, you would be well advised to send the travel agency a letter demanding the return of the money. If a satisfactory response is not forthcoming, you can sue for breach of contract in small claims court. Also, many state attorney general's offices have special units that deal with fraud within the travel industry. If this is so in your state, write the office describing your experience, and enclose copies of your correspondence with the travel agency. The attorney general's involvement in the case might lead to the return of your $50 along with sanctions against the agency.

Each of the above steps can be undertaken without aid of a lawyer, and each could lead to a quick settlement offer.

When your hotel room is unsatisfactory

Q. On vacation recently, my husband and I spent a night in a dirty, noisy hotel room, right above the hotel disco. When we complained to the manager, we were told there was no other room available. Are we entitled to a refund?

A. You might be. Legally, when you and your husband reserved the room, you entered into a contract. The hotel agreed to provide a room, and you agreed to pay for it. But unless it was stated to the contrary, the hotel had certain other obligations as well. For example, the hotel should have provided you with running water, electricity, and either a bed or a fold-out sofa suitable for sleeping. Likewise, you had the right to know in advance from the hotel management about conditions that would hinder your sleep during regular bedtime hours, and you were entitled to a room that met normal sanitation and cleanliness standards.

Send a letter to the hotel's general manager, clearly enumerating each of your complaints and requesting your money back. Then, if a satisfactory settlement can't be reached, you can file suit in a small-claims court in any county where the hotel regularly solicits or conducts business.

Are "non-refundable" airline tickets really non-refundable?

Q. Recently, I bought a special low-cost airline ticket that was "non-refundable." Then due to a death in the family, I had to cancel my trip. Am I legally entitled to get my money back?

A. Maybe. Since a consumer generally can't be bound by unusual contract terms which he or she is unaware of, whoever sold you the ticket should have advised you in advance that no refunds were allowed. If your travel agent failed to warn you, then he or she will most likely be obligated to make good on the refund. If you dealt directly with airline personnel, the responsibility will be theirs.

You also may be able to get a refund even if you were informed that the ticket was non-refundable, since most airlines have a policy of granting refunds or credit vouchers when serious circumstances—a death in the family, a summons for jury duty, or some other unavoidable obligation—cause travel plans to change. This isn't something airlines are required to do by law. They choose to do it as a matter of fairness and good customer relations.

In future situations like this, you should cancel your reservation as soon as possible. Then write to the customer relations division of the airline, explaining your problem. Enclose some sort of documentation (for example, a doctor's note saying you were in the hospital), and most likely the airline will act fairly. After all, it's in the company's best interest to keep customers satisfied.

What to do if you lose your airline ticket.

Q. Last month, while I was on vacation, my return airplane ticket was lost or stolen, and I had to buy a new one. Is there any way I can be reimbursed for this?

A. Quite possibly, yes. Unlike many areas involving the rights of air travelers (such as overbooking policies or smoking), no federal regulations govern lost tickets. Every airline has its own set of guidelines that become part of the contract you and the airline enter into when you buy your ticket. Slight variations exist, but the basic procedure is standard.

If your ticket is missing, report it immediately to the airline that issued the ticket—that is, the airline on whose form the original ticket was written. It doesn't matter how many different airlines you planned to fly; the airline you or your travel agent paid for this ticket is the one that counts. If the lost ticket is not used and not cashed in before the expiration date printed on the face of the ticket (usually 90 days to one year after the date of issue), you will be able to collect a full refund, minus a service charge (generally about $20). You will receive this refund the same way you paid for the original ticket. For example, if you paid for your ticket by check, you'll get a check in return. If either you or your travel agent knows the original ticket number, your refund may come back faster, provided your ticket hasn't been used. If, when you discover your loss, you find yourself stranded without the money to get home, most airlines will issue a second ticket and make individual credit arrangements for your return trip, although they are not required to do so. Either your travel agent or the airline you dealt with will be able to explain the specifics of your case.

Chapter 12

Neighbors

A neighbor's tree deprives our vegetable garden of sun. Can we force him to trim the tree?

Q. For many summers my husband and I have maintained a small vegetable garden on the edge of our property. However, in recent years a tree on our neighbor's land has grown to the point where it hangs over the garden and deprives our vegetables of sun. We've asked our neighbor to trim the tree, but he refuses to do so. Are there any legal steps we can take to force him to cut off the offending branches?

A. Yes, there are. There is an old dictum of law that states, "He who owns the soil owns the sky." This means that you have a property right in the air space above your land, and your neighbor is guilty of trespassing. Obviously, there are some limits to your "air space" rights. If the upper branch of a giant oak tree intruded one foot onto your property sixty feet above the ground, a court would be hesitant to rule in your favor. Likewise, you cannot stop a plane from flying across your property at a reasonable altitude. However, if your neighbor's tree actually hangs over your property and deprives your vegetables of the sun needed to survive, then the law is on your side.

As to how to enforce your property right, one possibility would be to seek relief through the courts. However, this can be expensive and time consuming. Thus, in your particular case, self-help (which is often impermissible under the law) might be in order.

As a general rule, in cases such as yours, the law provides that a property owner may cut off the offending branches of a neighbor's tree. The two prerequisites for such an action are that you give your neighbor reasonable advance warning of what you plan to do, and that you exercise due care in not injuring the rest of his tree.

Additionally, I should note that in most states a property owner is entitled to keep whatever fruit from a neighbor's tree extends over his or her own land.

Can I keep a neighbor from playing loud music late at night?

Q. I live in an apartment and am becoming increasingly upset with my next-door neighbor, who plays his stereo late at night. On several occasions I have asked him to turn down the volume. Sometimes he does and sometimes he doesn't. Either way, within a few nights the music is going full blast again. Are there any legal steps I can take against him?

A. Yes, there are. Your neighbor's actions, as you describe them, constitute a violation of civil and criminal law.

On the criminal side, playing loud music late at night amounts to disorderly conduct. And, while the police should not be called for every minor inconvenience, you would be within your rights in lodging a criminal complaint.

Civil steps can also be taken. You appear to have a cause of action under the law of "nuisance." In essence, this law provides that people have the right to reasonable comfort in their homes, and acts that might be perfectly proper under other circumstances become unlawful if they are carried out so as to interfere with enjoyment of this right. For example, a neighbor is entitled to cut down trees with a power chain saw—but not at midnight. Children can shout and play ball in the street in front of your house—but not at 5:00 A.M. The law holds that everyone must endure some degree of irritation, but there are limits, and your neighbor appears to have stepped over the line. Thus, you might be in a position to sue for both monetary damages and a court order that the offending conduct cease.

Other options are also available. Before taking legal action, you might first write your neighbor. A sternly worded letter could make him realize that the consequences of his late-evening record sessions will be troublesome for him as well as others, and that could lead to quieter nights. Also, you should send a letter of complaint to your landlord, who might take legal action on his own. In fact, if enough other tenants complain, the landlord might bring eviction proceedings against your tormentor.

Can I force my next-door neighbors to clean up their yard?

Q. Our next-door neighbors' yard is an unsightly mess. They never cut their grass; the lawn is littered with papers and tin cans; their house hasn't been painted in decades. It's gotten to the point where I'm afraid that the value of our property is going to go down because of their mess. Is there any way my husband and I can force these people to clean up their property?

A. I'm afraid that this is a case where the law leans toward the other side. Courts have traditionally held that "a man's home is his castle," and the situation you describe might be perceived by some as no different from a couple's painting their house bright orange with purple stripes. A paint job of that nature would be hideous but lawful.

Still, there are several steps you can take to try to improve the condition of your neighbors' property. First, you and several other neighbors might offer to pick up the litter and mow the lawn for them. This will remind the couple next door of their responsibilities and perhaps embarrass them into action.

Second, it is possible that the condition of your neighbors' yard represents a safety hazard, which would prompt local authorities to act. For example, if a decaying tree is leaning toward your property or in the direction of the street, a court might order its removal before it falls. The presence of tin cans and broken glass without an appropriate fence might be deemed a hazard to young children who could wander onto the property or be struck by blowing debris. A defective cesspool or bad plumbing could be considered a health hazard. Also, many municipalities have local ordinances that forbid hanging wash in the front yard and the like.

If your next-door neighbors fail to respond to your pleas for improvement, contact the municipal authorities in the area where you live. They will advise you as to whether or not legal action is appropriate.

Who is liable for damage caused by a natural phenomenon— such as a tree falling in a storm?

Q. Last month, during a thunderstorm, a large tree on our neighbors' property toppled onto our garage, causing several hundred dollars' worth of damage. Our neighbors have refused to reimburse us, claiming the accident was an "act of God." Are we entitled to payment for the damages?

A. You might be, but the chances are that you will have to prove negligence on your neighbors' behalf.

Some accidents are unavoidable, and the law is based on the belief that property owners cannot be held liable for every last thing that goes wrong with their land. And so, where damage is caused by a completely natural phenomenon (such as a tree falling in a storm), the injured party must usually show fault on the defendant's part in order to collect a judgment.

Were your neighbors negligent? That depends on the facts of your particular case. If they had noticed that the tree was rotting and did nothing about it, certainly they would be at fault. Likewise, if you had warned them that the tree was leaning precariously toward your garage and might topple in a high wind, they would have had an obligation to rectify the situation. Also, several states require owners to conduct periodic inspections of trees on their property to make certain they are safe. If such a requirement exists in your state and was ignored, you might have a cause of action. However, unless there was some delinquency on your neighbors' part, it is unlikely that you will be able to recover directly from them.

Having said all of this, I should add that this does not necessarily mean that you are without recourse if negligence cannot be proved. It is possible that your own homeowners' insurance policy (or your neighbors') will cover the accident. As a first step, I suggest that you read both policies carefully. It may well be that you are entitled to full reimbursement under one or both of them.

How can I make sure that our neighbors' fence is on their property, not mine?

Q. Our neighbors recently built a fence to divide our property from theirs. However, it appears to my husband and me that most of the fence is at least a foot over our side of the property line. Is there anything we can do to protect our property rights?

A. Yes, there is, but first you have to establish where the property line actually is. When you bought your house, you should have received a deed to the property. The same holds true for your neighbors. (If for some reason either of you no longer has a deed, copies are most likely on file at your county clerk's office.) From these deeds you and your neighbors should be able to agree on your joint boundary. If you are unable to reach agreement, a licensed surveyor can be retained to resolve the matter.

In the event your neighbors concede that the fence is on your property, you will have several options. Obviously, they can tear the fence down. Or, you can agree to sell them an "easement"—the right to keep the fence on your property—for a specified amount of money. The problem will become a bit thornier if they refuse to acknowledge your rights. Should this be the case, you can sue them for "trespassing." Provided you win such a suit, the court would be empowered to order the fence removed and award you a fair amount in monetary damages. However, since a legal battle of this nature could be lengthy, and costly to both sides, it would be in the best interests for all concerned to resolve the matter amicably between you.

How can we get our neighbors to treat their bug infested tree?

Q. Our next-door neighbors have a tree in their front yard that is infested with insects. On several occasions my husband and I have suggested they treat it, but they always refuse, and we're afraid that soon the bugs will spread to our own property. What legal steps can we take?

A. First, you should call local authorities to see if they will act on your behalf. The county Board of Health or state Department of Agriculture, for example, may consider the tree a health hazard and solve the problem for you. However, if your plea for assistance proves fruitless, there are other steps you can take.

Perhaps the most effective of these would be to file a lawsuit against your neighbors for maintaining a "nuisance." Under the law of nuisance, unless a person has reasonable justification, he cannot allow a condition to remain on his property if he knows that it is likely to harm a neighbor's interests. This is precisely what your neighbors appear to be doing. Their failure to control the insects threatens to damage your property and that of everyone living nearby. Whether or not your neighbors created the situation, it is within their power to control it and they are failing to do so.

Thus, you can sue for a court order to require your neighbors to treat their bug-infested tree or cut it down. If their continued refusal results in damage to your property, the court can also award you monetary damages.

What can we do to prevent our neighbor from mowing his lawn at eight o'clock on Sunday morning?

Q. Our next-door neighbor insists on mowing his lawn with a power mower at eight o'clock on Sunday morning. On numerous occasions we have asked him to choose a more decent hour, but he insists that this is "the only time" he can do it. Is he breaking any law?

A. He might be. You should first contact local authorities to determine whether municipal ordinances prohibit the use of power mowers at eight o'clock on Sunday morning. If they do, your problem is solved. Once you register a complaint, the police will take whatever steps are necessary to enforce the law.

If no such ordinance exists, your chances for success will rest on the earlier-mentioned law of "nuisance." In essence, this law provides that all people have the right to reasonable comfort in their homes. Thus, a perfectly proper act by someone else (such as mowing the lawn or playing phonograph records) can become unlawful if carried on in the wrong place or at the wrong time so as to interfere with your enjoyment of that right.

In the event you take legal action, the court will be called upon to balance the annoyance and inconvenience that results from your neighbor's conduct against the reasonableness of that conduct. This is an imprecise standard, to say the least, and, quite obviously, the judge will have great leeway to do what he thinks is "fair." However, if it turns out that the only reason your neighbor has "no other time" to mow the lawn is that he prefers to pursue his own leisure activities during the rest of the weekend, a court will probably find that your rest and relaxation is just as important as his. Should you prevail, you would be entitled to a court order stating that your neighbor mow his lawn at a more reasonable hour, and the judge would also be empowered to award monetary damages to you.

What can we do about neighbors who are carelessly ruining our flower beds?

Q. Each year my husband and I spend long hours cultivating our garden, which is separated from our neighbors' property by a fence. Our neighbors' children, however, have a basketball hoop set up in such a way that the ball comes over the fence and crushes our flowers with troublesome regularity. We've requested that the basket be moved, but our neighbors refuse. What can we do?

A. The law provides that all people have both the right to reasonable comfort in their homes and the right to keep their land free from unreasonable intrusions. By placing their basketball hoop where they have, your neighbors are interfering with your exercise of these rights. Accordingly, the hoop is an unlawful "nuisance," and your neighbors can be held liable for the "maintenance of a nuisance." Also, because the ball comes onto your property and the children undoubtedly come over to retrieve it, you are the victims of a trespass.

Your best first step would be to send a sternly worded letter to your neighbors, warning them that you will take legal action if the offending conduct does not cease. Often, statements in writing encourage action where oral requests have failed. Then, if you do not get a satisfactory response, you can file suit for a court order to have the basketball hoop moved as well as for a monetary award for damage to your garden.

Chapter 13

Pets

Can I prevent my neighbors from letting their dog run loose?

Q. Our next-door neighbors have a large, ill-tempered dog that they let run loose in the neighborhood. So far as I know, it has not yet bitten anyone, but on many occasions I have seen it snap and growl at passersby. My husband and I have two young children, and we are afraid that the dog might someday attack one of them. Are there any legal steps we can take to guard against this kind of thing happening?

A. There might be. It's possible that your state or community has a law that prohibits letting dogs run loose. Your local police will be able to advise you on this point, and, if the law is in your favor, they will enforce it.

Also, even if the dog has not caused any injuries or damage to property yet, the fear of a lawsuit might lead its owners to curb it. Almost half the states in the country have laws holding dog owners responsible for any harm inflicted by their pets. For example, the California Civil Code provides that "the owner of any dog is liable for the damages suffered by any person who is bitten by the dog while in a public place or lawfully in a private place, including the property of the owner of the dog, regardless of the former viciousness of the dog or the owner's knowledge of such viciousness."

Laws such as the above apply to virtually all situations, except where the injured party was reckless (for example, ignored a sign that read "Beware of Dog"), assumed the risk of injury (trespassed), or was guilty of willful provocation (teased the dog). Moreover, all of the remaining states in the country hold that an owner will be held liable for injuries caused by his or her dog if previously warned that the animal had vicious tendencies. My advice would be for you to send a letter to your neighbors stating your concern and asking that they no longer allow their dog to run loose. Make it clear that you are keeping a copy for your files, and if they do not comply with your request, send a second copy of the letter to the police. This should spur either your next-door neighbors or the authorities to action.

Must I pay veterinary costs if I run over a dog with my car?

Q. Last month, while I was driving to work, my car struck a dog in the street. Now the dog's owner insists that I pay the cost of all veterinary care arising from the accident. Do I have a legal obligation to do so?

A. Not necessarily. First of all, many states and counties have laws that forbid dog owners from letting their pets run free. Should this be true in the area where the accident occurred, it is highly unlikely that a court would rule against you.

If no such statute applies, however, the outcome of your case will probably hinge on whether or not you were negligent—that is, whether you exercised a reasonable amount of care. If you were driving carefully and the dog darted in front of your car, then the accident was not your fault and you cannot fairly be held liable. But if you were speeding around a curve at sixty miles an hour in a low-speed zone, it is likely that a court will rule against you.

At this point, both the burden of suing and the burden of proof rest with the dog's owner. If you were blameless, it is probably best to let the owner take the next step (if there is to be one). However, if the accident was your fault, you should consider making a fair settlement offer that will lay the matter to rest without potentially expensive and time-consuming litigation.

Reimbursement for "voluntary" veterinary care

Q. My neighbor's cat was hurt in a fall from an apartment window a few months ago. I found it lying in the courtyard and, since no one was home, took it to a veterinarian for treatment. The bill, which I paid, was $60. When my neighbor came home that night, I brought the cat to his apartment and gave him the bill. He thanked me, but said nothing about paying for the veterinary care. The cat has now completely recovered, but my neighbor still refuses to reimburse me. His last remark to me was, "No one made you do it." Does he owe me the $60?

A. The issue, in your case, is a close one, but chances are the owner of the cat will be forced to reimburse you for the veterinary bill.

Sometimes, a person like your neighbor receives a benefit for which he should pay even though no agreement regarding compensation was made. In such a situation, courts often find that an "implied contract" exists.

In order for an implied contract to be found in your case, three conditions must be met. First, your neighbor must have benefited from your act. Second, you cannot have paid more than the amount required to restore the cat to good health. And last, your performance must have been "necessary" rather than strictly voluntary.

The first two conditions are no problem in your case. The cat has fully recovered and its owner clearly benefited from your care. The amount paid was limited to the veterinarian's bill, which appears to have been reasonable. The major stumbling block you face is that your neighbor may claim your conduct was entirely voluntary and in no way was "necessary."

My guess is that a court will decide this last issue in your favor. While you had no legal obligation to care for the cat, there was a compelling moral obligation for you to do so. It is likely that a judge will rule your conduct was "necessary." After all, if you hadn't taken the cat to a veterinarian, your neighbor would have had to do so himself or made the cat suffer.

Responsibility for property damage caused by a pet

Q. My husband and I own a house in a suburban neighborhood and take great pride in our garden. We have just put in many bulbs and chrysanthemums. However, we're worried about a German shepherd owned by the couple next door. This dog rips up people's yards like a bulldozer, and I am sure it is only a matter of time until it uproots our garden. We have talked to the couple about the situation several times, and they say it's "not fair" to keep a dog as big as theirs indoors. When Fido gets around to demolishing our garden, what are our rights?

A. It might not be fair to keep Fido locked up indoors, but if your neighbors let him run wild, they are the ones who must pay for the consequences.

Some states have enacted laws holding dog owners liable for all damage done by their pets whether or not the owner had advance warning of the dog's behavior. This is a pretty strict rule, and not all states have chosen to follow it. However, every state that I am aware of does hold that a dog owner is liable for all damages caused by his pet if he has advance knowledge of the dog's propensity to do wrong and fails to guard against it.

Send a letter to Fido's owners politely stating that you have observed their dog digging up other people's lawns and would appreciate it if they no longer let him run off leash. Then, if Fido sees fit to dig up your garden, you will be in a position to file a suit for damages against the owners in small claims court.

Custody of pets

Q. My husband and I are planning to separate. Which of us will be entitled to custody of our dog?

A. Custody of pets is often a difficult issue to resolve. First, you and your husband should seek to settle the matter as you would any other property dispute. That is, if the dog has greater meaning to you, then you should be allowed to keep it in return for relinquishing something of equal sentimental value to your husband. While "trading" of this nature is often difficult, by the time you've finished negotiating such matters as alimony, allocation of household furnishings, and the division of bank accounts, custody of your dog may be easier to decide than it now appears.

If you cannot reach a settlement, the matter will be referred to court for trial. There, the judge will weigh such factors as which of you bore primary responsibility for the care and training of the dog, who the dog seems to prefer, and the like. However, after considering all of this, the judge can do no more than what he thinks is "fair." Since a trial will cost both you and your husband a great deal of time and money, it would be in your best interests to negotiate a fair settlement on your own without judicial intervention.

When a pet is willed to die

Q. An elderly neighbor of ours recently told me that her will contains a provision requiring that all of her pets be "put to sleep" when she dies. Will this provision actually be carried out?

A. When it comes to wills, the law generally provides that the wishes of a deceased person be fulfilled. However, provisions requiring the destruction of pets are frequently overturned by the courts, if not ignored by executors.

To begin with, there is a long-standing public policy against the destruction of property in accordance with a will. By way of example, courts have forbidden executors to tear down houses or burn money. And the destruction of a pet can be considered equally wasteful and capricious.

Second, in every state in the country, there is at least one statute protecting animals from cruelty and neglect. And the needless killing of a pet has been considered a violation of these local statutes.

Also, some courts have invalidated pet-destruction provisions after looking into the intent and state of mind of the pet owner when the will was written. Most often these provisions are included in wills drawn up for elderly people who live alone and fear their pets will suffer as strays or be whisked off to laboratories for scientific research. If a good home can be found for the animal, courts will often decide that, in these circumstances, the original owner would have wanted the pet to live.

If you're genuinely concerned about your neighbor's pets, you could offer now to take custody of the animals after her death. This could easily spur her to change her will. But if she dies without doing so, you can seek help and further advice from a local chapter of the Society for the Prevention of Cruelty to Animals.

How can we get our neighbors to stop mistreating their pet?

Q. Our next-door neighbors have a dog that they mistreat regularly. Last week, when my husband mentioned the matter to them, their answer was, "Mind your own business." We are not busybodies, but I hate to see a dog beaten and otherwise abused. Are there any legal steps we can take to stop it?

A. Yes, there are. Every state in the country has laws that forbid cruelty to animals, and, generally, the penalties for violation are severe. For example, in California any person who "cruelly beats" an animal; deprives an animal of "necessary sustenance, drink, or shelter"; "subjects any animal to needless suffering or inflicts unnecessary cruelty or in any manner abuses any animal" is guilty of a misdemeanor. The punishment is up to six months in prison and/or a fine of $500. Moreover, California law—like the law of most states—provides that once a court finds that a situation of abuse exists, it is the duty of any police officer, humane society, or public agency with jurisdiction over animal care to take in and treat an abused animal until it is redeemed by its owner, and that the owner shall be liable for the cost of the animal's care. Then, if upon the pet's return the owner continues to mistreat it, the court can order that the animal be taken away permanently.

Since your neighbors appear unable to take care of their own business, you should feel free to contact the police or your local Society for the Prevention of Cruelty to Animals. They will handle the matter from that point on.

Chapter 14

Breaking the Law Perpetrator and Victim

Handling harassing phone calls

Q. About a month ago I received a series of anonymous telephone calls which I have since learned came from a man who works in my office. What legal steps can I take against him?

A. Two types of remedies are available to you. Use of a telephone for purposes of harassment is a crime punishable by a fine and/or imprisonment. In addition, it is a violation of civil law and may enable you, as victim, to recover damages for harassment, intentional infliction of mental suffering, and, in some cases, even civil assault.

Your first step should be to contact the Annoyance Call Bureau of your local telephone company, which can be reached through its business office. The bureau will tell you how to file a criminal or civil complaint and what evidence you will need, including a log kept by you of telephone calls received, admissions of guilt by your caller to another person, and written statements. Once this information is gathered, the telephone company will advise you how to report the matter to your local district attorney. That office will handle whatever criminal proceedings are deemed appropriate.

You can also file a civil suit to recover damages instead of or in addition to the criminal action. However, if you do, you would be wise to wait until any criminal proceedings have been concluded, since the additional evidence that may have been obtained during the proceedings could prove helpful to you in the civil action.

Marijuana discovered in a friend's luggage

Q. A friend of mine was recently arrested after a routine airport security check when the authorities confiscated half an ounce of marijuana in his carry-on luggage. Are these seizures legal?

A. As a general rule, yes. The Fourth Amendment to the Constitution of the United States prohibits only unreasonable searches and seizures. Given the dangers posed by airplane hijacking, routine airport security checks are lawful.

The more pertinent question in your friend's case is whether or not the marijuana can be introduced as evidence against him at trial since, without it, there will likely be little evidence against him. Several courts have ruled that, when authorities conduct an airport search for weapons, any illegal drugs that are discovered may be confiscated but not used for purposes of criminal prosecution. Also, it is possible that the security guards violated some procedural requirement in conducting their search, and this, too, might mean the evidence could not be used at trial. If, for example, your friend's luggage was searched by hand solely because he had long hair and each of the other passengers was only subjected to a metal detection test, a court might rule that his rights had been violated.

Your friend needs a good criminal lawyer. If he does not know one, your local bar association will be able to refer him to one.

A workman steals your necklace

Q. Last week a workman came to my house to fix the television set in the bedroom. Minutes after he left I realized that my gold necklace, which I had put on top of the bureau, was missing. I called the repair company immediately, but the workman denies taking the necklace and the company refuses to reimburse me for it. Are there any legal steps I can take?

A. Yes. Keep in mind, though, that this is a case that will be difficult to win. Your best first step would be to file a criminal complaint with the police. Even if they fail to take action, you will have a record of the theft. Next, write a letter to the repairman and his employer asking for reimbursement.

If a satisfactory response is not forthcoming, you'll then have several options. You can see if your insurance policy covers the theft and accept the settlement; refuse to pay the repair bill (thereby reducing your loss somewhat and putting the burden of suit on the repair company); or file suit against the repairman and his employer.

Should you sue, you will be relying on "circumstantial evidence" that the repairman stole your bracelet. While such evidence is not conclusive, it could be enough for a court to rule in your favor. You would have a stronger case if the repair company or the police had a record of similar complaints that have been lodged against the workman and if you could testify to having seen the bracelet shortly before the repairman entered the bedroom.

Is a mugging victim entitled to compensation?

Q. Last month my husband was injured by an assailant during a mugging. The resulting medical bills totaled several thousand dollars, and he was unable to work for several weeks because of his injuries. Is there any way he can receive compensation for his losses?

A. There might be. In recent years, many states have enacted crime victim compensation laws. For example, the Uniform Crime Victims Reparations Act, which has been adopted in a number of states, establishes a state-financed program to compensate persons who suffer personal injury and the dependents of those who are killed as a result of criminal conduct. The suggested maximum allowance is $50,000 per victim, and losses of less than $100 are generally not considered. Reparations are determined by the degree of economic loss—including medical expenses, loss of earnings, and replacement costs incurred in obtaining services the injured victim would have otherwise been able to perform (such as child care). Property damage is not included. Some state laws have an amendment that limits reparations to instances where the victim has suffered genuine financial stress as a result of the crime. This amendment specifies that " a claimant suffers financial stress only if he cannot maintain his customary level of health, safety, and education for himself and his dependents without undue financial hardship."

To find out if your state has a crime victim compensation law, call or write your local attorney general's office. If you are covered by such a program, this office will be able to advise you on how to pursue your case. Also, check your insurance policy; many plans cover incidents of this nature.

It is unlikely that either of these remedies will fully compensate you and your husband for your losses, but they could help. You should also keep in mind that you might be able to deduct a portion of your losses when you file your federal and state income tax returns next April.

Is it possible to challenge an unfair speeding ticket?

Q. Last month I received a speeding ticket from a state trooper who said I was driving fifty miles an hour in a forty-mile-an-hour zone. I use this route to and from work every day and always drive under the speed limit. After the incident I took my car to a service station, where the speedometer was tested and found to be accurate. Is there any way I can challenge the ticket in court? I'm afraid that, since it is simply my word against the policeman's, his word will prevail.

A. You can challenge the ticket.

In order for law enforcement authorities to win their case against you, they must prove the accuracy of the policeman's assertion that you were speeding. For example, if he was using a radar device, they would be required to show both that the unit was accurate and that the policeman was properly trained in its use. Similarly, if the policeman gauged your speed by following you in his car, the accuracy of his speedometer could be called into question. In either instance, testimony by the gas station mechanic that your speedometer was in working order will be weighed in your favor, although, standing alone, it is not conclusive evidence.

Once, years ago, a New York woman went to court to challenge a speeding ticket given to her by a policeman whose radar unit had clocked her at a speed well in excess of the lawful limit. At trial, the judge ordered the unit tested and, much to the authorities' dismay, it was so inaccurate that it recorded a tree as traveling forty miles per hour! Needless to say, the charges were dismissed. Your case might have a similar ending.

Is there any legal action I can take against a store where I was falsely accused of shoplifting?

Q. Several weeks ago, as I was leaving a local department store, I was stopped by a security guard who said that "someone" had seen me slip a display necklace into my purse. The guard then insisted that I follow him to a security office where my purse was searched. There was, of course, no necklace and I was released. The entire experience was extremely humiliating. I did nothing wrong and would like to know whether I have a cause of action against the store for violating my rights.

A. You might have a cause of action for "false imprisonment." The first requisite for false imprisonment is genuine restraint. A mere obstruction (such as blocking one store aisle but allowing you clear access to another) does not suffice. Also, it is essential that the restraint be imposed against your will. Thus, if you agreed freely to accompany the guard and temporarily surrendered your freedom in order to clear yourself of suspicion, you do not have a cause of action.

Needless to say, it is often extremely difficult to determine whether restraint has been voluntarily or involuntarily imposed. Generally, a claim of false imprisonment will fail if it rests solely on the allegation that a security guard "exerted moral pressure," threatened "an embarrassing scene," or warned that he would call the police. However, if the guard took your purse and refused to return it or threatened you with physical force, or actually used such force to detain you, then the submission was "involuntary."

In many states, involuntary restraint by itself is sufficient to support a claim of false imprisonment (assuming, of course, that you did not shoplift or commit some other act that merited detention). However, because of growing losses suffered by retail establishments as a result of shoplifting, some states (such as New York) have enacted laws that grant immunity against suits for false imprisonment to a store that has "reasonable grounds" to detain a customer, and detains him or her "in a reasonable manner" for "not more than a reasonable time."

If your detention was truly involuntary and you wish to pursue the matter, you can proceed against the store on your own in small claims court. Obviously, if you choose, you may also retain a lawyer and sue in a higher tribunal. If you prevail, the court will be empowered to award you damages for loss of time, physical discomfort, mental suffering, humiliation, damage to credit or personal reputation, or any other loss you might have suffered.

Can we sue the police for failing to answer an alarm in time to stop a burglary?

Q. While my husband and I were away from home recently, a silent burglar alarm in our house went off in midday, signaling police headquarters that a burglary was in progress. But by the time the police arrived forty minutes later, the thieves had gone, taking thousands of dollars' worth of silverware and jewelry with them. Is there any way we can recover damages from the police, whose slow response enabled the thieves to escape?

A. There might be, but you will have several hurdles to leap. Most important, because some states and municipalities have laws that make them immune to suits of this nature, you should first get in touch with your attorney or local bar association to find out whether authorities in your area can be sued at all.

If the answer is "yes," you must prove negligence on the part of the police. Were they derelict in not answering the alarm more quickly? Maybe not! For example, if the only police cars on duty that day were actively engaged in lifesaving work (such as rescuing a drowning child), it is hardly reasonable to say that the police should have let the child drown in order to answer the alarm at your house. Similarly, if several burglaries occurred at the same time, the police couldn't respond to them all at once. Also, even if you succeed in proving negligence, a court might require you to show that the thieves would have been thwarted by a speedier police response. After all, it is possible that the alarm was tripped while the thieves were leaving, in which case a quick response would have made no difference.

In short, your case will not be easy to win, but you might prevail. Let me also add some words of caution. Even in areas where a state or city can be sued, there is frequently a requirement that the authorities be notified of a citizen's intention to sue within a relatively short period of time. (Negligence victims in New York City, for example, must announce their intention to sue the city within ninety days of the incident they are complaining of.) Thus, if you would like to sue, it is important that you consult an attorney at once.

Is it illegal to gamble in a friendly bridge game?

Q. Several friends and I play in a low-stakes bridge game where $2 or $3 change hands each week. Are we violating any law by gambling?

A. As a general rule, gambling laws are designed to penalize promoters, not casual players such as yourself. Thus, most states have laws similar to the New York statute that reads: "A person who engages in gambling solely as a contestant or bettor, without receiving any profit other than gambling winnings, and without rendering any material assistance to the establishment, conduct, or operation of the gambling activity" is not guilty of an offense. However, a small group of states takes a contrary view, and there gambling for anything of value is illegal. In Arkansas, for example, your bridge game would be against the law and you could be fined up to $25 for participating in it.

I should add that even in states where gambling as a "player" is legal, promotion (unless properly licensed) is against the law. And most state courts refuse to enforce gambling debts, regardless of their legality. Thus, if you win $10 next week and your friend refuses to pay, don't plan on suing her in small claims court. The judge would most likely rule that gambling, even where legal, is "against public policy" and your winnings would not be collectible.

Legal help for herpes victims?

Q. At a woman's discussion group I attended recently, someone mentioned that there are laws making it a crime to infect someone with herpes or any sexually communicable disease. There were some angry herpes victims in our group, and we wondered what really would be the possibility of taking legal action?

A. The answer to your question depends on several variables. In 1983, the Texas state legislature did pass a statute making it a criminal offense for an individual to expose another person knowingly to certain types of venereal disease. Violation of the law is punishable by up to six months' imprisonment and/or a $1,000 fine. However, the statute is limited to exposure occurring in Texas after the law went into effect.

In recent years, at least a dozen states have enacted similar statutes, but for now the best course of action in most jurisdictions is civil suit.

If a woman's boyfriend lied to her about having a venereal disease, she could sue for negligence, battery, and fraud. She still might be able to make a case for negligence even if she and her partner didn't openly discuss the herpes question at the outset of their relationship and even if he was ignorant of his condition.

But going to court on a matter of this nature is thorny business. First, there is the question of proof. A woman's lover might contend that he did in fact tell her about his condition; he could claim that she already had herpes or that she contracted it from another man; he could even argue that it was she who gave him herpes and not the other way around. Medical records and the testimony of former lovers can be mustered as evidence, but any way you look at it, a herpes trial could be exceedingly unpleasant.

Also, some courts are reluctant to award damages in cases of this nature, ruling that adults who consent to sexual activity assume certain risks—for instance, pregnancy—regardless of how many assurances they give each other. And so I would advise any herpes victim, no matter how angry, to think carefully and consult with a lawyer before deciding to file suit.

Should a woman—or man—sue and emerge victorious, the court will be empowered to award reimbursement for medical costs as well as reasonable compensation for pain and suffering.

Is it illegal to keep a bracelet I found on the street?

Q. Last week I found a gold bracelet on the sidewalk. Will I be breaking any law if I keep it?

A. In all probability, yes. Most states have laws that make it a criminal offense to keep lost property. The California Penal Code, for example, provides that "one who finds lost property under circumstances which give him knowledge of or means of inquiry as to the true owner, and who appropriates such property to his own use . . . without first making reasonable and just efforts to find the owner and restore the property to him, is guilty of theft." If the lost property is worth less than $200, the offense is considered petty theft, punishable by up to six months in jail and a fine of not more than $500. If it is worth $200 or more, the offense is grand theft, punishable by a sentence of up to one year.

As a practical matter, prosecutions of this nature are extremely rare. Indeed, it is highly unlikely that anyone will ever even learn that you have the bracelet. However, you might put yourself in the rightful owner's place for a moment and consider how she feels. Quite possibly, the bracelet has great sentimental value; it could have been a wedding gift or family heirloom. And, in any event, the rightful owner no doubt wants her bracelet back.

The lawful course of action would be to report your find to the police. This will show that you have tried in good faith to find the identity of the true owner. Then, if the bracelet is not claimed within a reasonable period of time, you will be entitled to keep it.

My coat was stolen from a checkroom. Is the restaurant liable?

Q. Last week I went to a restaurant with several friends and left my coat with the checkroom attendant. When it was time to leave, I presented my ticket to the woman on duty and was told that the coat had "disappeared." My coat cost $300, and the restaurant refuses to reimburse me for it. What are my legal rights?

A. Laws governing the liability of restaurants for misplaced or stolen items differ from state to state. But certain rules are widely recognized. The most common standard applied to cases such as yours is that a restaurant checkroom must exercise "reasonable care." If, for example, you left your coat check on the ladies' room floor and someone else picked it up and stole your coat, the restaurant would probably not be held liable. However, if the checkroom attendant left your coat unguarded and it was missing when she returned, the law would be on your side.

Your case will be somewhat more difficult to win if you live in a state that has a law limiting the liability of restaurants for property stolen from coat checkrooms. These laws are frequently posted on prominently displayed signs that read, "No Liability for Lost or Stolen Items," or, "No Liability in Excess of $50." However, even where such laws exist, courts have generally held that a patron may recover the full value of checked property if it has been lost due to the restaurant's "gross negligence."

The concept of gross negligence is a vague one, and may be interpreted differently by different judges. However, such oversights as leaving a checkroom unattended or giving a coat to a patron who claimed to have "lost" her check and did not show proper identification have been cited as examples of "gross negligence" by some courts.

Your best recourse would appear to be to file suit against the restaurant in small claims court. This will force its management to explain the circumstances under which your coat "disappeared," and may well lead to a fair settlement offer by the restaurant or a court order that reimburses you for the cost of your coat. Small claims courts are set up in such a way as to allow a plaintiff to proceed without hiring a lawyer. To make your case as strong as possible, bring as witnesses the friends who were with you in the restaurant as well as any documents that support your claim. This would include the coat check and any record (such as a bill of sale) that confirms the value of the missing coat.

I am tired of men who make obscene comments to me on the street. Is there any law to protect me?

Q. Like a lot of women, I'm sick and tired of walking down the street and hearing men make obscene comments and grunt noises at me. Are they breaking any law by behaving this way? And is there any legal action I can take?

A. Depending on their conduct and comments, they might be. Under New York law, for example, a person is guilty of disorderly conduct when he or she intentionally causes "inconvenience, annoyance, or alarm" by engaging in "tumultuous behavior," or using "abusive language," or making "an obscene gesture" in a public place. Similarly, virtually all states have laws against harassment, which encompasses a multitude of acts intended to harass, annoy, or alarm another person. If you find your "admirers' " conduct particularly threatening or abusive, you can lodge a criminal complaint against them, and the courts and district attorney's office will tend to the matter from then on.

Similarly, you might have a civil cause of action for harassment or assault. Civil assault (as opposed to its criminal counterpart) does not require the actual use of physical force. The law is violated if the offender intentionally threatens offensive bodily contact under circumstances that create a reasonable fear in your mind that he is about to follow through on his threat.

In recent years courts have upheld suits by women who were the unwilling recipients of "friendly" kisses on the cheek and pinches on the rear. Punishment for excessive verbal abuse would be consistent with these court rulings.

Drugs at a teen-age party

Q. My son, who is in high school, says that he does not experiment with illegal drugs. He admits, however, that many of his classmates do. If he is at a party or in some other situation where his friends are using drugs, can he be held criminally liable?

A. Technically, the answer is no, but the risks inherent are obvious. Should the police intervene, a chaotic scene could result and your son might be erroneously identified as a drug user. And, while the prosecutor would have the burden of proving in court that your son was guilty as charged, there is always the risk of an error.

Also, for future reference, you should keep in mind that parents who open their home to a party where illegal drugs are used expose themselves to criminal charges. For example, under the California Penal Code, any person who commits an act or omits the performance of any duty that "causes or tends to cause" a minor to violate the law is guilty of "contributing to the delinquency of a minor"—a misdemeanor punishable by a fine of up to $2,500 and/or one year imprisonment. New York has a similar statute under the heading "endangering the welfare of a child," and other states have comparable legislation.

Given contemporary mores, it may be next to impossible to provide a completely drug-free environment for teen-age children. But your son should be careful in choosing his friends—and the parties he attends.

How to curb a reckless driver

Q. My husband and I have young children and are concerned about a local resident who drives his car recklessly in our neighborhood. How can we curb his driving habits before someone is hurt?

A. A police officer can't issue a summons for a moving violation unless it's committed in his presence. Every state, however, has a procedure by which private citizens can file a criminal complaint.

The first thing to do is identify the offender. If, as you say, he's a local resident, you or a neighbor may already know his name. If not, check motor vehicle records against his license plate number to uncover his identity. Then, once you have his name, follow the recommended procedure in your state for filing a criminal complaint. In New York City, for example, violations have to be reported to the Criminal Court of the City of New York. Then the court issues a summons requiring the violator to appear in court and explain why criminal charges should not be filed against him. (The same procedure can also be used to enforce other laws, such as no-smoking or anti-littering ordinances.)

If you're serious about pursuing the matter, get in touch with the district attorney's office in your area to find out the proper procedure.

Are chain letters legal, and, if not, can anything happen to me if I get involved with one?

Q. Recently a friend tried to sell me a "chain letter" with a list of twelve names on it. According to his instructions, I was to pay $5 for the letter, send $5 to the top three names on the list, add my name to the bottom, resell the letter to four of my friends, and wait for the money to come rolling in. Are these chain letters legal, and, if not, what can happen to me if I get involved in the purchase and sale of one?

A. Chain letters such as the one you describe violate both state and federal law. This is because the "chain" is, in fact, not a chain but a geometrically progressing pyramid that cannot go on forever. Someone is going to lose money in the end, as evidenced by the fact that, with your particular scheme, over 268 million participants would have to be involved for the letter to work its way vertically through thirteen people. And, at that point, every citizen in the United States would be used up, so the remaining participants would have to sell the letter overseas to recoup even a portion of their initial investment.

Thus, the United States Postal Service takes the position that chain letters involving money or other items of value constitute an illegal lottery. Also, if the mails are used in any way to facilitate their sale or the transfer of money or other valuables, a participant can be fined up to $1,000 or sentenced to two years imprisonment. Similarly, virtually all states regard the circulation of chain letters as an unlawful lottery or fraud.

In truth, it's highly unlikely that you would be prosecuted for circulating the letter. However, your conduct would be against the law, and you are unlikely to make any money from it. Also, under federal law, the postal service can issue an order directing the postmaster of the station where you live to inspect your mail and return to the sender any money you might receive.

Erasing the record of childhood crimes

Q. When he was in his teens, my son pleaded guilty to a charge of possessing a small amount of marijuana. Is there any way that this conviction can be erased from his record so that it doesn't handicap him when he applies for jobs, credit, and the like?

A. Quite possibly, yes. Most states have laws that allow offenses by young wrongdoers to be deleted from their records. In New York, for example, any person who is charged with a crime he is alleged to have committed when over the age of sixteen but under nineteen is eligible for "youthful offender" status. Under this law, once the defendant has pleaded guilty, or a guilty verdict has been reached, the judge may decide that the interests of justice would be better served by removing the onus of a criminal conviction from the offender's record. Punishment—such as a fine or jail term—can still be meted out, but technically there is no conviction. Other states have comparable statutes, and, in most jurisdictions, minor drug offenses are treated in this fashion.

It is quite possible, then, that your son's criminal record no longer exists. If it does, however, you can seek a pardon, which, in the words of the United States Supreme Court, will mean that "in the eyes of the law, the offender is as innocent as if he had never committed the offense."

Your first step should be to check the court records to find out whether your son's conviction has already been erased. If it hasn't, you can write to the governor's office in your state for information on pardon procedures.

Can you be reimbursed if your purse is stolen from your office?

Q. Last week at work, my purse was stolen from my desk drawer. Someone told me I might be legally entitled to compensation from my company. Is this true?

A. There are several conditions under which you may be compensated for this loss. First, there's a possibility your employer has insurance covering thefts of this nature. If so, the office manager will know about it, and you will be reimbursed. It's also possible that your own insurance will cover the loss. Many homeowners have theft insurance, and sometimes these policies carry riders covering thefts away from home.

If you don't have insurance, your chances for recovery will rest on whether the building landlord or your employer was negligent. For example, if you could show that the landlord was repairing a door and left it wide open when it should have been locked at all times, a court could find that the landlord's negligence led to your loss. Likewise, if your company's receptionist saw a stranger roaming through the offices but did nothing in response, your employer might be found liable.

Once you've evaluated the circumstances and have decided who's at fault, small-claims court will be your best forum for action. Keep in mind, though, that suing your employer can be risky, and, unless you belong to a union that will help you, you'll most likely want to focus on the landlord if a lawsuit proves necessary.

Chapter 15

Lawyers

Can a person of modest means get sound, inexpensive legal help?

Q. On several occasions I've been in need of legal advice, but the cost of hiring an attorney was always more than I could afford. Is there any way a person of modest means can get sound, inexpensive legal help?

A. Legal advice can be expensive, but a surprising number of low-cost options are available. Perhaps the best known of these is the Legal Aid Society, which offers free legal services to people whose income is at poverty level. However, middle-class persons with incomes too large to qualify for Legal Aid will find a variety of other services.

Many bar associations operate legal referral services that offer consultations with a qualified lawyer for a nominal fee. Low-cost legal clinics have sprung up across the country. These are listed in the telephone directory under "Legal Services" or some similar heading, and frequently offer inexpensive counsel on a wide range of problems. Organizations such as the American Civil Liberties Union and Women's Law Project offer free legal advice on issues within their realm of interest. Labor unions frequently provide counsel for members on personal as well as job-related matters. And many lawyers will take a case on a contingency-fee basis—that is, if you win your case, they will receive a percentage of the award, but if you lose, they receive nothing.

In addition, most government agencies offer free advice within their own areas of expertise. State and local authorities are well versed in problems ranging from housing to abortion. The federal government has jurisdiction over an equally wide range of subjects. Before you spend any money on a lawyer, check the telephone directory under "United States Government" and your "State" and "City" government listings to see if an attorney employed by one of the agencies can answer your question for free. For example, if you have a problem making out your federal income tax return, the appropriate agency to call would be "United States Government—Internal Revenue Service." Government agencies are funded by your tax dollars; they have an obligation to perform on your behalf.

Phony lawsuits

Q. My husband and I are homeowners, and we have just been sued by a man we've never seen. This person, who is represented by counsel, alleges that while walking past our house four months ago, he slipped on the sidewalk. He is suing us for $20,000. When my husband called his lawyer to ask for details, the lawyer said, "Forget about details. We'll settle for $100. It will cost you a lot more than that just to hire an attorney."

To our knowledge, neither of us has ever seen this man before. He is simply trying to hold us up for $100, and his lawyer is right—it will cost us a lot more than $100 to hire counsel. Should we pay the $100 to get rid of them?

A. Absolutely not! The legal profession, like any other, has its share of unethical practitioners, and they should be dealt with firmly. Any claim of injury should, in the first instance, be reported to your insurance company. Then, if you do not have a policy that covers this specific type of incident, there are several steps to take.

First, you should consider retaining counsel. You appear to be dealing with unscrupulous adversaries and should be as well armed as possible. As for the man suing, he must supply the court with proof of his claim, and any court will think it strange that he waited four months before reporting the alleged accident. Check court records to see if the plaintiff or his lawyer has filed similar suits against other persons. Then, if they persist in bringing the case to court and offer inadequate proof to support it, you can file a grievance with the local bar association. This will lead to an investigation of the opposing counsel's overall fitness to continue practicing law. Also, if the facts of your case are as you portray them and the court finds that legal proceedings have been misused by your opponent for improper ends, you might well recover damages for all the aggravation and expense the suit has cost you, including your own attorney's fees.

How do lawyers determine their fees?

Q. Not long ago, I sought advice from an attorney regarding the possibility of filing a lawsuit for injuries I sustained in an accident. He told me that my case was a good one and offered to represent me. However, he says that I must pay all the litigation expenses and that, in addition, his fee will be 40 percent of whatever we recover. Is this standard practice for attorneys?

A. As a general rule, lawyers charge their clients in one of three ways—a set amount for the entire case, a specified hourly rate, or a contingency fee dependent on the amount recovered. In accident cases such as yours, the contingency-fee method is the most common.

As with many other legal services, no absolute standard for contingency fees exists. The most common practice is for a lawyer to charge one third of the net amount recovered after payment has been made by the client for such items as court transcripts and fees for expert witnesses. However, some lawyers charge more and others less.

In a few instances, the amount an attorney can charge is regulated by law. In many New York counties, for example, a lawyer who charges a contingency fee in personal injury suits must choose between two formulae: one third of the net amount recovered after payment of expenses; or a sliding scale, which gives the lawyer 50 percent of the first $1,000 recovered, 40 percent of the next $2,000, 35 percent of the next $22,000, and 25 percent of anything over $25,000.

Needless to say, a lawyer can charge less than the formula allows if you and he agree to it. Also, where circumstances warrant, he can apply to the court for permission to charge slightly more.

Ask your local bar association for the names of several lawyers who are qualified to handle personal injury cases. After speaking with each of them, you should be able to find a lawyer you trust who will agree to handle your case at a price you think is fair.

Getting your money's worth from your lawyer

Q. Two years ago I hired a lawyer to represent my interests in a financial dispute. Since then, though I have paid him a fairly large retainer fee, he has done next to nothing on my behalf. Is there any way that I can get my money back?

A. There might be, but before you try, you should make certain you have all the facts.

The cornerstone of good litigation is extensive behind-the-scenes research, which takes time. Also, lawsuits move very slowly, and it is not at all uncommon for several years to elapse before a case goes to trial. Thus, your attorney may well be performing conscientiously on your behalf, even though you have seen no results.

I should add, though, that there are occasions when a lawyer will decide that a case isn't "worth his while" and will stop trying. This can occur when a plaintiff's injuries turn out to be less severe than originally thought. The complexity of a case or the obstinacy of a particularly difficult opponent also may cause an attorney to lose heart. But excuses like these are not valid. When you hire a lawyer, he becomes obligated to act in a professional manner on your behalf.

Your best first step would be to explain your concern to your lawyer. Ask him what he's done and what he plans to do. Then, if you still feel he has failed to live up to his obligation and you can't resolve the matter directly with him, there are several steps you can take. Virtually every bar association in the country has a committee on grievances, which examines charges of professional misconduct against attorneys who practice within its area of jurisdiction. If you wish to report your attorney to this committee, it will investigate your complaint and take disciplinary action, if appropriate. You can also retain another lawyer and file suit for breach of contract or legal malpractice. Either way, if you succeed, you will most likely be awarded an amount equal to the retainer fee you paid, in addition to compensation for whatever damage has resulted from your attorney's improper conduct.

What can I do if my lawyer's fee seems too high?

Q. Six months ago my husband died and left an estate of just under $100,000. There were no trust funds, no challenges to the will, and no beneficiaries other than myself. In short, it was an extremely simple estate, but the lawyer who probated the will charged me $3,000. I realize that attorneys often take a percentage of the estate as their legal fee, but wasn't this exorbitant?

A. It depends on several factors. Fees are determined by a number of variables, including an attorney's ability, his professional standing, and the amount of work done in connection with the estate. In your case, the critical question may well be, "How much work did the attorney do?"

Three thousand dollars might seem high for probating a simple uncontested will (that is, filing it with the court and getting court approval). But it is possible that your lawyer did quite a bit more work than you realize. Did he (or she) administer the estate? Did he prepare estate-tax returns? Did complications arise in the course of probate? He might have spent long hours that you weren't aware of.

As a practical matter, an attorney's fee should be discussed before the job is done, which would also allow you to compare the rates and services of other lawyers. In your case, it is too late for that. Thus, I recommend that you express your sentiments to your attorney and try to agree on an amount that seems fair to both of you. Then, if he is unwilling to compromise and you continue to feel that the fee is too high, you can refuse to pay the bill, which would force your attorney to file suit. In the litigation that followed, it would be up to the court to determine whether the fee was fair and reasonable.

How to use small claims court

Q. On several occasions, I've wanted to sue someone to vindicate my rights. But each time, I've been intimidated by the thought of going to court. How do small claims courts work?

A. Each year, roughly four million Americans turn to small claims court for help. It's a quick, inexpensive way to solve minor legal problems, and you don't even need a lawyer. Your chances of prevailing in court, however, will be significantly better if you know how it works and what to expect.

If you want to file a case, you must first find the proper court. Check your local telephone directory under "Courts," "City of . . .," etc. The name of the court will vary, depending on where you live: "Small

Claims Court," "Justice Court," "Magistrates Court" and "Court of Common Pleas" are often synonymous. Once you find the listing, telephone the court clerk to make sure it's the right place. Generally, you'll have to sue in the county where the defendant lives or conducts business. If the defendant is a corporation, the county court will advise you of the corporation's proper legal title.

When you arrive at the court for the first time, a clerk will give you a complaint form to fill out. The fee will generally be between $2 and $10. On the form, you will have to write your name and address, the defendant's name and address, a brief description of why you're suing and the damages claimed. The amount for which you can sue will vary from state to state but is generally in the neighborhood of $1,000. Small claims courts award only money; they cannot order a defendant to take a specific action.

The clerk will then assign you a hearing date and notify the defendant by mail of your complaint. Most likely, the hearing will be held within two weeks of filing. Some small claims courts hold sessions in the early evening, others during regular working hours.

Prior to the hearing date, there are several things you should do to build a strong case. Gather as much evidence as possible—contracts, photographs, accident reports, cancelled checks and similar documents are likely to be effective in court. If possible, arrange for the presence of witnesses who can support your contentions. Organize your thoughts so you'll be able to make a coherent presentation of your case. Working with a written outline may help.

Make certain you get to court on time for your hearing. At the appointed hour, the court clerk will read a list of cases to be heard, and either side may request an adjournment to a later date. If there are valid grounds for the request, it will be granted. If the adjournment is viewed as a stalling or harassing tactic, however, it will be denied.

Next, there will be an important decision for you to make. Most small claims courts are staffed by a single judge. Often there are dozens of cases to be heard in a given session. It's impossible for one person to handle all of them, so you and your adversary will be asked to submit your controversy to arbitration. This is a procedure by which you present your dispute to an impartial third party—usually an attorney—who rules on it. The advantage to arbitration is that it is quicker than waiting for a judge. Under most circumstances, it's the common-sense move to make. If you decide to arbitrate, however, the arbitrator's decision is final. You won't be able to appeal it to a judge or to a higher court.

The procedure for arbitration is the same as when you go before a judge. As a plaintiff, you'll be called upon to testify first. Tell your story in the simplest, most straight-forward way possible, citing any documents you have to bolster your claim. If you're cross-examined, the following guidelines will work to your benefit:

1. Listen carefully to each question, and don't answer unless you understand it completely. If necessary, ask that a question be rephrased or repeated.

2. Don't volunteer information or go off on a tangent. Answer only what's asked.

3. Don't be misled by a cross-examining attorney. If a lawyer (or anyone else) begins a question with the phrase "Is it not a fact that…," answer "no" if it's not a fact.

4. If your memory fails you, say so. "I don't know" or "I forget" are sometimes the only honest answers.

5. Don't joke or spar with your questioner. Just politely answer the questions.

After you've finished presenting your case, your opponent will be given the opportunity to speak.

Should you fail to appear for your court date, the case will be dismissed. If the defendant fails to appear, you'll be sent before an arbitrator who will listen to your testimony and award you appropriate damages. Generally, these damages will include repayment of your filing fee, interest, and the award itself.

Most small claims courts notify the parties by mail within several days of the court's judgment. If you've won and the defendant fails to pay up, send him or her a letter requesting payment. Then if a satisfactory response is not forthcoming, telephone the court clerk, who will advise you regarding the use of law-enforcement personnel to collect your judgment.

Chapter 16

Insurance

Suing for additional payment after a settlement is "final"

Q. Several years ago, when I was injured in a car accident, the driver's insurance company paid for my medical expenses and gave me several hundred dollars "for damages." Now I've discovered that my injuries are more severe than I originally realized, but the settlement bars me from seeking further payments. What are my legal rights?

A. This is an instance in which it will be difficult, but not necessarily impossible, for you to receive further compensation. If you signed the release that insurance companies generally require before settling a claim, your chances for additional recovery from the company are slight, unless you can prove that you were induced to settle by fraud or some other unlawful tactic.

But, even if the insurance company is immune to suit, other potential defendants exist. The doctor who treated you after the accident may have seriously misdiagnosed your injuries. If so, and if the settlement was based on his misdiagnosis, you could file a claim against him for medical malpractice. Likewise, if your lawyer mishandled the case and reached a settlement agreement that was patently against your best interests, he might be liable for legal malpractice.

No matter how you challenge them, insurance settlements are extremely difficult to overturn, but the possibility for success does exist. Your best first step would be to consult an attorney. Then, armed with more detailed legal advice, you may proceed as you see fit. (And think twice before signing your rights away in the future.)

Flood insurance

Q. Last year a number of homes in our county were damaged by floods and, as a result, our insurance broker says that flood insurance is no longer available. Is this lawful?

A. Quite possibly, insurance will be available to you under the National Flood Insurance Act. Under this act, residents and businesses in participating communities can purchase federally subsidized flood insurance at reasonable rates. Coverage for single-family residences can go as high as $185,000 for structural damages plus an additional $60,000 for contents. Nonresidential properties are insurable for up to $250,000 for structural damage and an additional $200,000 for contents.

The key to participation in the federal flood insurance program is that your *community* must participate. This can be done by local officials submitting an application to the Federal Emergency Management Agency (FEMA), which is headquartered in Washington, D.C. 20472, and has regional offices across the country. FEMA will then review your community's application and determine what steps are required for eligibility. Usually this entails a commitment by local officials to modify building codes, zoning ordinances, and the like in a manner that will curtail flood damage in the future.

Local insurance brokers and municipal officials in your area should know whether your community is already entitled to insurance benefits under the National Flood Insurance Act. If it is not, you and your neighbors should consider petitioning local government officials to participate.

"No-fault" automobile insurance

Q. Recently I suffered minor injuries in an automobile accident that was my fault. However, I am told that under "no-fault" automobile insurance statutes, I might be entitled to recover damages anyway. What are my legal rights?

A. That will depend on the law of the state where your car was insured. Traditionally, the party at fault in an automobile accident was liable for damages. If you were to blame, you recovered nothing. However, in recent years about half the states have adopted "no-fault" automobile insurance statutes. Under these laws, a person can collect for medical bills and lost wages from his or her own insurance company, no matter who was to blame for an accident. However, in return, you as an insured driver forfeit several rights. You cannot sue another party to the accident unless your medical expenses exceed a given amount (which varies from state to state) or unless you sustain a fractured bone, permanent injury, or disfigurement. Also, each state with no-fault insurance has put a limit on the amount a driver's own insurance company is required to pay pursuant to a no-fault policy. This limit ranges from $2,000 to $50,000, depending on the state. If your damages exceed that amount, you must sue the party responsible for the accident in order to recover. Similarly, many no-fault statutes do not cover property loss. If your car was damaged, the old rule of "who was at fault" will govern.

Your first step—as with any accident—should be to report the matter to your insurance company. A company representative will advise you regarding your no-fault rights.

Can an insurance company that is investigating my accident question friends about my personal habits?

Q. Three months ago I was injured in an accident at work. I filed a lawsuit and, almost immediately, an insurance company investigator began questioning my neighbors, coworkers, and friends about my personal habits. The investigator tells people that I was "involved in an accident," and then asks whether I get drunk, use drugs, give wild parties, or "sleep around." All of this seems irrelevant to my case, and I resent it very much. Is this sort of questioning legal?

A. Unfortunately, there are very few curbs on the investigative practices of insurance companies. Like other organizations, they must obey the law, which means that investigators cannot trespass onto your property, hide a microphone in your bedroom, and so forth. But they are allowed to gather general information that relates directly to your accident or that might be used to impeach your credibility at trial.

Perhaps your best remedy lies in the hands of the jury. Jurors represent a cross section of the community and have the same likes and dislikes as other people. Should they learn at the trial about the manner in which the insurance company investigated your case, it might well be reflected in their verdict.

How can we prove the value of our stolen possessions to an insurance company?

Q. My husband and I returned from a vacation to find that our house had been robbed. We estimate the value of our loss (which included jewelry, clothes, and appliances) to be $8,000, but the insurance company says we "lack proof" and refuses to settle for more than half that amount. Is there a way we can prove our claim?

A. There are several ways of proving the value of your possessions to an insurance company. The most reliable of these is inspection and valuation by an independent appraiser. Many persons, particularly those with valuable jewelry or artwork, commission appraisals of this sort, and insurance companies are generally responsive to them.

In your case, of course, you can no longer order an appraisal since the theft has already occurred. However, there are several other ways you might be able to prove your loss. First, you should gather together as many cancelled checks and bills relating to the stolen merchandise as possible. If your records are incomplete, ask your bank to send you copies of the cancelled checks. Similarly, the stores where you bought the merchandise should have copies of past invoices dating back several years. These papers will prove the original cost of at least some of the stolen items. Next, make a list of friends, relatives, and business acquaintances who saw any of your possessions before the theft. These people can file statements with the insurance company on your behalf.

In all likelihood, some compromise on your part will be necessary. But, if the insurance company refuses to make what you feel is a fair settlement offer, you do have the option of filing suit for the full value of your loss. If this becomes necessary, the above-mentioned items of proof should help substantiate your case in court.

Am I ineligible for theft insurance if I live in a high-crime neighborhood?

Q. I have several thousand dollars' worth of jewelry, a television, and a stereo system that I would like to insure against theft. However, an insurance agent I contacted told me that I could not get theft insurance because my apartment is located in a high-crime neighborhood. Is he correct?

A. Probably not. In 1970, Congress passed Title VI of the Housing and Urban Development Act. It authorizes the Department of Housing and Urban Development to make crime insurance available at affordable rates to residents of any state in which a critical unavailability of insurance exists. Pursuant to this statute, insurance is available in amounts from $1,000 to $10,000 and, in a single policy, combines coverage against:

1. Theft of property from your home by means of forcible entry;

2. Stealing of personal property in your presence and with your knowledge, either inside or outside your home (for example, a mugging); and

3. Damage to premises caused during the course of an attempted or actual break-in.

Claims for reimbursement under the act are subject to a small deductible amount. Also, to qualify, your house or apartment must be equipped with appropriate locks on all doors and first-floor or basement windows. A description of the required locks and further policy information can be obtained from the Federal Insurance Administration (an agency of the Department of Housing and Urban Development) by writing Federal Crime Insurance, Post Office Box 6301, Rockville, Md. 20849. Most insurance brokers are also familiar with the program. Premium rates vary according to the area in which an insured premises is located. A $1,000 policy will cost about $32 annually, and a $10,000 policy will cost about $126.

Is it legal for our insurance company to make us take a lie-detector test?

Q. Part of our home was destroyed recently by fire. When my husband and I put in our claim for reimbursement, the insurance company told us that both the fire and our list of losses were "suspicious" and we would have to take a lie-detector test before they paid us. Can such a test be lawfully required?

A. No, it cannot.

Basically, your case boils down to a question of proof. The insurance company has the burden of proving that the "suspicious" nature of the fire somehow precludes recovery under the insurance policy (for example, that the fire was set by you or on your order). You and your husband will have the burden of proving the value of the items lost. However, you cannot be required to take a lie-detector test in either instance. In fact, many states do not even allow the results of lie-detector tests to be admitted as evidence at trial.

Your first step should be to try to work out a fair settlement with the insurance company. Then, if you are unable to do so, you have the option of filing suit for the amount of your loss within the limits of your policy coverage. To prove your case, you should gather together as many checks and bills relating to your losses as possible. Testimony on your behalf from building contractors, real-estate agents, appraisers, and friends regarding the amount of damage caused by the fire will also help.

What can I do if my medical insurance company doesn't reimburse me properly?

Q. Recently I underwent minor surgery at my doctor's office for the removal of a cyst. This type of operation is covered by my medical insurance. However, the insurance company now says that its schedule of payments is far less than my doctor's bill, and they will only reimburse me for 20 percent of the cost. What are my legal rights?

A. That depends on a number of factors. First, and most important, is the exact wording of your insurance contract. What does it say about surgery of this nature? Is office surgery covered only up to a certain percentage of the doctor's charge? Many health-insurance contracts reimburse their holders on a set schedule of allowances for particular types of operations. Is that the case with your policy? If the insurance contract is limited in scope, you might not be entitled to further reimbursement.

Also, you have to consider the reasonableness of the doctor's fee. Maybe the bill was exorbitant, in which case neither you nor the insurance company would be obligated to pay it.

But there are instances where a doctor's bill is reasonable and the insurance company falls to fulfill its obligations under the insurance policy. Sometimes this occurs when the company simply ignores a provision in the contract. Other times, the company may rely on an unreasonably low schedule of surgical rates not previously made available to the policyholder. In such instances, you have every right to sue the company for breach of contract. This action can be brought in small claims court, or in a higher court if the amount is large enough. Should you sue, the court will be empowered to award you whatever amount the judge (rather than the insurance company) thinks is equitable. Also, once suit is filed, the insurance company might make a reasonable settlement offer that will end the case without further effort on your part.

Most unions and corporate employers have a staff expert on medical insurance contracts. If such a person is available for consultation where you work, seek out his or her advice. In the future, be sure to read your insurance contract carefully before it becomes effective. That way, you will be secure in knowing that you have the type of medical coverage you want.

Homeowners' insurance

Q. My husband and I have just bought our first home. What type of homeowners' insurance is it advisable to get to protect our investment?

A. The purchase of a house is the largest investment most couples ever make, and it's important to safeguard it properly. The first rule of thumb is to deal with a reputable insurance agent—someone known in the community and backed by a secure company. Ask the agent to explain all available options. Make sure the policy you choose covers fire, theft, water damage, and other occurrences which pose a realistic danger to your home. Most homeowners' policies include a personal liability option which protects you in the event a non-family-member is injured in your home. This protection is advisable.

Generally, your house should be insured for at least 80 percent of its replacement value, and you should make certain that the policy covers the contents of your home as well. Some policies exclude jewelry, artwork, and other valuables, but, at a minimum, you'll want furniture, clothes, and other necessities to be included. Make sure you understand the policy, so you know exactly what you're entitled to. And pay close attention to the policy "deductible"—that is, the amount of loss you must absorb yourself from each incident before insurance company payments begin. Compare premiums (the cost of the insurance policy)—both for different policies offered by the same agent and similar policies offered by different agents.

Once your policy is in place, keep a list of personal belongings which are insured, and consider having them formally appraised if any are particularly valuable. That way, you'll be better able to prove your losses should the need arise. And review your insurance policy periodically to make sure it covers inflation, home improvements, and other changes in the value of your home.

When you borrow a car, are you covered by insurance?

Q. Every once in a while I borrow my friend's car. If I'm ever in an accident, will her insurance cover the damage?

A. It might. The answer lies in the extent of coverage on your friend's insurance policy. In many states, the owner of a motor vehicle is liable only for his or her own negligence or—if he or she is the head of a household—the negligence of a family member. Therefore, it is possible that the policy will not protect you, even though you're driving with your friend's permission. This would mean that, if you were sued after an accident, you would have to hire your own lawyer and pay any amount awarded by the court to the injured party.

Also, many people carry insurance that's financially inadequate. For example, if someone were seriously injured while you were driving and your friend's policy had a $10,000 limit, you could be liable for any damages above $10,000—even if you were covered by her policy. Ask your friend for the details of her coverage the next time you borrow her car. Also, if you own a car, check your own policy. Some policies have riders extending liability insurance coverage in the event that the policy holder is driving someone else's vehicle.

Is legal insurance a good bargain?

Q. Recently I was offered a prepaid legal plan guaranteeing services for an annual fee of about one hundred dollars. Are these plans a good bargain?

A. That depends on many factors—how much the plan costs, what it covers, and the quality of lawyers involved.

According to the American Bar Association, almost seven million Americans have some form of legal coverage, usually as part of employee benefits. This insurance is similar to health insurance in that you pay a fixed amount in exchange for service benefits to be used as needed.

The costs and coverage of these plans vary widely. If you are considering legal coverage, first find out what type of service is provided. Virtually all plans offer free telephone consultations, but will you be entitled to office visits as well? Will plan attorneys review loan applications and purchase agreements? Will they draft wills and letters to landlords? Does the plan provide counseling on matters of divorce, traffic violations, and worker's compensation?

You should also ask if the company has a full-time legal staff or if counseling comes from an outside firm. Can you choose your own attorney? Is there a limit to the number of hours spent on your behalf? Will there be easy access to the plan's lawyers, and do they have an office nearby or a toll-free telephone number?

There are many legal-service companies and plans being offered, so you can afford to be selective. Read each company's literature carefully. Speak to other policyholders to see if they are satisfied. For further information, get in touch with either The American Prepaid Legal Services Institute, 750 North Lake Shore Drive, Chicago, IL 60611; The National Resource Center for Consumers of Legal Services, Post Office Box 340, Gloucester, VA 23061; or your state bar association.

Chapter 17

Social Security

How to qualify for social security benefits

Q. I worked full time before getting married and, in the years since, have had occasional part-time jobs. Am I eligible for Social Security benefits?

A. In general, there are two prerequisites you must fulfill to receive Social Security benefits. First, you or your husband must have held jobs covered by the Social Security system. And second, one of you must have worked long enough in covered jobs to acquire "insured status."

As for the first prerequisite, well over 90 percent of the jobs in the United States (including self-employment) qualify as "covered." (Workers in jobs not covered by the Social Security system, such as employees of the federal government, usually have some alternative form of retirement benefits.)

To fulfill the second prerequisite—"insured status"—you must have been employed in covered jobs for a certain number of calendar quarters and paid the required Social Security taxes during that period. The number of quarters you will need to receive maximum benefits will vary, depending on your year of birth and the age at which you seek Social Security benefits. However, not more than forty quarters can be required. Workers who lack the quarters they need to receive full benefits can accumulate additional quarters with part-time covered jobs that pay $570 or more per quarter.

These are the general guidelines. To find out the exact extent of your own coverage, contact a Social Security Administration office in the area where you live. Also, many unions and corporate employers have benefits departments that advise present and past employees on the status of their retirement benefits.

Can you work and still collect Social Security?

Q. Though my father is sixty-five, he would like to continue in his present job. Can he do so and still begin receiving his Social Security benefits?

A. Social Security benefits are intended as a substitute for earnings lost as a result of retirement. If your father wants to begin collecting his full retirement benefits now, he will have to limit his earnings over the next five years. For people ages sixty-two through sixty-four, the earnings limit is $7,440 annually; for ages sixty-five through sixty-nine, it is $10,200. For individuals seventy and over, there is no limit.

If your father's earnings exceed the amount allowed for his age group, his benefits will be reduced by $1 for every $3 earned over the limit. For recipients ages sixty-two through sixty-four the reduction is $1 for every $2. But this applies only to "earned income"—wages and tips, for instance. Your father can receive any amount of "unearned income" (stock dividends, interests, and so forth) without reducing his Social Security benefits.

Can Social Security benefits be attached?

Q. My parents' debts are greater than their financial assets, and one creditor is threatening to attach their Social Security benefits. Would this be lawful?

A. No. The federal government can take Social Security checks to collect unpaid taxes, and a court can attach the benefits to enforce an alimony or child-support order. But the Social Security Act provides that Social Security checks cannot be attached for any other purpose by any creditor—be it a corporation, individual, or even the government.

Moreover, most states have laws that shelter other assets as well. In New York, for example, 90 percent of a person's salary is exempt from attachment, as is 90 percent of the income from most trusts. Protection also applies to the cash surrender value of most life insurance policies and to personal property of an essential nature, such as clothing, furniture, and kitchen appliances.

In some instances, pension benefits can be attached, but usually only to pay alimony or child support. In the majority of cases, the federal Employee Retirement Income Security Act and related state statutes preclude attachment.

Obviously, it would be in your parents' best interest to stabilize their financial situation. One way they can do so is to negotiate settlements with their creditors that will provide for partial payment now in return for a release from all further obligations. But if a satisfactory settlement cannot be reached, the law will provide them with some protection.

Making sure your employer pays your Social Security

Q. My employer deducts money from my weekly paycheck for Social Security. However, I am concerned that he might not be making the proper payments to the federal government. Do I have a legal right to inspect his books to check up on this?

A. You do, but there's a much easier way to handle this problem. All you have to do is call or write the district office of the Social Security Administration in the area where you live. At your request, they will send you a form titled "Request for Statement of Earnings." Simply fill out the form with your name, address, Social Security number, date of birth, and signature, and mail it to the Social Security Administration, Baltimore, Md. 21235. The government will then send you a statement of all payments made to your Social Security account by your present and past employers.

This service is free of charge, and your employer will not even be told about the request. Then, once the statement is received, if you still have doubts about the propriety of your employer's conduct, you can refer the matter to the Social Security Administration district office in your area. They will investigate the matter further on your behalf and see to it that your employer makes whatever contributions to your account are required by law.

Will I be entitled to a share of my husband's Social Security benefits if we divorce?

Q. My husband and I have been married for twenty years and, regrettably, are now contemplating a divorce. If we go through with it, will I ever be eligible to receive part of his Social Security benefits?

A. Yes. Under the present law, a divorcée is entitled to benefits as soon as she turns sixty-two and her ex-husband starts to collect retirement or disability payments, provided that she was married to him for at least ten years. Moreover, if the ex-husband dies, she may begin collecting benefits at age sixty (age fifty, if she is disabled). These rules hold true even if the husband has remarried.

Keep in mind, though, that if you have worked for a substantial portion of your adult life, you might be entitled to Social Security payments based on your own work record. Whenever a person is eligible for benefits on more than one account, the larger amount is payable. When you apply for retirement benefits, you may choose between a share, computed on the basis of your ex-husband's benefits (usually about 50 percent of what he is entitled to), or whatever you have earned in your own right.

Social Security regulations can be extremely complex. Any time you have questions about them, look in your local telephone directory under "United States Government—Social Security Administration," and call for advice. You can also ask for free pamphlets, entitled *Your Social Security* and *A Woman's Guide to Social Security.*

Social security benefits for disabled children

Q. My 12-year-old daughter is physically handicapped and has extremely expensive medical and supervisory needs. Is she entitled to Social Security or some other form of disability payment?

A. She might be. Under the Supplemental Security Income program (SSI), governed by the Social Security Administration, the federal government provides monthly payments to aged, blind, and disabled people who have little or no income and financial resources. Under this law, a person 18 or older is considered "disabled" if a physical or mental impairment prevents him or her from doing substantial, gainful work and is expected to last for at least 12 months. A child under 18 (such as your daughter) is considered disabled if he or she has an impairment of comparable severity.

On request, a local office of the Social Security Administration will refer you to rehabilitation service agencies and will also send you copies of two booklets—*A Guide to Supplemental Security Income* and *SSI for Aged, Disabled and Blind People.*

In addition, you should be aware of a number of other federal and state benefits. For example, in 1975 Congress passed the Education for All Handicapped Children Act. Among other things, this act requires that 1) handicapped children be identified, evaluated, and provided with a free and appropriate education; 2) handicapped children be involved to the fullest extent possible in regular educational programs; 3) nondiscriminatory procedures be used to evaluate and place handicapped children in appropriate classes, with parents actively involved in the decision-making process; 4) an individualized education program be developed for each child, to be reviewed and revised annually; and 5) handicapped children be placed in private schools or tutored at home at no cost to parents when an appropriate public school program is unavailable.

Your local board of education will provide you with special-education information for your daughter.

Epilogue

This book began with the caveat that it's not a do-it-yourself legal guide, but rather an aid in making legal decisions a person is likely to face in everyday life. Several more items covered in the preceding pages also bear mention:

1. In determining the outcome of a particular claim, courts look to specific facts as much as to the law that governs them.

2. Litigation is expensive, and judgments are sometimes difficult to collect. Thus, it's generally best to try settling a case before resorting to litigation. You can always negotiate amicably and—if a fair compromise is impossible—litigate later. The converse is considerably harder.

3. Many small claims can be resolved without a lawyer's help. Most big ones should not be addressed without advice from an attorney.

This book ends, then, with the hope that it has fulfilled its purpose—to make you more aware of your legal rights and how to enforce them.

Index

free-lance employees and benefits, 21-22

and health problems, 8-9

And jury duty, 23

job security, suit for, 11-12

negligence of employer, suing for, 10

non-payment, 16-17

overpayment, 12-13

overtime and extra pay, 7-8

personnel file, access to, 9-10

poor reference, unfounded, 20

pregnancy leave and seniority, 19

rights of nonsmokers, 22-23

salespersons and business losses, 18

severance pay, 22

sexual harassment, 12, 15-16

Joint bank accounts, and divorce, 71

Joint house purchase, unjoining, 48-49

Jury duty, 23

Juvenile offenders and prosecution, 121

L

Landlords, 25-41

and apartment alterations, 39

and apartment sharing, 37-38

and building conversion, 53-54

and children, 32-33

and crime, 29-30

discrimination in renting, 32-33

emergency repairs, 34-35

group rentals, 27-28

heating, 38-39

and home businesses, 33-34

and insects, 33

late rent payment, 30

lease breaking, 26-27, 33, 39

liability for stolen property, 40, 216

overcharging, 35

and painting, 36-37

and repairs, 28-29, 31-32, 34

security deposits, 25-26, 27

sex discrimination, 32, 35-36

and subletting, 27

summer house, sharing, 27-28

unlawful entry, 40-41

withholding rent from, 31, 33, 37, 39

Landscaping, refunds, 46-47

Lawyers and counsel, 6, 217-223, 241

fees, determining, 219, 220-221

house, buying, 43, 47, 48, 49

insurance settlements, challenging, 226

lawyers' misconduct, 220

low-cost, 217-218

money's worth from, 220

Lease, breaking, 26-27, 33, 39

Legal help and counsel, 217-218

(*See also* Lawyers)

Legal Insurance, 232-233

Libel by employer, 20

Lie-detector tests, 229-230

Limited warranties, 92

Litigation, expense and difficulty, 241

Living-together contracts, 57-58

Living wills, 177-178

Loans

bank, 135

and bankruptcy, 142

to friends, 135-136, 140

Long-term contracts, breaking, 86-87

Lost airline tickets, 187-188

Lost property and finders, 210-211

Lost wills, 168-169

Lotteries, illegal, 214

Lump-sum divorce settlement, 79

M

Mailing, 84, 94-95

chain letters, 214-215

mail-order houses, cancellation of merchandise, 110-111

unordered merchandise, 97-98

Unsafe toys, 119
Unsafe working conditions, 11
Used cars and dealers, 91-92, 93-94
Usury, 30
Utility bills, 90

V

Vacation homes, weekend, 27-28
Vandalization by children, 117
Venereal disease, exposing others to, 209-210
Veterinary care of another's pet, 199
Visitation rights, holiday, 78
Vocational training school refunds, 102-103

W

Wage and Hour Division, Department of Labor, 7-8
Wages, reporting, 131
Warranties
  appliance, 92
  express oral, 89, 91
  homeowner, transfer of, 50
  implied, 88, 89, 92, 95, 97, 109
  limited, 92
Warranty registration cards, 94-95
Wedding photographers, 109-110
Weekend vacation homes, 27-28
Wills
  challenging, 162, 164-165
  and destruction of property, 201
  estate division, 168
  and inheritance taxes, 166
  law of, 163,164
  and lawyers' fees, 220-221
  leaving tax-free money, 166
  lost, 168
  and moving to another state, 167
  no will, and inheritance, 161, 162-163
  pets, willed to die, 201

probating, 167, 221
and remarriage, 167-168
review and change, 167
and tax benefits, 161
undue influence, 166
validation, invalidating, 162, 165-166
witnessing, 162, 166
writing one's own, 162
(*See also* Inheritance)
Withholding tax requirements, 131
Woman's Guide to Social Security, A, 238
Women's Law Project, 217
Workers' compensation programs, 10

Z

Zoning ordinances, 27, 43, 51, 226